David Clarke

Besser in

Englisch

Textarbeit

Oberstufe

Cornelsen
SCRIPTOR

Über den Autor:
David Clarke ist Brite. Er hat langjährige Erfahrung als Englischlehrer an deutschen Gymnasien und arbeitet jetzt als Schulbuchautor. Er ist Verfasser zahlreicher wegweisender Lehrwerke und Übungsprogramme.

Bibliografische Information der Deutschen Nationalbibliothek
Die Deutsche Nationalbibliothek verzeichnet diese Publikation in der Deutschen Nationalbibliografie; detaillierte bibliografische Daten sind im Internet über http://dnb.d-nb.de abrufbar.

1. Auflage

Bibliographisches Institut GmbH, Mecklenburgische Straße 53, 14197 Berlin

Redaktionelle Leitung: Simone Senk
Redaktion: Claudia Fahlbusch
Herstellung: Annette Scheerer
Layoutkonzept: Horst Bachmann, Weinheim
Umschlaggestaltung: glas AG, Seeheim-Jugenheim
Satz/Layout: Dagmar & Torsten Lemme, Berlin (Teil I), Ines Schiffel, Berlin (Teil II)
Druck und Bindung: Heenemann GmbH & Co. KG, Bessemerstraße 83–91, 12103 Berlin
Printed in Germany

ISBN 978-3-411-87070-7

Grundlagen der Textarbeit

TEIL I

Vorwort

Ziel von *Besser in Englisch – Textarbeit* ist es, Sie so effektiv wie möglich in die Methoden der Textarbeit in der Oberstufe einzuführen.

Aufbau des ersten Teils

Der erste Teil *Grundlagen der Textarbeit* besteht aus 13 Kapiteln. Sie stellen die in der Oberstufe gängigen Textsorten und Aufgabentypen dar, die Sie mit der Bearbeitung dieser Aufgaben einüben können. Der Lösungsteil beinhaltet voll ausgearbeitete Modelllösungen zum Vergleich mit Ihrer eigenen Antwort.
Die Kapitel – außer Kapitel 2 – umfassen drei Bereiche, und zwar:

A Text und Aufgabenstellung
B Praktische Hilfe und Arbeitsschritte, inklusive nützlicher sprachlicher Mittel
C Arbeitsblatt für die eigene Beantwortung der Aufgabe(n)

Einheitliche Prüfungsanforderungen (EPA)

Der Band basiert auf den bundeseinheitlichen Prüfungsanforderungen (EPA). Die EPA schreiben drei „Anforderungsbereiche“ vor, die anhand von sogenannten Operatoren (*operative verbs*) umgesetzt werden sollen. Dies klingt sehr kompliziert, ist aber in der Praxis nicht so schwierig.

▷ **Was heißt „Anforderungsbereich“?**
In der Oberstufe werden drei unterschiedliche Anforderungen an Sie gestellt:

1. das Verstehen und Wiedergeben des Inhalts eines Textes
2. die analytisch interpretierende Auseinandersetzung mit dem Text
3. die eigene Stellungnahme zu dem Text und die Bewertung des Textes

In den Klausuren, die Sie in der Oberstufe schreiben, und in der Abiturprüfung spiegeln sich diese drei Anforderungsbereiche (AB) in drei unterschiedlichen Teilaufgaben wider:

1. Comprehension (AB I)
2. Analysis of language and structure (AB II)
3. Evaluation: comment or recreation (AB III)

▷ **Was heißt „Operatoren“?**
Operatoren sind Arbeitsanweisungen, z. B. ***Summarise*** *the text* oder ***Analyse*** *the cartoon.* Obwohl es viele verschiedene solcher Operatoren gibt, sind die folgenden am gängigsten und daher für Sie am wichtigsten:

GOOD TO KNOW **Die gängigsten Operatoren**

1. **describe** *beschreiben* – eine detaillierte und möglichst konkrete Darstellung geben (AB I), z. B. ***Describe*** *the setting of the story and its effect on the characters' state of mind.*
2. **outline** *umreißen* – nur die Schwerpunkte eines Themas präsentieren, ohne ins Detail zu gehen (AB I), z. B. ***Outline*** *the author's views on the effects of globalisation.*

3. **state** *darlegen* – klar und unmissverständlich sagen/schreiben (AB I), z. B. ***State** briefly the problems faced by ethnic minorities in the UK.*
4. **point out** *herausstellen* – gewisse Aspekte eines Themas herausfiltern und erklären (AB I), z. B. ***Point out** the writer's attitude to artificial insemination.*
5. **summarise** *zusammenfassen* – eine kurze Darstellung der Schwerpunkte eines Textes geben (AB I), z. B. ***Summarise** the author's position on climate change.*
6. **analyse** *analysieren*; ***examine*** *untersuchen* – gewisse Aspekte und/oder Merkmale eines Textes beschreiben und erklären (AB II), z. B. ***Analyse** the opposing views on professional sport. **Examine** the author's use of language.*
7. **characterise** *charakterisieren*; ***write a characterisation*** *eine Charakterisierung schreiben* – die Charaktere beschreiben und untersuchen, wie sie präsentiert werden (AB II), z. B. ***Characterise** the main characters in the play. **Write a characterisation** of the main protagonists in the story.*
8. **explain** *erklären* – beschreiben und im Detail darlegen (AB II), z. B. ***Explain** the protagonist's obsession with making money. **Explain** how the pie chart and the line graph support the writer's view.*
9. **interpret** *interpretieren* – die Bedeutung verdeutlichen (AB II), z. B. ***Interpret** the message that the author evidently wishes to convey.*
10. **compare** *vergleichen* – Ähnlichkeiten und Unterschiede ermitteln und aufzeigen (AB II), z. B. ***Compare** the protagonists' attitude to the war.*
11. **comment** *kommentieren* – die eigene Meinung zu einem Thema ausdrücken und begründen (AB III), z. B. ***Comment** on the author's views on the role of women in society.*
    Beachten Sie: Es kommt häufig vor, dass ein Kommentar in Form eines ***Leserbriefes*** (*letter to the editor, reader's letter*) verlangt wird.
12. **discuss** *diskutieren* – ein Thema argumentativ untersuchen mit Gründen dafür und dagegen (AB III), z. B. ***Discuss** the effects of globalisation as described in the press article.*

Wie kann man Textaufgaben am besten bearbeiten?
Keiner kann Ihnen eine Zauberformel nennen, mit der Sie – ohne Ihr eigenes Zutun – von heute auf morgen keine Probleme mit der Textarbeit mehr haben. Hier sind aber acht Arbeitsschritte aufgeführt, die Ihnen zumindest helfen können, das Beste aus Ihren eigenen Fähigkeiten und Anstrengungen zu machen. Sobald Sie einen Schritt wirklich verstanden haben, setzen Sie einen Haken ☑ in das entsprechende Kästchen.
Wenn alle Kästchen abgehakt sind, müssen Sie sich über die Textarbeit keine Sorgen mehr machen.

Step 1: Read the whole text right through to get the general sense. Don't worry if you cannot understand every word, and don't start looking up words yet. ☐

Step 2: Read the text a second time. Underline the words you can't understand. Don't look up words yet. ☐

Step 3: Look at the words you have underlined. Pick out the sense transmitters *(sinntragende Wörter)*. These will be nouns and verbs, sometimes qualified by adjectives and adverbs.Ignore the rest. ☐

Step 4: Find out the meaning of the sense transmitters. ☐
Don't look into your dictionary yet. Try it this way:
- ▷ Look at the annotations at the end of the text. Perhaps the examiner has given you some of the words here.
- ▷ Is there a word like it in German? (Be careful about 'false friends'!)
- ▷ Can you work out the meaning from the context? (But don't just guess!)

Step 5: Now read through **all** the questions. ☐
- ▷ What does the examiner want to know? Make brief notes *(Stichpunkte)*.
- ▷ What part or parts of the text do you need to answer each question? Mark the text with a textmarker or by underlining.

Step 6: Now answer each question one by one. Make a draft *(Entwurf)* on rough paper *(Konzeptpapier)*. Answer each question fully, but do not repeat yourself or put in unnecessary material. **Use your own words whenever possible!** ☐

Step 7: Check your rough answers for language mistakes, for example: ☐

Vocabulary mistakes
- ▷ spelling, especially of words from the text or those given in word lists
- ▷ verb + preposition combinations, e.g. *(to) take part* ***in*** *sth*, *(to) divide sth* ***up***

Grammar mistakes
- ▷ tenses, particularly sequence of tenses *(Zeitenfolge)*
- ▷ word order, particularly of adverbs
- ▷ tense combinations in *if*-sentences
- ▷ agreement *(Übereinstimmung)* of verbs and their subject
- ▷ verbs followed by the infinitive, e.g. *(to) want* ***to go,*** or the *-ing* form, e.g. *(to) avoid* ***meeting*** *sb*
- ▷ use of the definite article

Step 8: When you are satisfied with your draft answers, make a fair copy *(Reinschrift)*. Be careful not to make little mistakes when copying. ☐

Viel Spaß und Erfolg beim Arbeiten mit **Besser in Englisch!**
Der Autor

1 Inhaltsfragen beantworten

A Text und Aufgaben

Bei diesem Pressebericht aus dem *Observer*, einer britischen Sonntagszeitung, handelt es sich um den Zusammenhang zwischen Obdachlosigkeit und Drogenkonsum. Laut einer Untersuchung ist die Situation in Großbritannien um ein Vielfaches schlimmer, als Drogenexperten bisher angenommen haben. Anhand konkreter Zahlen, Expertenmeinungen *(expert opinion)* und zweier kurzer Fallstudien *(case studies)* beschreibt der Bericht die besorgniserregende Situation und schlägt Gegenmaßnahmen *(countermeasures)* vor.

Homeless in drugs epidemic

Addiction[1] figures for street sleepers beyond 'worst dreams' of experts

by Ben Summerskill and Dino Mahtani

Four out of five homeless people in Britain are regular drug users – and almost half have used heroin or crack in the last month. The figures, far higher than previously acknowledged[2], have shocked homelessness experts.

'We knew of drug use among people we work with,' said Shaks Ghosh of Crisis, which commissioned[3] the research[4]. 'What we never expected, in our worst dreams, was this level of use and addiction.'

One in four of Britain's homeless use cocaine or ecstasy, researchers found. One in three use tranquillisers[5]. Only four percent do not use either drugs or alcohol at all.

James Edwards has been homeless in London for more than ten years. Now 32, he has been a heroin addict for almost all of that time. 'I've tried to get off it time and again,' he said. 'But when you finish rehab[6], there's no aftercare[7]. The last time I tried to get help they told me there was a six-month waiting list. In most cases, you just end up in a hostel with lots of other junkies.'

Not only are two in three heroin users among the homeless taking the drug on a near-daily basis, but the study found that drug dependence[8] rose steadily the longer a person was homeless. If a housing crisis lasts more than three years, there is a two-in-three chance that the person involved[9] will have become dependent on their main drug of choice.

Tim, a 46-year-old former soldier who has lived on London's streets since he left his family six years ago, said: 'I've tried to stop drinking. I had a temper[10] the last time. Because of that they wouldn't let me go back to my hostel. You just end up here again with people drinking.'

Large numbers of the homeless say they do not use services such as night shelters or hostels because of the high levels of drug use, violence and chaos they meet there.

The research will increase concern that it may be almost impossible for homeless people to kick addictions[11] to drugs or alcohol. 'On a typical day, four in five spent

time with other homeless people, and half said these had similar levels of drug use to their own,' Jane Fountain of the National Addiction Centre, which carried out the Crisis study, said.
The research will confirm the view of the Government's controversial[12] 'Homelessness Tsar'[13], Louise Casey, that money given to beggars[14] is often spent on drugs. In the run-up to Christmas 2000, Casey launched a campaign[15] asking people not to give money to street sleepers. Many charities, including Shelter, distanced themselves from the campaign.
Campaigners are calling for a boost[16] in provision for the treatment and care of homeless drug users. In spite of the levels of addiction discovered by the survey, only one in seven alcoholics had received help for their habit in the four weeks prior to interview.
Needle exchange was a popular service for drug addicts, but just three per cent had been in a detox unit[17] in the last month. More than half of alcoholics seeking help had not received any in the previous year.
'Getting a vulnerable[18] person with a serious mental health problem to recognise that they have an addiction is not simple,' Ghosh said. 'When people turn that corner and decide they are determined[19] to become clean, it's a major step forwards. But finding out that help is not available is a crushing blow[20] that can leave a person bitter and uninterested in coming off drugs.'

582 words

1 addiction = Sucht, 2 (to) acknowledge = *(hier)* zugeben, 3 (to) commission = in Auftrag geben, 4 research = Forschung(sarbeit), 5 tranquilliser = Beruhigungsmittel, 6 rehab = Rehabilitation, 7 aftercare = Nachbehandlung, 8 drug dependence = Drogenabhängigkeit, 9 (to be) involved = *(hier)* betroffen (sein), 10 (to) have a temper = jähzornig sein, 11 (to) kick an addiction = eine Sucht überwinden, 12 controversial = umstritten, 13 'Homelessness Tsar' = *(hier, iron.)* Regierungsbeauftragte, die für Obdachlose verantwortlich ist, 14 beggar = Bettler/in, 15 (to) launch a campaign = eine Aktion starten, 16 boost = *(hier)* Zunahme, 17 detox unit = Entgiftungsstation, 18 vulnerable = *(hier)* gefährdet, 19 determined = entschlossen, 20 crushing blow = vernichtender Schlag

ASSIGNMENTS

1. Describe the reaction of drug campaigners to the new addiction figures.
2. Explain how the homeless react to their sense of hopelessness.
3. Point out the reasons why the homeless often reject the help available to them.
4. Analyse the connection between the research findings and the opinion of Louise Casey, the 'Homelessness Tsar'.
5. Give the opinion of many drug activists on possible government action in view of the new situation.
6. Comment on Shaks Ghosh's attitude to the fight against drugs.

B Praktische Hilfe und Arbeitsschritte

Inhaltsfragen, meist in Form einer Aufforderung mit Operatoren (*operative verbs*), sind die gängigste Methode, einen Text inhaltlich auszuwerten. Damit will man herausfinden, ob Sie einen Text wirklich verstanden haben.

Inhaltsfragen verlangen meist eine umfangreiche Antwort, was die Auswertung verschiedener Textstellen erfordert. Fragen, die mit dem bloßen Abschreiben von ein oder zwei im Text vorformulierten Sätzen leicht zu beantworten sind, sollten zumindest in der Oberstufe nur selten vorkommen.

Methode

Schritt 1: Lesen Sie den Text mindestens zweimal aufmerksam durch – einmal, um den allgemeinen Sinn zu begreifen, und ein zweites Mal, um die Einzelheiten zu erfassen. Es ist übrigens durchaus nützlich, die wichtigsten Aussagen bzw. Argumente (*key statements, key arguments*) schon beim Lesen zu markieren. Dieses Verfahren kann viel Zeit sparen.

Schritt 2: Lesen Sie jetzt alle Inhaltsfragen durch. Vergewissern Sie sich, dass Sie die Fragen wirklich verstanden haben. In einer Klausurarbeit können Sie ruhig den Aufsichtslehrer um Hilfe bitten, wenn Sie aufgrund der Fragestellung unsicher sind. Es ist äußerst wichtig, dass Sie sich die Zeit nehmen, alle Fragen durchzulesen, bevor Sie mit der Bearbeitung der ersten beginnen. Sonst kann es sehr leicht passieren, dass Sie für eine Frage Textmaterial verwenden, das zu einer späteren Frage gehört.

Schritt 3: Jetzt können Sie mit der Bearbeitung der Fragen beginnen. Sie sollten dabei eine Schlüsselfrage ständig im Kopf haben: ***Was genau will der Prüfer von mir wissen?*** Schwächen bei der Bearbeitung von Inhaltsfragen sind weniger auf Unvollständigkeit, als vielmehr auf das Aufführen von Nebensächlichkeiten und Ungefragtem zurückzuführen. Manchmal sieht es so aus, als habe der Schüler einfach alles aufgeschrieben, um ganz sicherzugehen, dass er „irgendwo und irgendwie" dabei auch die richtige Antwort erwischt hat. Bemühen Sie sich also immer, eine präzise und genaue Antwort zu geben. Wenn Sie mehr als vier oder fünf Sätze geschrieben haben, können Sie bei den meisten Inhaltsfragen davon ausgehen, dass Sie auch ungefragtes Material verwendet haben.

Schritt 4: Beachten Sie bei der Formulierung Ihrer Antwort folgende wichtige Hinweise:

▷ Benutzen Sie dieselbe Zeitform, die in der Aufgabenstellung vorkommt. Meist wird dies eine Form des Präsens sein.

EXAMPLES

Point out the reason why the homeless often ***reject*** the help ...
→ The homeless **tend** to refuse help because ...

Explain what the government ***has done*** to solve ...
→ Ministers **have introduced** new laws to control ...

▷ Schreiben Sie über einen Text (Sprache, Struktur) oder über die Absicht des Autors, dann benutzen Sie – wie im Deutschen auch – grundsätzlich das *simple present*.

EXAMPLES

The author/writer **claims** that ...
The article **is divided** into three parts, namely ...
The first part (ll. 1–20) **deals with** the problem of ...

▷ Schreiben Sie nicht wörtlich vom Text ab, auch nicht in Form von unnötig langen Zitaten. Die Anwendung der eigenen Sprache – hauptsächlich durch den Gebrauch von geeigneten Synonymen – ist das höchste Gebot.

USEFUL VOCABULARY

(to) be unemployed/homeless/without a permanent home/income

(to) feel depressed/hopeless/isolated

(to) consume/use alcohol/crack/drugs/heroin/...

(to) be vulnerable/exposed to risk because of mental illness/instability

(to) be/become dependent/hooked on alcohol/drugs/...

(to) do one's best/try to break/stop the habit of ...

(to) avoid/ignore/not make use of/reject night shelters/hostels because ...

(to) be disappointed by the lack of aftercare/help/rehab services

(to) demand a big boost/increase/rise in funding/money for helping drug addicts/the homeless/...

C Arbeitsblatt

1. Describe the reaction of drug campaigners to the new addiction figures.

2. Explain how the homeless react to their sense of hopelessness.

3. Point out the reasons why the homeless often reject the help available to them.

4 Analyse the connection between the research findings and the opinion of Louise Casey, the 'Homelessness Tsar'.

5 Give the opinion of many drug activists on possible government action in view of the new situation.

6 Comment on Shaks Ghosh's attitude to the fight against drugs.

2 Zusammenfassungen schreiben

Praktische Hilfe und Arbeitsschritte

Das Schreiben einer Textzusammenfassung ist vielleicht die von Lehrer/innen am häufigsten eingesetzte Aufgabenstellung, um festzustellen, ob Sie den Inhalt des Textes in allen Einzelheiten erfasst haben. Die *summary* ist deshalb fast immer Bestandteil des Prüfungsteils *Comprehension*.

GOOD TO KNOW **Mögliche Aufgabenstellungen**

Es gibt verschiedene sprachliche Möglichkeiten, die Anweisung *Summarise the text* zu geben. Hier ist eine Auswahl:

Write a summary/precis/abstract of the text.
Summarise the text in not more than ... words.
Write an abstract/precis of the text using not more than ... words.
Reduce the text to about one third of its original length.
Point out the author's/writer's main arguments/thoughts.
Say what happens in the story/narrative in about ... words.

Eine Zusammenfassung *(summary, precis, abstract)* ist eine verkürzte Fassung eines Textes in fortlaufender, zusammenhängender Form. Sie ist also keine Auflistung wichtiger Inhaltspunkte.

Früher wurde ein *precis* bzw. ein *abstract* als eine besondere Form der Zusammenfassung betrachtet. Der Text sollte auf etwa ein Drittel seiner ursprünglichen Länge gekürzt werden – eine Aufgabe, die manchmal sehr schwierig war. Heute jedoch scheint dieser Unterschied zur normalen *summary* nicht mehr zu existieren. Die Begriffe *precis, abstract* und *summary* können also als gleichbedeutend verstanden werden.

Ein Text wird gekürzt, indem

1. Sätze, Textstellen und Wörter weggelassen werden, die hinsichtlich der wesentlichen Argumente, des Gedankenganges bzw. der Erzählung des Autors entbehrlich sind,
2. die Textteile, die übrig geblieben sind, neu formuliert werden, und zwar mit möglichst wenigen Wörtern.

Wenn Ihr/e Lehrer/in Ihnen sagt, dass Sie „eigene Formulierungen" verwenden sollen, heißt dies nicht, dass Sie das Original vollständig neu verfassen müssen. Viel wichtiger als das bloße Auswechseln einzelner Wörter ist, dass Sie versuchen, **andere sprachliche Möglichkeiten zu finden,** denselben Inhalt knapper auszudrücken.

Methode

Schritt 1: Lesen Sie den Text mindestens zweimal aufmerksam durch, einmal, um den allgemeinen Sinn zu verstehen, und ein zweites Mal, um die Einzelheiten zu erfassen. Geraten Sie nicht in Panik und setzen Sie sich nicht selbst unter Druck! Sie werden nie eine gute Zusammenfassung schreiben, wenn Sie diesen Schritt auslassen bzw. sich dafür zu wenig Zeit nehmen.

Schritt 2: Jetzt lesen Sie den Text ein drittes Mal durch, Satz für Satz. Setzen Sie alle Sätze, Satzteile und Wortgruppen, die nicht unmittelbar zum wesentlichen Gedankengang des Autors beitragen, in Klammern (...). Konkret heißt das, dass Sie die folgenden Textelemente einklammern:

- ▷ Statistik, Ziffern, Daten
- ▷ Einleitungen für Beispiele: *for example, for instance, e.g., as in the case of, as when* usw.
- ▷ Einleitungen für eingeschobene Gedankengänge: *By the way, ..., Incidentally, ..., Furthermore, ..., Moreover ..., I remember when ..., That reminds me of the story of ..., We should not forget the ...* usw.
- ▷ Stilmittel wie Gleichnisse *(similes)*, Metaphern *(metaphors)*, Wiederholungen *(repetition)*, Ironie *(irony)*, bitterer Spott *(sarcasm)*, Alliteration *(alliteration)*, Übertreibung *(hyperbole)*, Personifizierung *(personification)*, Aufzählung *(enumeration)* usw.
- ▷ Einleitungen für Zitate: *As ... points out/remarks/says/writes ..., ... once said/ wrote that ...* usw.
- ▷ Einleitungen für allgemeine Lebensweisheiten, Redensarten usw.: *As everyone knows, ..., As the proverb/saying goes/has it, ...* usw.
- ▷ Namen und Einzelheiten untergeordneter Figuren

Schritt 3: Schreiben Sie die nicht eingeklammerten Textteile auf ein Blatt Konzeptpapier. Prüfen Sie, ob Sie tatsächlich alle unnötigen Textstellen weggelassen haben.

Schritt 4: In diesem Stadium der Arbeit haben Sie eine Reihe von Wörtern, Satzteilen und Sätzen zusammengestellt, die die wesentlichen Gedanken des Autors beinhalten, die aber noch als fortlaufender Text in grammatikalisch richtigem Englisch formuliert werden müssen.

Schritt 5: Wenn Sie fertig sind, überprüfen Sie Ihren Entwurf auf sprachliche Fehler. Schenken Sie den folgenden Punkten besondere Aufmerksamkeit:

- ▷ Rechtschreibung, besonders bei den Wörtern, die im Text vorkommen
- ▷ Zeitformen (verwenden Sie dieselben Zeitformen wie im Text)
- ▷ Wortstellung, besonders von Adverbien
- ▷ Verwendung des bestimmten Artikels
- ▷ Verben + *ing*-Form oder Infinitiv

USEFUL EXPRESSIONS Zusammenfassungen

at the beginning of the	article, essay, leader, report, story, text,	the	author essayist reporter writer	argues asserts claims explains says states writes	(that) ...

introducing	her his their	argument discourse essay report text	the author(s) *(Name)*	argue(s) assert(s) claim(s) explain(s) mention(s) point(s) out	(that) ...

in the	middle concluding final	section	we	are given information about ... are informed about/that ... are told that ... hear ... read ...

the	opening middle closing concluding final	part section	is devoted to is given over to	data evidence information statistics	about ... on ...

developing	her his	argument(s) ideas line of thought theme topic chain of thought	the	author writer	argues asserts claims points out	(that) ...

the	author writer	analyses discusses examines	the argument that ... the assertion that ... the question of ...	by	pointing out (that) saying

in conclusion, the	author writer	summarises	her his	argument by saying (that) ... case

3 Struktur von fiktionalen Texten

A Text und Aufgaben

Die folgende Kurzgeschichte befasst sich mit dem Antiquitätenhändler Mr Price. Mr Price wohnt allein in einer Wohnung über seinem Geschäft und befürchtet ständig, dass nachts in seinen Laden eingebrochen wird. Er hat dort viele wertvolle Antiquitäten sowie Bargeld. Am Ende eines Geschäftstags stellt sich immer wieder das Problem, was mit dem vielen Geld passieren soll.
In der Geschichte lesen wir, wie Mr Price sich mit seiner hysterischen Angst vor Dieben quält. Dann – tief in der Nacht – klopft jemand an die Tür ...

The Antique Dealer

Mr Price, the antique dealer[1], lived alone in a small flat above his shop. Because of the many valuable[2] articles he kept on the premises[3], he was always afraid that one night someone would break in and rob him. Years before, when he had first come to live there, he had shutters[4] fitted to all the ground-floor windows and strong locks put on all the doors. In addition, he locked up most of his valuable articles in a cupboard, which he had had specially made for this purpose[5]. But, in spite of these precautions[6], he never felt safe, particularly when he had a lot of money in the flat after a good day's business.

One Saturday night, when he counted the money after closing the shop, he found that he had taken nearly £200 that day. This was an exceptionally[7] large sum and the thought of keeping it in the house made him feel nervous. He knew that it would be better to take it to his son's house, where there was a small safe[8], but it was a foggy evening and his son lived on the other side of town. In the end, he took the money with him to his bedroom, put it in the pocket of one of his overcoats[9] and locked the wardrobe door. He put the key under his pillow and went to bed.

Mr Price lay awake for a long time, wondering if his money was really safe, and it was well after midnight before he fell asleep. Almost immediately, or so it seemed, he was woken up by the loud ringing of the shop doorbell. He sat up in bed. Could he be dreaming? Surely, he thought, no one could want to see him at this hour of the night. The doorbell rang again, echoing through the silent house. He could not help thinking about the story he had heard about a man who had been attacked and robbed when he went to answer the door at night. Once again the doorbell rang, more persistently[10] this time.

Mr Price got out of bed and went across to the window. The fog had cleared slightly. He opened the window and looked out. He could just make out[11] the shadowy[12] figure of a man standing on the pavement below. "What do you want?" Mr Price called out in a nervous voice. The figure stepped back until it was standing under the street lamp. It was a policeman. "Sorry to disturb you, sir," said the policeman, "but there is a light on in your shop. I think you have forgotten to turn if off."

437 words

1 antique dealer = Antiquitätenhändler/in, 2 valuable = wertvoll, 3 premises = Gebäude, 4 shutters = Fensterläden, 5 for this purpose = zu diesem Zweck, 6 precaution = Vorsichtsmaßnahme, 7 exceptionally = außerordentlich, 8 safe = Tresor, 9 overcoat = Mantel, 10 persistently = beharrlich, 11 (to) make out = ausmachen, 12 shadowy = schemenhaft

ASSIGNMENTS

❶ Describe the setting of the story.
❷ Describe Mr Price's feelings. When does the writer make use of explicit characterisation and when does he use implicit characterisation?
❸ From whose point of view is the incident described? Who tells the reader the story?
❹ By using the line numbers, try and find the structure of the story: exposition – rising action – climax/turning point – falling action.

B Praktische Hilfe

Die Nummern ❶–❹ beziehen sich auf die Aufgabennummern oben.

❶ *Setting* ist der Rahmen einer Geschichte, eines Theaterstückes oder eines Romans, in dem die Handlung stattfindet. Wenn Sie aufgefordert werden, das *setting* zu beschreiben, stellen Sie sich die folgenden Leitfragen:

1. Wo findet die Handlung statt?
2. Wie sieht der Handlungsort aus?
3. Wann findet die Handlung statt?
4. Wie ist das Wetter?
5. Welche Personen sind anwesend?

Sehr häufig spiegelt das *setting* den Gemütszustand der Hauptperson wider.

▷ Unterstreichen Sie alle Wörter, Ausdrücke und Sätze, die den Rahmen der Geschichte darstellen, mir einer Farbe.

❷ Der Gemütszustand der Hauptperson(en) stellt einen weiteren wesentlichen Bestandteil einer Handlung dar. In der Übersicht auf Seite 21 finden Sie geeignete Adjektive, mit denen Sie den Gemütszustand von Mr Price beschreiben können.

REMEMBER **Direkte und indirekte Charakterisierung**

Vergessen Sie nicht, dass wir zwischen direkter und indirekter Charakterisierung *(explicit and implicit characterisation)* unterscheiden.
Explicit characterisation bedeutet, dass der Leser/Hörer beispielsweise Informationen erhält, weil ein Dritter etwas über eine Figur aussagt.
Implicit characterisation bedeutet, dass der Leser/Hörer Informationen über den Gemütszustand oder die Persönlichkeit der Hauptperson(en) erhält, weil die Figur selbst etwas tut oder sagt.
In dieser Geschichte wird Mr Price teils direkt und teils indirekt charakterisiert.

▷ Unterstreichen Sie mit einer anderen Farbe alle Wörter, Ausdrücke, Ereignisse usw., die den Gemütszustand von Mr Price verdeutlichen.

▷ Sehen Sie sich jetzt die Textteile genauer an, die Sie in der zweiten Farbe unterstrichen haben. Unterteilen Sie diese Textteile in zwei Kategorien: direkte (= wir werden darüber von einem Dritten unterrichtet) und indirekte (= wir leiten ab) Charakterisierung.

❸ Wie wir als Leser oder Hörer („Empfänger") auf eine Schilderung reagieren, dafür ist die Erzählerperspektive *(point of view)* entscheidend. In *The Antique Dealer* hätten wir den Vorgang wahrscheinlich ganz anders wahrgenommen, wenn wir ihn mit den Augen des Polizisten oder gar des Sohnes gesehen hätten.

Der Autor beschreibt den Vorgang in der dritten Person als Beobachter *(third person narrator)*. Der Erzähler ist nicht Mr Price selbst, sondern der Autor. Der Autor aber weiß alles über Mr Price – er kennt nicht nur sein äußeres Leben, zum Beispiel, was Mr Price macht und wie sein Laden aussieht, sondern auch sein Innerstes, seine Gedanken, Ängste und Gefühle. Der Erzähler ist also allwissend *(omniscient narrator)*. Im Gegensatz zum *third person narrator* (Beobachter) liegt der Vorteil eines *first person narrator* (Ich-Erzähler) darin, dass das Erzählte lebendiger wirkt. Deswegen wird letztere Erzählweise in der Unterhaltungsliteratur bevorzugt.

Das Problem des Ich-Erzählers ist jedoch die mangelnde Glaubwürdigkeit. Der Ich-Erzähler kann zwar eigene Gedanken und Beweggründe lebendig und plastisch darstellen, ist aber nicht in der Lage, Gedanken und Beweggründe anderer Figuren ebenso darzustellen. Der Ich-Erzähler kann nicht glaubhaft gleichzeitig als Hauptfigur einer Erzählung und als allwissender Erzähler fungieren.

❹ Von der Struktur bzw. dem Aufbau her weisen Kurzgeschichten generell vier klar definierte Unterteilungen auf:

1. **Exposition**
   Die *exposition* ist eine Art Einleitung. Der Autor stellt den Rahmen (Ort, Zeit usw.) seiner Erzählung dar und stellt dem Leser die Hauptperson(en) vor.

2. **Rising action**
   Nach der *exposition* folgt ein Abschnitt, der durch steigende Spannung *(rising action)* gekennzeichnet ist. Der Autor beschreibt eine Schlüsselsituation *(key situation)*, in der sich die Hauptpersonen befinden. Der Autor kann dies direkt tun, indem er dem Leser – wie in der Geschichte *The Antique Dealer* – die Situation der Hauptperson(en) schildert. Er kann jedoch die Spannung auch indirekt steigern, indem er eine Situation oder ein Ereignis kommentarlos darstellt. Es bleibt dem Leser überlassen, die Bedeutung der Handlung zu bewerten. Die indirekte Methode des Spannungsaufbaus ist ein wichtiges Merkmal der modernen amerikanischen Kurzgeschichte.

3. **Climax**
   Climax bezeichnet den Spannungshöhepunkt einer Erzählung, den Punkt, an dem die Situation, mit der die Hauptpersonen konfrontiert sind, gelöst wird. Der *climax* bildet einen Wendepunkt *(turning point)* im Leben der Figuren.

4. **Falling action**
   Der Schluss einer Erzählung ist durch eine abrupt abnehmende Spannung *(falling action, release of tension)* charakterisiert.

Beachten Sie: Wenn Sie einen Text erläutern, verwenden Sie wie im Deutschen immer Zeitformen des Präsens.

EXAMPLE

In the story, we **read** of Mr Price, who **is** an old antique dealer. He **lives** in a flat above his shop ...

Vergessen Sie nicht, dass das *present progressive* und das *present perfect – simple* und *progressive* – auch Zeitformen sind, die die Gegenwart ausdrücken.

EXAMPLES

Mr Price **is lying** in bed when suddenly the doorbell rings.
The man **has heard** stories of robberies at night, and this makes him nervous.
The antique dealer **has been living** alone for many years.

Am wichtigsten sind aber das *present simple* und das *present perfect simple*.

USEFUL EXPRESSIONS **Struktur/Aufbau**

the	exposition introduction	goes from line/l. ... to line/l. ...			
in the	exposition, introduction,	we	experience hear read	how	Mr Price ... the antique dealer ... the protagonist ...
		the	author writer	sets the scene by	saying ... ...
line ... to line ... is		characterised marked	by	rising action falling action	
the tension a sense of danger		begins to	build up increase decrease fall	as we	hear read	that ...
the	climax highest point turning point	is	achieved reached	between line ... and line ...	
the	last ... lines concluding part final section	are characterised is marked	by	falling action a release of tension	

USEFUL VOCABULARY **Setting und Gemütszustand**

afraid, dark, foggy, frightened, frightening, gloomy, heavy, isolated, lonely, loud, mysterious, nervous, persistent, safe, shadowy, small, strong, threatening, valuable, ...

antique, article, doorbell, lock, Saturday night, safe *(Tresor)*, shop, shutters, ...

attack sb, be broken into, be robbed, echo, feel, frighten, hide, lie (awake), make sb/sth out, remember, ring, think (nervous thoughts), wonder, ...

C Arbeitsblatt

1. Describe the setting of the story.

The setting of the story is

2. Describe Mr Price's feelings. When does the writer make use of explicit characterisation and when does he use implicit characterisation?

The writer tells us about Mr Price's state of mind by both _____ *and* _____ *characterisation.*

3. From whose point of view is the incident described? Who tells the reader the story?

4. By using the line numbers, try and find the structure of the story: exposition – rising action – climax/turning point – falling action.

exposition: ll. _____ – _____

rising action: ll. _____ – _____

climax: ll. _____ – _____

falling action: ll. _____ – _____

4 Atmosphäre in fiktionalen Texten

A Text und Aufgaben

Dieser Text ist ein Auszug *(extract)* aus *Life at the Top* von John Braine. Der Roman *(novel)* wurde 1962 als Fortsetzung der Geschichte von Joe Lampton veröffentlicht, die in Braines erstem Roman *Room at the Top* (1957) begonnen wurde.
Joe, der aus einfachen Verhältnissen stammt, heiratet Susan, die Tochter eines erfolgreichen Unternehmers. Joe bekommt eine Stelle in der Firma seines Schwiegervaters. Dank des Geldes seiner Frau wohnt er im besten Viertel der Stadt. Er wird Mitglied im Golfclub und wechselt auch seine politische Partei. Trotzdem wird Joe nicht glücklich. Er ist unzufrieden in seiner Ehe, die nur scheinbar funktioniert. Sein Sohn, privat erzogen an einer teuren Schule auf Kosten der Großeltern, verachtet ihn. Die Arbeit bei seinem Schwiegervater erfüllt ihn auch nicht: Jeder weiß ja, wie und warum er seine Stelle als Chef der Buchhaltung bekam. Endlich erkennt Joe, dass seine frühere Überzeugung, dass der Besitz von Geld kulturelle und klassenbedingte Unterschiede überbrücken kann, falsch war.
In diesem Auszug macht Joe einen Abendspaziergang durch die Stadt. Er denkt über sein Leben nach.

Life at the top (*extract*)

After about half an hour of fast walking I began to enjoy myself. It was a long time since I'd walked in the rain, a long time since I'd walked around Warley; and longer still, it seemed, since I'd been alone.

I found myself standing by the bridge in Snow Park watching the river. It was swollen [1] with the last two days of heavy rain; another day like today, I thought dreamily, and it would burst its banks [2]. I pulled my hat down farther over my eyes. There was something profoundly [3] satisfactory about the idea of a flood [4], of the black cold water engulfing [5] first the park, then the town. It wouldn't happen; it couldn't happen because the town was too high above the river, but it ought to happen; the river had its rights as the town had, the black cold water eddying [6] and swirling [7] under the iron bridge was alive as the town was alive.

The guard rail [8] was waist-high [9]; I leaned over it, the iron cold under my hands. There was a gas lamp at the entrance to the bridge; I could see the rain dimpling [10] the water. To my left I could see only the vague outline [11] of Warley Forest; to my right the trees on the skyline hid the bandstand and the tennis courts. I was alone watching the river, the trees around me, and now, by some trick of light, the water appeared not black but silver. It was flowing [12], flowing between the trees, flowing away from the town, flowing to wherever rivers flow to, but flowing away. And now the wind was stronger; I could catch the smell of the river, rank [13], canine [14], a mastiff [15] coming out of the darkness.

287 words

1 swollen = angeschwollen, 2 burst its banks = über seine Ufer treten, 3 profoundly = (geistig) tief,
4 flood = Überschwemmung, 5 (to) engulf = *(fig.)* verschlingen, 6 (to) eddy = strudeln,
7 (to) swirl = herumwirbeln, 8 guard rail = Brückengeländer, 9 waist-high = hüfthoch,
10 (to) dimple = sich kräuseln, 11 outline = Umriss, 12 (to) flow = strömen, 13 rank = sauer,
14 canine = wie Hunde, 15 mastiff = englische Dogge, eine Art Kampfhund

ASSIGNMENTS

1. Describe what happens in the extract.
2. Read the description of a) Snow Park and b) the river. Give your own impression of these places.
3. Looking at both the introduction to the text and the extract from the novel, describe Joe Lampton's appearance and mood.
4. Point out how the author establishes a unity of place and person. Support your opinion by quoting from the text.

B Praktische Hilfe und Arbeitsschritte

In der Literatur ist das Verhältnis zwischen dem Handlungsort *(setting)* und der/den Hauptperson(en) oft wichtig. Der Autor kann entweder über die Beschreibung des Ortes den Gemütszustand *(state of mind)* der Person(en) widerspiegeln oder – weniger häufig – einen Kontrast darstellen, um den Gemütszustand der Person(en) hervorzuheben. Dieses Wechselspiel zwischen Handlungsort und Hauptperson(en) bestimmt den Hintergrund der Atmosphäre eines fiktionalen Textes.

Methode

Schritt 1: Betrachten Sie zunächst den **Ort der Handlung** genauer. Diese Leitfragen werden Ihnen dabei helfen:

1. Findet die Handlung drinnen *(indoors)* bzw. in einem begrenzten Raum *(within a very limited area)* oder draußen *(outdoors)* statt?
2. Wann findet die Handlung statt? Zu welcher Jahreszeit? Zu welcher Tageszeit?
3. Wie ist das Wetter? Betrachten Sie die Lichtverhältnisse und die Temperatur besonders genau.
4. Sind andere Personen anwesend? Wenn ja, sind sie fröhlich und aktiv oder zeigen sie eher eine bedrückte, passive Stimmung?
5. Werden Tiere erwähnt? Wenn ja, was sind das für Tiere? Haustiere? Nutztiere? Wildtiere? Wie wird das Tier normalerweise charakterisiert?

In der folgenden Tabelle finden Sie ein paar Ideen, die einen Anhaltspunkt bieten können.

GOOD TO KNOW **Handlungsort – Gemütszustand**

Beschaffenheit	Mögliche Bedeutung
Raum	
stark begrenzt	Gedanken der Person eher nach innen und auf sich selbst gerichtet; Person fühlt sich eingeengt/isoliert
unbegrenzt	Gedanken und Wahrnehmung der Person eher nach außen und auf andere gerichtet; Person fühlt sich frei, ihren Weg selbst zu bestimmen
Zeit [1]	
Frühling/Sommer/Tag	Gemütszustand eher optimistisch und zukunftsorientiert
Herbst/Winter/Nacht	Person eher pessimistisch, nachdenklich, bedrückt, vergangenheitsorientiert
Wetter	
stürmisch	erregte, oft unbeherrschbare Gefühle; extrem emotionsbetont
neblig, wolkig	unklare, verschwommene Gedanken bzw. Gefühle; unsicher, bedrohlich
kühl, regnerisch	gefühlskalt; zurückhaltend; wenig Verständnis – oder Interesse – für die Gefühle und Belange anderer Menschen
Schnee, Eis	menschliche Isolation; Unfähigkeit, eine menschliche Beziehung einzugehen bzw. aufzubauen; neigt dazu, die Situation anderer Menschen misszuverstehen oder zu verkennen; egozentrisch; starke Neigung zur Selbsttäuschung
sonnig, trocken	fröhlich; herzlich; verständnisvoll
Personen [2]	
spielende Kinder	Unschuld; Arglosigkeit; Harmlosigkeit; Unverdorbenheit
fröhliche Menschen	Fröhlichkeit; Ausgelassenheit; frei von Sorgen/Kummer
zurückhaltende Menschen	Schüchternheit; oft beobachtend
herumlungernde Menschen	Langeweile; Oberflächlichkeit; Trägheit
aggressive Menschen	Gewalt; Drohung, Aggression; triebhaft

Beschaffenheit	Mögliche Bedeutung
Tiere[2]	
Haustiere	Treue; Abhängigkeit; Geduld; Menschenersatz; Ausgleich für fehlende menschliche Kontakte/Wärme
Nutztiere	Ausnutzung; mangelnde Wärme; Unfreiheit; Bevormundung; Stumpfsinnigkeit
Wildtiere	Freiheit; Selbstbestimmung; Entfaltung

1 Achten Sie hier darauf, dass gerade die Zeit einer Handlung oft **kontrastiv** als Betonungsmittel verwendet wird. (Eine Person, die an einem schönen Frühlingstag traurig ist, wirkt trauriger als jemand, der sich an einem grauen, nasskalten Wintertag so fühlt.)

2 Personen und Tiere, die eine reine Statistenrolle spielen, können entweder den Gemütszustand der Hauptperson(en) widerspiegeln oder ihn kontrastiv hervorheben *(highlight)*. Besonders bei Tieren wird deren hervorstechendes Merkmal häufig verwendet, um menschliche Einstellungen, Motivationen und Vorhaben zu verdeutlichen und zu untermalen.

Schritt 2: Jetzt schauen Sie sich die **Hauptperson(en)** genauer an.

1. Wie ist die äußere Erscheinung (Kleidung, Gesichtsausdruck, Körperhaltung)?
2. Wie würden Sie den Gemütszustand der Person(en) beschreiben? Fröhlich und ausgelassen? Verstimmt? Nachdenklich? Euphorisch? Optimistisch oder pessimistisch? Zukunftsorientiert oder in der Vergangenheit verhaftet?

▷ Ideen und Anregungen finden Sie beim Sprachmaterial unten.

Schritt 3: Nun geht es darum, diese zwei Elemente, also

1. die Beschaffenheit des Handlungsortes und
2. den Gemütszustand der Hauptperson(en), zusammen zu betrachten.

Die Leitfragen dabei heißen:

1. Wo gibt es Ähnlichkeiten oder Gemeinsamkeiten?
2. Wo gibt es Unterschiede oder Kontrastmomente?

Um diese Leitfragen zu beantworten, vergleichen Sie die Adjektive und andere Formen der Beschreibung *(similes, metaphors)*, die Sie bei der Bearbeitung der Schritte 1 und 2 oben gesammelt haben. Ziel ist es, sinnverwandte Wörter/Ausdrücke *(synonyms)* und Wörter/Ausdrücke von gegenteiliger Bedeutung *(antonyms)* zu identifizieren. Dies geht am einfachsten anhand einer Gegenüberstellung in Listenform. Links listen Sie die Beschaffenheiten des Handlungsortes auf, rechts tragen Sie die Personenmerkmale entsprechend ein, wie in der folgenden Tabelle gezeigt.

Handlungsort	Person(en)	
	ähnlich	gegenteilig

Schritt 4: Nach dieser Vorbereitung sind Sie jetzt in der Lage, die Atmosphäre der Geschichte oder des Vorganges näher zu bestimmen. Sehen Sie sich das Sprachmaterial unten an, nicht nur um eigene Ausdrucksmöglichkeiten zu erweitern, sondern auch um Ideen und Anregungen zu bekommen.

USEFUL EXPRESSIONS **Handlungsort und Hauptpersonen**

Allgemein verwendbares Material *(transport vocabulary)*

at the beginning in the middle at the end	of the	extract, passage, text,	we the reader	hear(s) read(s) get(s) the impression	that ...

in line ...	it says the reader is told we are told	that ...

between line ... and line ... the	author writer	tells	us ... the reader ...

the ... is	compared with a ... contrasted to ...

the	author writer	establishes a	connection relationship	between ... and ...
		draws a parallel		

the	mood state of mind	of the main character is	mirrored reflected	by ...

the	author writer	contrasts compares	*(Name)*'s	mood to that of ... feelings to those of ... state of mind with that of ...

(Name)'s	emotions feelings mood state of mind	is are	emphasised highlighted made clear stressed	by ...

Raum ***(space)***

the	action (chain of) event(s) series of) incident(s) story	happen(s) occur(s) take(s) place	indoors out of doors outside		
			in a	confined enclosed limited	space area

Zeit ***(time)***

the	action (chain of) event(s) (series of) incident(s) story	happen(s) occur(s) take(s) place	during the day	
			in	the evening the afternoon (the) winter June
			at	night the weekend

Wetter ***(weather)***

the weather is	chilly damp foggy frosty icy		
throughout the	course of the action episode incident	the weather is	sunny wintery misty

the	action event(s)	take(s) place happen(s)	on a	cold foggy	day in	February spring

Personen *(characters)*				
there are no other	characters people		present to be seen	
the only other	person present people		is a ..., who ... are ...	
the main character(s)	is are	alone during the	entire whole	episode incident

Tätigkeit, Körperhaltung *(activity, position of the body)*				
the	(main) character(s) women		is are	lying in bed and ... leaning over a ... and ... sitting in
(Name)				
(Name) is	sitting standing	with	lowered eyes/head rounded shoulders, fists/hands clenched	

Äußere Erscheinung *(outer/outward appearance)*							
the main character(s) *(Name)*		is are	wearing	casual clothes dirty old clothes a heavy overcoat a business suit			
we	gather (that)	he she they	is are	fat			
	hear read understand			of	average medium	build height size	
				heavily lightly	built		

(Name) is	attractive good-looking ordinary-looking plain		
(Name) is	young		
	in	early late	middle age
		her early his late	20s 40s

Gemütszustand *(state of mind)*	
(Name) is	aggressive calm deep in thought depressed full of joy happy thoughtful

Atmosphäre *(atmosphere)*			
the atmosphere is	full of	suspense foreboding	
		suppressed	aggression emotion violence
	heavy with	menace foreboding	

C Arbeitsblatt

1 Describe what happens in the extract.

2 Read the description of a) Snow Park and b) the river. Give your own impression of these places.

Snow Park:

The river:

Personal impression:

3 Looking at both the introduction to the text and the extract from the novel, describe Joe Lampton's appearance and mood.

4 Point out how the author establishes a unity of place and person. Support your opinion by quoting from the text.

5 Analyse von Gedichten

A Text und Aufgaben

Das folgende Gedicht stammt aus einer Sammlung von Gedichten über Chicago mit dem Titel *Early Moon* von Carl Sandburg. Die Sammlung wurde erstmalig 1916 veröffentlicht und ist ein gutes Beispiel für die Arbeiten amerikanischer Poeten des 20. Jahrhunderts, die Poesie einer breiteren Leserschaft zugänglich machen wollten.
Sandburg, der als Journalist bei der *Chicago Daily News* arbeitete, verwendet eine einfache, alltägliche Sprache, um vertraute und bekannte Szenen realistisch zu beschreiben.

Lost
Desolate[1] and lone
All night on the lake
Where fog trails[2] and mist creeps[3],
The whistle of a boat
Calls and cries unendingly,
Like some lost child
In tears and trouble
Hunting[4] the harbor's breast
And the harbor's eyes.

[1] desolate = verlassen, [2] (to) trail = *(hier)* ziehen, [3] (to) creep = kriechen, [4] (to) hunt = *(hier)* suchen

ASSIGNMENTS

1. Describe the scene portrayed in the poem.
2. Analyse Sandburg's use of imagery, e.g. the boat and the harbor.
3. The poem falls into three parts. Use line numbers to identify each part and explain its function.
4. Sandburg uses the stylistic devices *simile, alliteration* and *personification* to express his vision. Find an example of each.

B Praktische Hilfe und Arbeitsschritte

Gedichte unterscheiden sich von Prosa dadurch, dass sie etwas in knapper Form mitteilen möchten. Die Kürze und Bündigkeit eines Gedichts verlangt eine Sprache, die auf zwei Ebenen gleichzeitig wirksam ist: der Ebene der Oberfläche bzw. der reinen Beschreibung *(level of exterior meaning, level of apparent meaning)* und der Ebene der tieferen Bedeutung *(level of interior meaning)*.

Inwiefern - und ob überhaupt - ein Gedicht grundsätzlich formelle Merkmale wie Reimschema, Rhythmus, Metrik und eine charakteristische äußere Form aufweisen muss, bleibt umstritten. Die gängigste Meinung unter Literaturwissenschaftlern ist, dass sich Poesie von Prosa weniger durch solche traditionellen Merkmale unterscheidet als vielmehr durch die oben beschriebenen zwei Bedeutungsebenen.

Bei der Interpretation eines Gedichts geht es im Grunde also darum, a) die Bedeutungsebenen zu identifizieren und zu erläutern, b) die Intention des Dichters zu erkennen und c) die Struktur *(structure)* und Stilmittel *(stylistic devices)* zu erkennen und zu erläutern, die der Dichter verwendet, um seine Intention deutlich zu machen.

Methode

Schritt 1: Normalerweise werden Sie zuerst aufgefordert, die Oberflächenebene *(exterior meaning, apparent meaning)* zu beschreiben. Um diese Ausgabe zu erfüllen, stellen Sie genau das dar, was in dem Gedicht vordergründig steht. Versuchen Sie an dieser Stelle nicht, das Gedicht zu „interpretieren“ oder irgendwelcher Symbolik näher nachzugehen.

Schritt 2: Im zweiten Schritt müssen Sie die tiefere Bedeutung des Gedichts darlegen. Diese wird fast immer mit einem Vergleich *(comparison)* zum Ausdruck gebracht.

GOOD TO KNOW **Sinntragende Wörter und Ausdrücke**

Viele Schüler/innen finden es schwierig, den tieferen Sinn - also die Symbolik - eines Gedichts zu erkennen. Eine Methode ist, sich die sinntragenden Wörter und Ausdrücke (Substantive, Verben, Adjektiv-Substantiv-Kombinationen) genauer anzusehen. Fallen die sinntragenden Wörter und Ausdrücke eindeutig in zwei oder mehr unterschiedliche Themenbereiche oder Wortfelder? Wenn ja, gibt es irgendwelche Gemeinsamkeiten zwischen diesen Wortfeldern oder *poles*? In Sandburgs Gedicht sind die *poles boat/harbor* und *child/mother* problemlos zu erkennen.

Schritt 3: Nun sollten Sie die Stil- und Sprachmittel, die der Autor verwendet, finden und erklären. Die in der Poesie am häufigsten vorkommenden Stilmittel sind die folgenden.

1. Das ***simile*** (Gleichnis) wird immer durch *like* oder *as* eingeleitet:

   My mistress' eyes are nothing like the sun,
   Coral is far more red, than her lips' red,
   ...

   (Shakespeare, *Sonnet 130)*

2. ***Alliteration*** (Alliteration/Stabreim) heißt, dass mehrere Wörter mit gleich klingenden Anfangsbuchstaben oder -lauten beieinanderstehen. ***Assonance*** (Assonanz) ist dagegen der Gleichklang nur der Vokale (mindestens von der letzten betonten Silbe an):

What passing-bells for these who die as cattle?
Only the monstrous anger of guns.
Only the stuttering rifles' rapid rattle
Can patter out their hasty orisons.
...

(Wilfried Owen, *Anthem for Doomed Youth)*

EXAMPLE

... rifles' rapid rattle
... rapid rattle
Can patter out ...

3. ***Personification*** (Personifizierung) heißt, dass der Dichter einer Sache oder einem Ding menschliche Merkmale verleiht:

This is the Night Mail crossing the border,
Bringing the cheque and the postal order,
Letters for the rich, letters for the poor,
The shop at the corner, the girl next door.
Pulling up Beattock, a steady climb:
The gradient's against her, but she's on time.
Past cotton-grass and moorland boulder,
Shovelling white steam over her shoulder.
Snorting noisily as she passes
Silent miles of wind-bent grasses.
...

(from W. H. Auden, *Night Mail*)

▷ locomotive = woman

4. ***Repetition*** (Wiederholung) ist die bewusste Wiederholung derselben Idee oder Sprache und wird zur Betonung verwendet.

...
And gossip, gossip from all the nations,
News circumstantial, news financial,
Letters with holiday snaps to enlarge in,
Letters with faces scrawled on the margin,
Letters from uncles, cousins and aunts,
Letters to Scotland from the South of France,
Letters of condolence to Highlands and Lowlands,
Written on paper of every hue,
...

(from W. H. Auden, *Night Mail*)

5. ***Enumeration*** (Aufzählung) ist eine Auflistung von mindestens drei Personen, Sachen oder Ideen und wird ebenfalls zur Betonung verwendet:

...
Written on paper of every hue,
The pink, the violet, the white and the blue,
The chatty, the catty, the boring, the adoring,
The cold and official and the heart's outpouring,
...

(from W. H. Auden, *Night Mail*)

Schritt 4: Im abschließenden Schritt wird von Ihnen oft erwartet, dass Sie Ihre Meinung über bestimmte Aspekte des Gedichts – Form, Inhalt, Intention – frei äußern.

USEFUL EXPRESSIONS **Analyse eines Gedichts**

the poem is	devoted to ... given over to ...	
the poem	comprises ... is divided into ... is made up of ...	parts sections lines

the	introductory middle concluding	part section	extends goes	from line ... to line ...		
when the poet		says ..., writes ...,	we	are aware understand	he she	is referring to ...
the poet	compares the ... with/to a ... contrasts ... to ...					
	draws establishes	a	comparison contrast	between ... and ...		
the ... may be	assumed seen	to	represent ... stand for ...			
have suggest	a	deeper hidden interior	meaning in so far as ...			
there is an example of	alliteration enumeration	in line ... when ...				
an example of	metaphor simile	can be found in line ... when ...				
the final	sound syllable	of	every every second	line rhymes		
the poet does not	employ make use of use	complex images difficult language a rhyme scheme				
the poet	employs uses	colloquial everyday formal	language			

USEFUL VOCABULARY

look out for/search for the entrance to the harbor; try to find/make out the harbor lights
show/signal to other ships/shipping where one is going/heading/sailing
warn other ships/shipping of one's presence by sounding a whistle/foghorn
be about/deal with ordinary people/everyday events/life; describe events/scenes from everyday/ordinary/working life

C Arbeitsblatt

1. Describe the scene portrayed in the poem.

2. Analyse Sandburg's use of imagery, e.g. the boat and the harbor.

3 The poem falls into three parts. Use line numbers to identify each part and explain its function.

4 Sandburg uses the stylistic devices *simile, alliteration* and *personification* to express his vision. Find an example of each.

6 Autorenabsicht I: *narrative texts*

A Text und Aufgaben

Dieser Bericht aus der *Daily Mail*, einer britischen Boulevardzeitung, ist ein Beispiel für einen chronologischen Erzähltext *(chronological narrative text)*. Solche Texte versuchen die fünf journalistischen Fragen *(journalistic questions)* – was?, wer?, wo?, wann? und warum? – zu beantworten.
Der Bericht beschreibt, wie Kamel Bourgass dem Untersuchungsrichter vorgeführt wird. Bourgass wird vorgeworfen, den Polizisten Stephen Oake mit einem Messer getötet und vier weitere Polizisten zum Teil schwer verletzt zu haben, als sie ein Haus in Manchester durchsuchten. Hintergrund des Polizeieinsatzes war der Verdacht, Bourgass und seine Mitstreiter hätten einen terroristischen Anschlag mit hochgiftigem Rizin in London geplant.

As seven armoured[1] officers guarded him, he was calm and still

by Paul Harris

They held the man's arms so tightly in the dock[2] that he could barely move. Terrorist suspect[3] Kamel Bourgass was handcuffed[4] and restrained[5] now and there wasn't a single police officer in court who did not understand the significance[6] of that.
Four days earlier this small anonymous figure with a pouting lip[7] and staring eyes[8] was alleged[9] to have gone berserk[10] with a knife in a flat, leaving one police officer dead and four others injured. There were no handcuffs then. There was no mistake now.
The 27-year-old Algerian was appearing[11] in Britain's most secure court at Belmarsh in South London on charges[12] of murdering Special Branch Detective Constable Stephen Oake and trying to kill four other officers.
To look at him yesterday, it took some imagination[13] to picture how. He was a short, not particularly aggressive looking man and his bowed[14] head gave him an almost apologetic air[15]. You had to keep reminding yourself[16] that this was the man accused[17] of a few seconds of frenzy[18] that turned a supposedly straightforward police operation into a catastrophe. The charges told the rest of the story.
The clerk of the court read out only the rank[19] and number of each of the four officers that Bourgass is accused of attempting[20] to murder. The words fell coldly in the small court. But they read Detective Constable Stephen Oake's name aloud and Bourgass was charged with murdering him on January 14.
The 40-year-old, who was married with three children, died from multiple stab wounds[21] to his upper body and chest.
The police were searching the flat in Crumpsall, Manchester, as part of an investigation[22] into Al Qaeda links.
More than an hour after carrying out the raid, and detaining[23] three men, they suddenly made a connection with the hunt for a most-wanted suspect alleged to have

been involved in the ricin poison plot[24] that was uncovered in London last week. Yesterday - 200 miles from Manchester and a long way from his homeland - Bourgass made his first appearance[25] before magistrates[26].

He was surrounded by seven uniformed policemen, unarmed but wearing full armoured clothing. He was dressed in a Manchester police issue forensic suit, an all-in-one white paper overall with a hood drawn tightly around his head - his clothes are understood to have been sent for scientific tests. Only a glimpse[27] of short, black hair was visible beneath the top of the hood, and the face had several days' growth of stubble[28].

He was dwarfed[29] by the closest two officers as they gripped[30] his arms at the elbow. His hands, one of which is believed to have been injured, were secured[31] behind his back. He remained calm and perfectly still.

Bourgass spoke through an Arabic interpreter, and then only to give his name and confirm[32] his date of birth - May 5, 1975.

District judge Timothy Workman, who conducted the 15-minute formal hearing, was told that police were still working to confirm whether Kamel Bourgass was his real name. He made an order banning[33] photographs or sketches that might identify the defendant[34], saying they could prejudice[35] separate proceedings or police investigations.

Prosecutor[36] Susan Hemming said Bourgass had no permanent address or any form of income in the UK.

Manchester solicitor[37] Patrick Regan, defending, made no application for bail[38]. Bourgass was remanded in custody[39] to the Central Criminal Court on January 27.

555 words

1 armoured = bewaffnet, 2 dock = *(hier)* Anklagebank, 3 suspect = Verdächtige/r, 4 handcuffed = in Handschellen, 5 (to) restrain = *(hier)* bändigen, 6 significance = Bedeutung, 7 pouting lip = Schmollmund, 8 staring eyes = starrende Augen, 9 (to) allege that sb has done sth = jdm vorwerfen, etwas getan zu haben, 10 (to) go berserk = durchdrehen, 11 (to) appear = erscheinen, 12 charge = Anklage, 13 imagination = *(hier)* Vorstellungskraft, 14 bowed = gebeugt, 15 apologetic air = bedauernde Haltung, 16 (to) remind oneself = sich selbst erinnern, 17 (to) accuse = beschuldigen, 18 frenzy = Wahnsinn, 19 rank = *(hier)* Dienstgrad, 20 (to) attempt = versuchen, 21 multiple stab wounds = zahlreiche Stichwunden, 22 investigation = *(hier)* Ermittlung, 23 (to) detain = verhaften, 24 ricin poison plot = Rizingiftanschlag, 25 appearance = *(hier)* Auftritt, 26 magistrate = Untersuchungsrichter/in, 27 glimpse = kurzer Blick, 28 stubble = Stoppeln, 29 (to) dwarf = klein erscheinen neben, 30 (to) grip = festhalten, 31 (to) secure = *(hier)* fesseln, 32 (to) confirm = bestätigen, 33 (to) ban = verbieten, 34 defendant = Angeklagte/r, 35 (to) prejudice = *(hier)* beeinflussen, 36 prosecutor = Ankläger/in, 37 solicitor = Anwalt/Anwältin, 38 bail = Kaution, 39 (to) be remanded in custody = in Untersuchungshaft bleiben müssen

ASSIGNMENTS

1. Describe the sequence of events *(Reihenfolge der Ereignisse)* leading up to Kamel Bourgass's arrest in Manchester.
2. Pick out concrete details from the text. Why may the reporter have included these? What effect do they have on the reader's understanding of the event?
3. Analyse how the reporter's use of language makes it clear to the reader that this is a neutral account of a real event.

B Praktische Hilfe

Die Nummern 1–3 beziehen sich auf die Aufgabennummern oben.

1. Die Informationen, die Sie benötigen, um diese Aufgabe zu lösen, sind im ganzen Text verstreut. Zum Beispiel war die Entdeckung des Gifts Rizin in einer Londoner Wohnung das anfängliche Ereignis *(initial event)*, das den Polizeieinsatz in Manchester erst ins Rollen brachte (l. 26). Geben Sie also keine unvollständige Antwort.

2. In Erzähltexten werden konkrete Einzelheiten über Ort, Zeit, Person(en) und Beweggründe gegeben, um die Glaubwürdigkeit *(plausibility)*, die Realitätsbezogenheit *(realism)* und das Leserinteresse *(reader's interest)* zu erhöhen. Fehlen solche Einzelheiten, wirkt ein Erzähltext flach *(two-dimensional)* und farblos *(bland)*. Interessant und vielsagend ist es übrigens, solche Einzelheiten durch allgemeine Aussagen zu ersetzen.

COMPARE

- ▷ The 27-year-old Algerian was appearing in Britain's most secure court at Belmarsh in South London on charges of murdering Special Branch Detective Constable Stephen Oake and trying to kill four other officers.
- ▷ The accused was appearing in Britain's most secure court on charges of murdering a police officer and trying to kill several others.

Die zweite Aussage verstößt gegen die Grundregel, dass alle möglichen Fragen des Lesers – z. B. *Who's the accused?* und *Where's Britain's most secure court?* – beantwortet werden sollten.
Um die Frage oben zu beantworten, sollten Sie alle im Text erwähnten Einzelheiten heraussuchen und nach ihrer Art – also Ort, Zeit, Personenbeschreibung, Sachbeschreibung, Beschreibung eines Vorganges – kategorisieren. Dann beantworten Sie anhand der Information oben die weiterführenden Fragen.

❸ Der Reporter schildert die Gerichtsverhandlung und ihre Hintergründe weitgehend wertfrei. Sprachlich wird dies hauptsächlich durch die Verwendung des Passivs, z. B. „was handcuffed and restrained“ (l. 2); „was alleged to have“ (l. 5), realisiert. Das Passiv verleiht dem Bericht Objektivität, da es die Tat statt den bzw. die Täter in den Vordergrund stellt. Der Reporter äußert keine eigene Meinung zu dem Vorgang bzw. zu den angeblichen Straftaten des Angeklagten und wählt ein sachliches, wertneutrales Vokabular, um rein äußerliche Erscheinungen zu beschreiben, z. B. „... short anonymous figure with a pouting lip and staring eyes ...“ (l. 4); „... a short, not particularly aggressive looking man ...“ (ll. 11/12).

USEFUL EXPRESSIONS

in	line ... the first paragraph		of the	report article press item	
at the end					
get receive	an accurate		idea impression	of ...	
describe	people events	in detail			
give provide	details of	time place		by	saying ... describing ...
	concrete hard	information about ...			
answer possible questions satisfy the reader's curiosity		by	writing giving	an interesting report a complete picture a comprehensive account	

C Arbeitsblatt

1 Describe the sequence of events *(Reihenfolge der Ereignisse)* leading up to Kamel Bourgass's arrest in Manchester.

2 Pick out concrete details from the text. Why may the reporter have included these? What effect do they have on the reader's understanding of the event?

3 Analyse how the reporter's use of language makes it clear to the reader that this is a neutral account of a real event.

7 Autorenabsicht II: *persuasive texts*

A Text und Aufgaben

Diese ganzseitige Anzeige der britischen Reederei P&O Cruises erschien in ausgewählten britischen und irischen Zeitungen und Zeitschriften. In der Anzeige handelt es sich um die ersten Kreuzfahrten des neuen Luxusliners Adonia auf dem Mittelmeer, der Ostsee und in den norwegischen Fjorden.
Die Anzeige ist teils rein **informativ**, z. B. *departures from Southampton, brochure request line*: 0870 5 726 726, teils **instruktiv**, z. B. *to find out more call …*, und teils **überzeugend**, z. B. *Adonia, Britain's latest superline, is ready to take you on an unforgettable holiday*. Die Aussage *(message)* der Anzeige wird anhand von Grafiken und Text zum Ausdruck gebracht.
Diese Anzeige wurde gemäß der **AIDA**-Formel erstellt. Diese vier Buchstaben bedeuten *attract **A**ttention* (auf sich aufmerksam machen), *arouse **I**nterest* (Interesse wecken), *create **D**esire* (Wünsche hervorrufen) und *make **A**ction easy* (Handeln leicht machen).

A stunning[1] addition to our fleet.

D epartures from Southampton.

30% **O** ff bookings made before the end of February.

N o children on board.

I naugural season[2].

A brochure request line: 0870 5 726 726

Adonia, Britain's latest superliner, is ready to take you on an unforgettable holiday. Enjoy the best in live music at the 'All That Jazz' bar, relax[3] with a magazine and a capuccino in the 'Easy Like a Sunday' lounge or swim in one of Adonia's four pools.

This summer you can be one of the first to experience[4] life on this superb super-liner as she takes in the best of the Mediterranean, the Baltic and the Fjords. To find out more call our brochure line quoting[5] reference PZ1, clip[6] the coupon or visit www.pocruises.co.uk.

Title

Forename

Surname

Address

Postcode

Telephone

Email

Post to: PO Box 66, Cleveland, BS21 7QX

Have you ever taken a cruise before?
Yes No

Have you cruised with P&O Cruises before?
Yes No

Life doesn't get much better than this. P&O Cruises

WE HAVE SET ASIDE[7] CABINS THAT ARE AVAILABLE[8] AT A DISCOUNT OF 30% ON 2012 CRUISES IF BOOKED BEFORE 28.02.12. ONCE SOLD THE FARE WILL REVERT[9] TO THE NORMAL BROCHURE FARE. NOT AVAILABLE AT EVERY GRADE[10] OR ON EVERY CRUISE. SUBJECT TO AVAILABILITY[11]. ABTA V8764

1 stunning = umwerfend, 2 inaugural season = Eröffnungssaison, 3 (to) relax = entspannen, 4 (to) experience = *(hier)* erleben, 5 (to) quote = *(hier)* angeben, 6 (to) clip = *(hier)* ausschneiden, 7 (to) set aside = *(hier)* reservieren, 8 available = verfügbar, 9 (to) revert = zurückkommen, 10 grade = *(hier)* Preisstufe, 11 subject to availability = abhängig von Verfügbarkeit

ASSIGNMENTS

1. Why is it possible to say that this advertisement (ad) is a good example of the use of the AIDA formula?
2. Using two colours, underline those parts of the advertisement that are mainly informative, and those that are intended to persuade. Is it always possible to separate these two functions?
3. Some of the informative elements you have underlined are instructive, i.e. they tell the reader what to do. Show this by looking at the language.
4. How would you characterise the language of the more persuasive elements in the ad, for example "A stunning addition to our fleet" (l. 1)?

B Praktische Hilfe

Die Nummern 1–4 beziehen sich auf die Aufgabennummern oben.

1. Hier geht es darum, die vier Absichten, also 1) *attract attention*, 2) *arouse interest*, 3) *create desire* und 4) *make action easy,* zu identifizieren. Beachten Sie, dass es besonders bei den Absichten 2 und 3 zu einer gewissen Vermischung kommen kann.

2. Anzeigen können je nach Absicht und Zielgruppe in zwei Hauptgruppen unterteilt werden. Erstens gibt es Anzeigen, die einen weitgehend informativen Charakter haben. Dies gilt zum Beispiel für Kleinanzeigen, für die Anzeigen von Behörden und sehr viele Anzeigen für Freizeitveranstaltungen. Natürlich hofft der Herausgeber solcher Anzeigen, das Interesse der angesprochenen Menschen zu wecken, denn sonst hätte es wenig Sinn, die Anzeige überhaupt zu schalten. Trotzdem bleibt die Information das Hauptziel.

   Bei der zweiten Gruppe steht die Absicht im Vordergrund, den Verbraucher dazu zu bringen, ein bestimmtes Produkt zu kaufen. Solche Anzeigen weisen auch informative Elemente auf, aber das wirkliche Ziel ist nicht zu informieren, sondern zu überzeugen.

   In dieser Aufgabe geht es zunächst darum, diese Elemente, also *information* und *persuasion*, zu identifizieren. Es ist nicht immer möglich, die beiden Absichten klar zu trennen. Es ist ja gerade die Kunst eines Anzeigentextes, durch geschickte Wahl von Wörtern und Grafiken das Element *persuasion* unterschwellig und versteckt arbeiten zu lassen.

❸ In der Anzeige haben einige der informativen Elemente die Funktion, dem Leser zu sagen, was er tun soll, um weitere Informationen zu erhalten. Sie sind sprachlich gekennzeichnet durch die Verwendung der Befehlsform *(the use of the imperative)* und des Stilmittels Aufzählung *(enumeration)*.

❹ Durch positive Wörter, meist Adjektive, versuchen Anzeigen ein Produkt so preisgünstig und begehrenswert wie möglich darzustellen. Die *Adonia* ist zum Beispiel „stunning" (l. 1) und mit „four pools" (l. 13) ausgestattet; Passagieren wird „an unforgettable holiday" (ll. 8/9) und „the best of live music" (l. 9) versprochen. Zur Beantwortung dieser Aufgabe sollten Sie zunächst solche positiven Adjektive und Aussagen heraussuchen und auflisten. Dann sollten Sie sagen, welchen Eindruck *(image)* der Leser dadurch von einer Kreuzfahrt auf diesem Schiff gewinnt.

USEFUL EXPRESSIONS

the elements	are	combined ill-defined unclear mixed-up	
	interact with each other		
have a	favourable positive good	impression of ...	
refer to describe	the	product user consumer	as being ...
try seek	to create give	a positive image good impression	
the	copy writer's advertisement's	use of positive	adjectives language
use	concrete hard	information	as a means of ... for the purposes of ...

C Arbeitsblatt

1 Why is it possible to say that this advertisement is a good example of the use of the AIDA formula?

2 Using two colours, underline those parts of the advertisement that are mainly informative, and those that are intended to persuade. Is it always possible to separate these two functions?

3 Some of the informative elements you have underlined are instructive, i.e. they tell the reader what to do. Show this by looking at the language.

4 How would you characterise the language of the more persuasive elements in the ad, for example “A stunning addition to our fleet” (l. 1)?

8 Autorenabsicht III: *informative texts*

A Text und Aufgaben

Im deutschen Sprachraum sind regionale Akzente weitgehend ‚neutral', d. h., sie sagen in der Regel nichts Nennenswertes aus über die soziale Herkunft oder gar Klassenzugehörigkeit des Sprechers. Im Gegenteil sind viele Menschen stolz auf ihren regionalen Akzent und auf die Besonderheiten ihres Sprachgebrauchs. Bislang war die Situation in Großbritannien ganz anders. Die englische Entsprechung von Hochdeutsch – *'Received Pronunciation'* oder einfach *'RP'* – war nicht nur eine absolute Voraussetzung des beruflichen Erfolgs, sondern bestimmte auch die gesellschaftliche Stellung.
Jetzt aber hat sich die Situation verändert. *RP* hat zugunsten regionaler Akzente, die von der Wirtschaft wegen ihrer höheren Kundenakzeptanz zunehmend bevorzugt werden, an Ansehen verloren. Diese Veränderung ist jedoch nicht ohne Probleme. Da britische Akzente oft stark von *RP* abweichen, werden sie außerhalb Großbritanniens – wo in Schulen durchweg *RP* gelernt wird – nur schwer oder gar nicht verstanden. Daher die wachsende Beliebtheit von Sprachtrainern, die versuchen, zumindest die ‚Höhen und Tiefen' regionaler Akzente zu glätten.

We want to talk proper [1]

Why so many British people are taking elocution lessons [2]

NOW that Britain's public-school elite [3] is in retreat [4], is the way it talks disappearing too? For years social levellers [5] have been celebrating the decline of Received Pronunciation (RP), the clipped, cut-glass way of talking often known as Oxford or BBC English. Once the confident [6] accent of the ruling class, it is now, supposedly, attracting contempt [7] rather than respect.
But it's not as simple as that. Certainly, RP, as it once was, no longer rules. The BBC likes to use regional accents; in Hollywood, a posh [8] British accent is a cliché for brutality, arrogance and stupidity [9]. Consumers [10] no longer see it as a sign of trustworthiness [11] and authority. Peter Trudgill, a leading sociolinguist, says that some call centres prefer [12] regional accents to RP because of the negative reactions RP arouses [13]. Although there is little solid [14] research, linguists think that RP speakers may have fallen from 5% of the population to less than 3%. "There may well be more RP speakers abroad than here," says David Crystal, the country's best-known authority on the English language.
And RP has changed. Today's version is closer to accents that were once thought plebeian [15]. The queen's mother spoke differently from the way she talks. Princess Diana's speech was different again – closer to the general southern accent sometimes called 'Estuary English' [16]. Modern RP includes, for example, some glottal stops – an example is 'Gatwick' pronounced without the 't'.
Yet (...) there is a large and growing demand for 'better' speech. Ann Jones, the general secretary of the Society of Teachers of Speech and Drama, estimates that more

than 10,000 people take elocution lessons every year. "In the last five or six years it's really taken off," she says. Her members (...) have as much work as they want. The director of the London Language and Drama School, Sarah Mann, says that all speech training courses are full, and some 200 people are paying £45 ($71) an hour for one-on-one coaching.

Most people taking lessons are not trying to learn classic RP, but to make their verbal skills match their other business tools - such as the visuals in a slide presentation. A typical aim is to dilute[17] regional accents to the point that they will be readily understood by people from elsewhere. Ms Mann says that it can take as little as six one-hour lessons to help a motivated student to replace glottal stops with 't's in words like 'water', and to pronounce a missing 'l' in words such as 'old', 'cold' and 'gold'.

She does not necessarily try to eliminate[18] regional accents as long as the speaker learns to eliminate 'lazy' speech such as slurring, and annoying verbal tics[19], such as 'know what I mean?', 'sort of' or 'like'. "You can get away with[20] even quite a marked accent if you are an interesting speaker (...)," she says.

There is a strong business case for all this. A survey of company directors by the Aziz Corporation, which calls itself the country's leading independent spoken communications consultancy, says that 31% think that a strong regional accent is a disadvantage in business.

But why the growth in demand? One reason is globalisation. Foreigners typically learn RP, or something like it, and are often mystified[21] by Britain's stronger regional dialects. Dealing with them means speaking some sort of standard English.

A second reason is the growing emphasis on better presentation skills in business. Managers who are willing to spend a lot of money on public relations, speech writers, coaches and so on are more likely to want their Ps and Qs fixed too.

A third reason is changes within companies. Jayne Comins, a speech coach in London, notices a big increase in clients with a computing background. "Talking's not what they are really about," she says. "A lot of men in IT didn't start out wanting a job working with people, but when they become successful they often have to talk at board meetings[22], give presentations and sell their product."

661 words

1 (to) talk proper = richtig sprechen, 2 elocution lessons = Sprechunterricht, 3 public-school elite = auf Privatschulen erzogene Führungsklasse, 4 in retreat = auf dem Rückzug, 5 social leveller = Verfechter/in des Egalitarismus, 6 confident = selbstbewusst, 7 contempt = Verachtung, 8 posh = vornehm, 9 stupidity = Dummheit, 10 consumer = Verbraucher/in, 11 trustworthiness = Vertrauenswürdigkeit, 12 (to) prefer = bevorzugen, 13 (to) arouse = erwecken, 14 solid = *(hier)* fundiert, 15 plebeian = plebejisch, 16 Estuary English = ursprünglich der in der Themsemündung gesprochene Dialekt, jetzt in ganz Südostengland, 17 (to) dilute = *(hier)* entschärfen, 18 (to) eliminate = beseitigen, 19 tic = Eigenart, 20 (to) get away with sth = *(hier)* sich etwas erlauben können, 21 mystified = verwirrt, 22 board meeting = Vorstandssitzung

ASSIGNMENTS

1. Say how British people's perception *(Wahrnehmung)* of 'Received Pronunciation' (RP) has changed, and what effect this has had.
2. Why are the British, particularly men in the IT industry, becoming increasingly interested in taking elocution lessons?
3. What use does the writer make of linguists and speech trainers? Why do you think he or she does this?

B Praktische Hilfe

Die Nummern 1–3 beziehen sich auf die Aufgabennummern oben.

1. Nur selten ist ein Text rein informativ *(informative)*, argumentativ *(argumentative)* usw. Meistens können wir nur eine mehr oder minder starke Tendenz ausmachen, z. B. hauptsächlich informativ mit beurteilenden Elementen *(mainly informative with evaluative elements)*. Auch der vorhandene Text ist nicht rein informativ, obwohl die Hauptabsicht des Verfassers offensichtlich ist: den Leser über die zunehmende Beliebtheit von Sprechunterricht in Großbritannien sachlich aufzuklären.

   Um diese Aufgabe zu lösen, sollten Sie
   - die wesentlichen Aussagen über den veränderten Status der früher allgemein gültigen Aussprache *(Received Pronunciation, RP)* heraussuchen und
   - die Auswirkung dieser Veränderung auf die britische Gesellschaft kurz schildern.

   Listen Sie dabei nicht bloße Informationsbrocken auf, sondern schreiben Sie einen zusammenhängenden Text. Möchten Sie wörtlich zitieren, dann achten Sie darauf, dass Sie nur den wirklich relevanten und zutreffenden Teil einer Aussage wiedergeben. Zeilenlange Zitate, in denen die eigentliche Aussage irgendwo „begraben" ist, gehen meistens an der Fragestellung vorbei. Beachten Sie auch, dass Ihre Lösung streng textbezogen bleiben soll – also nicht Ihre eigene Meinung zu dem Sachverhalt enthalten darf. Verwenden Sie aber möglichst eigene Worte und Formulierungen.

2. Hier gelten dieselben Hinweise wie unter 1 oben. Beachten Sie aber, dass die Informationen, die Sie für eine vollständige Antwort benötigen, an unterschiedlichen Stellen im Text zu finden sind.

3. Der Verfasser ist Journalist. Um seinem Bericht eine gewisse Autorität und Glaubwürdigkeit zu verleihen, zitiert er entweder direkt ("...") oder indirekt einige Linguisten und

Sprachtrainer, die er meist namentlich mit Angaben zu ihrer Tätigkeit bzw. Stellung erwähnt. In Presseberichten werden wertende Aussagen bzw. Behauptungen des Autors typischerweise unmittelbar durch eine Expertenmeinung untermauert (s. z. B. II. 9–10). Um Frage 3 zu beantworten, suchen Sie zunächst alle direkten und indirekten Zitate in der Reihenfolge ihres Vorkommens heraus. Danach identifizieren Sie die Aussagen des Verfassers, die durch die Zitate gestützt werden. Schließlich sagen Sie, welche Wirkung dies auf den Leser haben mag (s. Absatzbeginn).

USEFUL VOCABULARY

(to) alter/change one's opinion/perception/view of sth

(to) become an object of contempt/criticism/ridicule

(to) be despised

(to) no longer be held in respect/be respected

(to) create/give rise to a negative reaction

(to) prefer regional accents/dialects

(to) find sth less threatening/more pleasant/more trustworthy

(to) be more complex/complicated

(to) not be as simple/straightforward as it sounds

(to) take a more differentiated approach

(to) improve one's spoken language/verbal skills

(to) express oneself/speak more clearly/understandably

(to) enunciate/pronounce words clearly

(to) correct/get rid of glottal stops such as the ... in words like ...

(to) find it difficult/hard to understand sb

(to) need a standard form of language like High German/...

(to) do sth for good/sound business reasons

(to) be another/further result of globalisation

C Arbeitsblatt

1. Say how British people's perception *(Wahrnehmung)* of 'Received Pronunciation' (RP) has changed, and what effect this has had.

2. Why are the British, particularly men in the IT industry, becoming increasingly interested in taking elocution lessons?

3. What use does the writer make of linguists and speech trainers? Why do you think he or she does this?

9 Autorenabsicht IV: *instructive texts*

A Text und Aufgaben

Dieser Text ist ein Auszug aus der Bedienungsanleitung für einen DVD-Receiver. Der Verfasser verwendet die Befehlsform (Imperativ), um dem Benutzer zu sagen, wie er den DVD-Player, die Lautsprecherboxen und das TV-Gerät an den Receiver anschließen soll. Achten Sie auf die gelegentliche Verwendung des Passivs. Trotzdem verleiht der Gebrauch der Kurzform - z. B. *you're, doesn't* - dem Text einen fast ungezwungenen Ton *(conversational tone)*.

Quick Start Guide [1]

1) Hook up [2] **your DVD player, speakers, subwoofer and TV.**

First, look on the back of your DVD player and figure out [3] if it has an optical output [4] (if you're not sure, consult [5] the manual [6] that came with your DVD player). If it does, hook up your DVD player to this receiver with this digital terminal. If your DVD player doesn't have an optical digital output, hook the player up with the analog terminals. Then, hook up the speakers you want to use with this receiver. This receiver can be used with just two speakers but it's better to have five speakers to get accurate [7] surround sound [8]. See *page 14* for more details on connecting [9] your speakers. Next, hook up your powered subwoofer if you have one. For all speakers make sure to connect the positive (+) and negative (–) terminals on the receiver and speakers with the same wire (positive to positive, negative to negative).

Before hooking up your speakers affix [10] the colour-coded sticker with the appropriate [11] name (for example, "front right") to the speaker wire so you always know which speaker that wire is connected to.

While pressing down [12] the speaker tab [13] push the speaker wire into the terminal and release [14] the speaker terminal tab.

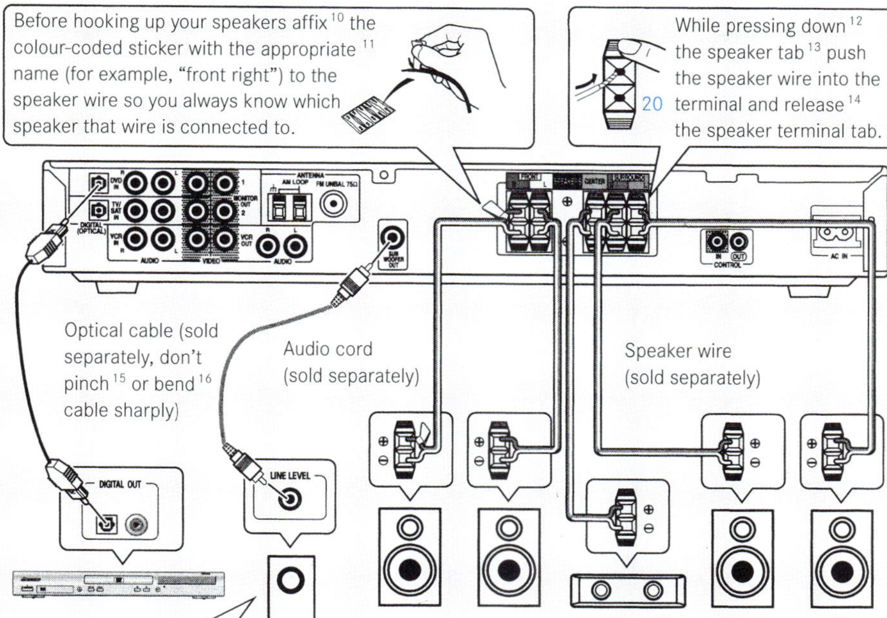

When you're hooking up your subwoofer make sure its power cord [17] is disconnected.

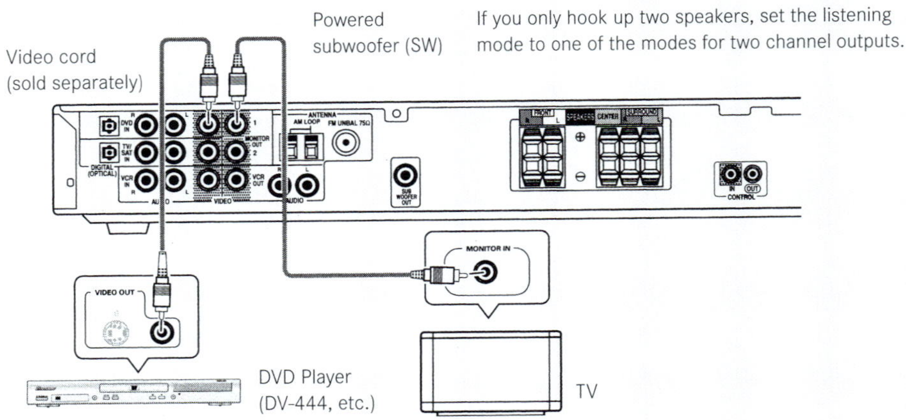

Lastly, hook up your DVD player to the DVD IN VIDEO and your TV to the MONITOR OUT VIDEO terminals as shown above.

Automatic speaker setup (receiver automatically configures [18] Front, Center Surround speakers and Subwoofer)
Once you have completed the above tasks, the receiver will automatically detect [19] which speakers you have connected and configure your speaker settings according to that. You don't have to do anything. This setup establishes [20] the size and configuration of the speaker system you have connected and is the easy way to set up your speakers for surround sound. If you don't have surround speakers or want to make more exact speaker settings, you should go to *page 25*.

394 words

1 Quick Start Guide = Kurzanleitung, 2 (to) hook up = anschließen, 3 (to) figure out = *(hier)* feststellen, 4 optical output = optischer Ausgang, 5 (to) consult = *(hier)* lesen, 6 manual = Bedienungsanleitung, 7 accurate = *(hier)* voll, 8 surround sound = Surroundklang, 9 (to) connect = anschließen, 10 (to) affix = anbringen, 11 appropriate = *(hier)* entsprechend, 12 (to) press down = nach unten drücken, 13 speaker tab = Lautsprecherklemme, 14 (to) release = *(hier)* loslassen, 15 (to) pinch = *(hier)* einklemmen, 16 (to) bend = knicken, 17 power cord = Stromkabel, 18 (to) configure = konfigurieren, 19 (to) detect = *(hier)* feststellen, 20 (to) establish = *(hier)* festlegen

ASSIGNMENTS

1. Looking at the language, show that this is an instructive text.
2. A friend has lost the operating instructions for his or her DVD receiver. Write down what you would say to your friend when telling him or her how to connect up the equipment. Then compare the language you have used with that of the written operating instructions.

B Praktische Hilfe

Die Nummern ❶ und ❷ beziehen sich auf die Aufgabennummern oben.

❶ Diese Bedienungsanleitung für einen DVD-Receiver ist rein informativ in Form von Instruktionen. Was sind die sprachlichen Merkmale solcher Texte?

- ▷ Verwendung der **Befehlsform** (des Imperativs): ***Hook up*** *your DVD player*, ...
- ▷ Verwendung des **Passivs**, wenn beschrieben wird, was mit einem Gerät gemacht werden kann/soll: *This* ***receiver can be used*** *with ...*
- ▷ Gebrauch des Stilmittels **Aufzählung** *(enumeration)*: *first, then, next, before, ...*
- ▷ Verwendung von **Zeichnungen** *(drawings)*, oft mit **Abkürzungen** *(abbreviations)*
- ▷ Verwendung von **drucktechnischen Mitteln** wie Fettdruck *(bold)*, Kursivdruck *(italics)*, Versalien *(upper case)* usw.

USEFUL VOCABULARY

be clearly/unmistakably ... because ...
express ... by ...
know sth because of .../on account of ...
make use of bold type/dashes/italics/symbols ...
writer's use of ...

❷ Wenn Sie Freunden erklären möchten, wie sie ihren DVD-Receiver bedienen müssen, würden Sie bestimmt eine andere Sprache als die der schriftlichen Bedienungsanleitung wählen. Hier sind einige Vorschläge, um Ihnen bei der Umschreibung des Textes zu helfen:

- ▷ Statt der Befehlsform können Sie Strukturen wie *You have to/must ..., You should ..., It's a good idea to ...* usw. verwenden.

- ▷ Statt des Passivs verwenden Sie das **Aktiv**, da es weniger formell und verbindlicher klingt: *This receiver can be used with ... → You can use this receiver/it with ...*

- ▷ Verwenden Sie immer wieder Ausdrücke, mit denen Sie **Anweisungen strukturieren** können, um die Reihenfolge der einzelnen Schritte zu erklären, z. B. *To begin with ...,*
First of all ..., After (you've done) that you ...,
Then you ..., Now you can ..., Finally/Last of all you ...

▷ Benutzen Sie nach Möglichkeit eine **zwanglose Sprache**, die Sie auch in Gesprächen verwenden würden.

USEFUL VOCABULARY

Wörter, die Aufmerksamkeit erregen *(attention catchers)*, wie *Look, ...; Listen, ...; Now then, ...*

kurze Rückfragen *(check questions)* wie *..., okay?; ..., all right?; ..., got it?*

Frageanhängsel *(question tags)* wie *..., isn't it?; ..., has it?*

einleitende Wörter *(introductory words)* wie *Well, ...; Now, ...*

▷ Wählen Sie statt quasitechnischer Sprache eine **alltägliche Ausdrucksweise**, z. B.: *consult* → *look at, affix* → *stick, appropriate* → *right, release* → *let go*

C Arbeitsblatt

1 Looking at the language, show that this is an instructive text.

2 A friend has lost the operating instructions for his or her DVD receiver. Write down what you would say to your friend when telling him or her how to connect up the equipment. Then compare the language you have used with that of the written operating instructions.

10 Autorenabsicht V: *argumentative texts*

A Text und Aufgaben

In folgendem Beitrag aus der *Times* berichtet der Fachredakteur für Erziehungsfragen Glen Owen über einen angekündigten Vortrag von Dr Giles Mercer, dem Vorsitzenden des Verbandes der privaten katholischen Schulen *(Catholic Independent Schools Conference)*.
Dr Mercer ist der Überzeugung, dass die Trivialität und Einseitigkeit *(one-sidedness)* des britischen Fernsehangebotes für Jugendliche – das im Wesentlichen aus Soaps, Popmusik und Quizsendungen besteht – eine gesellschaftliche und politische Bedrohung darstellt. Das Fehlen von Sendungen, die sich mit Tagespolitik *(politics of the day)* und aktuellen Fragen *(current events)* jugendnah befassen, bedeutet, dass eine ganze Generation quasi ihres Wahlrechts beraubt wird *(become disenfranchised)*.

TV trivia is our weakest link [1], says head
by Glen Owen, Education Correspondent

Programmes such as *The Weakest Link* are damaging pupils and threatening [2] the stability of society says the headmaster of a leading Catholic school.
Giles Mercer, Headmaster of Prior Park College in Bath and chairman of the Catholic Independent Schools [3] Conference, believes that teachers are being forced [4] to work overtime to undo the damage done to pupils by 'mindless' [5] television.
"In the media-driven world of popular entertainment, random [6] facts, rather than deeper understanding, are at a premium [7] – literally so in endless game shows such as *The Weakest Link* and *Who Wants to be a Millionaire?*," he will say at the conference in Bournemouth later today.
"As well as these trivial programmes, 'list mania' rages [8]: top tens, rich lists, poor lists, what's in, what's out, even a list of so-called Greatest Britons, none of whom can be compared [9] to any of the others.
"Together with soaps and other undemanding [10] entertainment, they make up a large part of the viewing diet. They are not balanced by serious news and political programmes designed to attract teenagers."
He worries that the BBC, which makes *The Weakest Link* presented by Anne Robinson, and ITV, which shows *Who Wants to be a Millionaire?* presented by Chris Tarrant, risk spawning [11] a generation of disenfranchised [12] school-leavers.
"Our schools will have to work increasingly hard to compensate for this vacuum in helping our young people to make well-informed judgements about the world around them and to avoid [13] the temptation [14] of becoming passive and cynical about politics."
Dr Mercer believes that broadcasters should engage [15] the interest of teenagers by designing more topical [16] programmes for them. "There seems to be nothing between the BBC's *Newsround*, designed for nine-to-ten year olds, and *Panorama*, for adults.

Teenagers are very worried about the state of the world - things like terrorism, pollution and homelessness [17] - but there is nothing to satisfy this."
He admits [18] that a few programmes do stimulate and broaden [19] pupils' minds and points to *The Life of Mammals* on the BBC as an example.
"If they can do programmes like that with natural history, then they should be able to do it in the political sphere [20]. But my fear is that the mindless ones have taken root [21]. Parents are very worried."
"Voter apathy, especially among the young, is surely one of the biggest political dangers we face. The failure to educate the young to think well for themselves risks creating [22] a vacuous [23] and unstable society."
"Many young people no longer believe in rebellion, but don't believe in conforming [24] either. They don't believe in the protest culture [25], but don't really want meaningless [26] pop either." John Dunford, the general secretary of the Secondary Heads Association, agreed.
"When surveys [27] are carried out into the amount of time pupils spend watching television, teachers are horrified [28] by the results," he said. "And it is the poor quality, as much as the large quantity, which bothers [29] them."
A recent survey found that children aged under 18 watch an average of two-and-a-half hours of television every day, and 36 per cent of under-4s and 52 per cent of under-16s have a television in their bedroom.
Neither Celador, which makes *Millionaire*, nor the BBC wanted to respond [30].

525 words

1 weakest link = schwächstes Glied, 2 (to) threaten = bedrohen, 3 independent school = Privatschule, 4 (to) force = zwingen, 5 mindless = geistlos, 6 random = zufällig, 7 at a premium = hoch im Kurs, 8 (to) rage = *(hier)* toben, 9 (to) compare = vergleichen, 10 undemanding = anspruchslos, 11 (to) spawn = hervorbringen, 12 disenfranchised = ohne Wahlrecht, 13 (to) avoid = vermeiden, 14 temptation = Versuchung, 15 (to) engage = *(hier)* wecken und wach halten, 16 topical = aktuell, 17 homelessness = Obdachlosigkeit, 18 (to) admit = zugeben, 19 (to) broaden = *(fig.)* erweitern, 20 sphere = *(hier)* Bereich, 21 (to) take root = Wurzeln schlagen, 22 (to) create = schaffen, 23 vacuous = *(hier)* geistlos, 24 (to) conform = sich anpassen, 25 protest culture = Protestbewegung, 26 meaningless = bedeutungslos, 27 survey = Umfrage, 28 horrified = entsetzt, 29 (to) bother = *(hier)* beunruhigen, 30 (to) respond = *(hier)* Stellung nehmen

ASSIGNMENTS

1. According to Glen Owen, what does Dr Mercer find worrying about the present situation, and what does he think should be done about it?
2. Examine how Dr Mercer's use of language expresses the aim of the speech he intends to give before other head teachers.

B Praktische Hilfe

Die Nummern ❶ und ❷ beziehen sich auf die Aufgabennummern oben.

❶ Die Hauptabsicht eines argumentativen Textes *(argumentative text)* ist es, sich mit einem umstrittenen Thema *(controversial topic)* argumentativ auseinanderzusetzen. Daher weisen solche Texte meistens drei Elemente *(structural elements)* auf. Am Anfang der Argumentation wird die eigene Position bzw. Meinung dargestellt. Dann werden Gründe und Belege dafür möglichst überzeugend präsentiert. Am Schluss werden oft korrektive Maßnahmen vorgeschlagen.

Um die gestellte Frage zu beantworten, sollten Sie daher zunächst folgende Informationen anhand des Textes sammeln:

- ▷ Dr Mercers Meinung zu der jetzigen Situation,
- ▷ seine Begründung mit entsprechendem Beleg,
- ▷ die angebliche Auswirkung der aktuellen Situation auf britische Jugendliche und
- ▷ was dagegen unternommen werden sollte und könnte.

Wenn Sie alle relevanten Informationen gesammelt haben, verwenden Sie das Material in dem Kästchen unten, um eine vollständige und zusammenhängende Antwort zu schreiben.

USEFUL VOCABULARY

according to …/in …'s opinion/view …; mindless/trivial/vacuous TV programmes such as …; (to) damage pupils; (to) act against the interests of/threaten society; (to) be forced to do sth; (to) correct/heal the damage done by sth

game show/soap/list/league table; (to) be obsessed by sth/have an obsession with sth; (to) place a high value/premium on sth; factual knowledge/deeper understanding; (to) not balance sth with sth else

(to) give rise to a situation; (to) disenfrachise sb; (to) be interested/not interested in sth; to cause apathy/lack of interest in sth; to act against a healthy democracy/…; to demand that sb does sth; to want sb to do sth

❷ Dr Mercer will seine Zuhörer von der Richtigkeit seiner Meinung überzeugen. Daher verwendet er die typische Sprache argumentativer Texte. Besonders wichtig dabei sind folgende sprachliche Mittel:

B Praktische Hilfe

- ▷ Wendungen zum Ausdruck der persönlichen Meinung wie *I think ..., in my opinion ...* usw.
- ▷ Mittel zur Betonung wie *there can be no doubt that ..., we must ..., it is clear ..., whichever way you look at it ...*
- ▷ rhetorische Fragen
- ▷ das Zitieren von Belegmaterial wie Statistiken, Zahlen usw.
- ▷ *should/ought to* als Ausdruck einer dringenden Empfehlung
- ▷ *will* (indirekte Rede: *would*), um auszudrücken, dass eine gegebene Situation mit Sicherheit in der Zukunft eintreten wird
- ▷ die Verwendung des Komparativs *(better than ..., more informed)*
- ▷ die Verwendung von Vergleichen wie *On the one hand, ... but on the other (hand) ...* usw.

Um diese Aufgabe zu lösen, sollten Sie solche Sprachmittel aus dem Text heraussuchen.

USEFUL EXPRESSIONS **Autorenabsicht und -einstellung**

the	author writer	hopes tries	to	convince persuade	the reader that ...	
(Name) tries to bring		the reader us		round to	her his	point of view
(Name)	attacks calls into question makes fun of pokes fun at ridicules		the	idea notion proposition suggestion	that ... by pointing out ...	
(Name)	questions the		sense of ... wisdom of ...		by	recalling ... referring to ...
the author presents convincing			arguments evidence		to support the ...	
the writer	cites quotes	accurate data accepted authorities recognised experts			in support of ... to support his view that ...	
(Name)	employs makes use of uses	doubtful data selective evidence unconfirmed statistics			when	he she	claims ...

the author tends to	exaggerate make sweeping statements think in black and white terms					
the writer	displays expresses shows	a/an	extremely rather very	biased one-sided prejudiced unbalanced	view opinion	when …
he she	concentrates on … while			ignoring the … overlooking the fact that … forgetting …		
when *(Name)* uses	expressions language phrases words graphs			like …, it is clear that …		

USEFUL VOCABULARY

ask a rhetorical question; be convinced that …; call into question; conclude that …; doubt; draw a conclusion; emphasise a point about …; highlight an argument …; make use of …; present a case for …; question the government's policy on … by asking …/by pointing out …; refer to comparative statistics on …; stress; use; the writer's use of …

C Arbeitsblatt

1 According to Glen Owen, what does Dr Mercer find worrying about the present situation, and what does he think should be done about it?

2 Examine how Dr Mercer's use of language expresses the aim of the speech he intends to give before other head teachers.

11 Grafiken beschreiben und deuten

A Grafik und Aufgaben

Die Marktforschung über die Wirksamkeit von Callcentern zeigt, dass Kunden auf regionale Akzente unterschiedlich reagieren. Einige Akzente werden als relativ oder sogar sehr vertrauenswürdig empfunden, während andere eher Misstrauen hervorrufen. Das Diagramm unten stellt dar, von welchem Prozentanteil der Befragten zehn regionale und nationale Akzente englischer Sprache als vertrauenswürdig empfunden werden.

Speak up

Accents perceived[1] as very/fairly honest, 2002, %

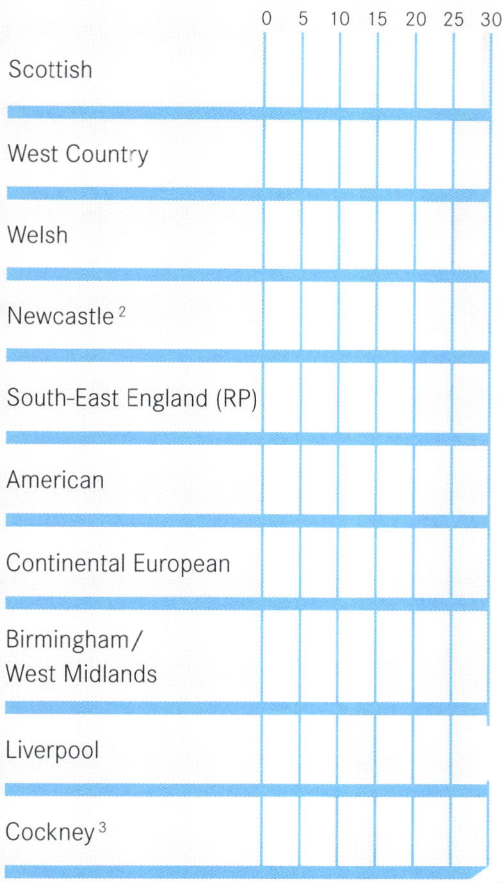

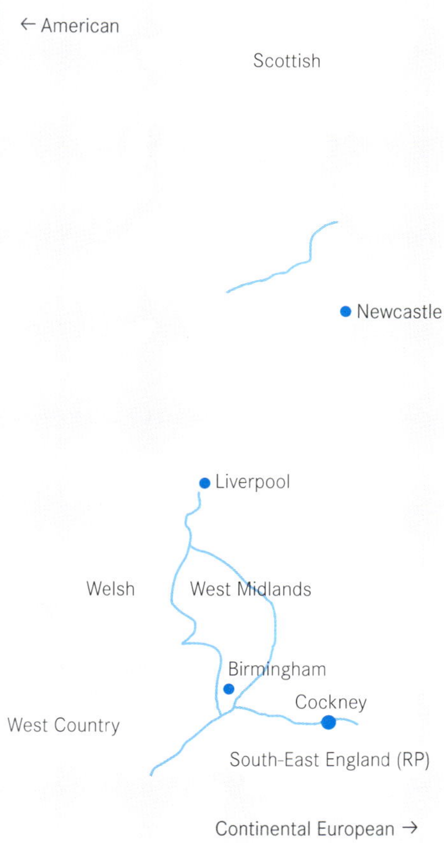

1 (to) perceive = wahrnehmen,
2 Newcastle = Hafenstadt in Nordostengland,
3 Cockney = Ostlondoner Arbeiterdialekt

Source: Aziz Corporation

ASSIGNMENTS

❶ Describe the bar chart and say what its purpose is.
❷ Interpret the information in the bar chart.

B Praktische Hilfe

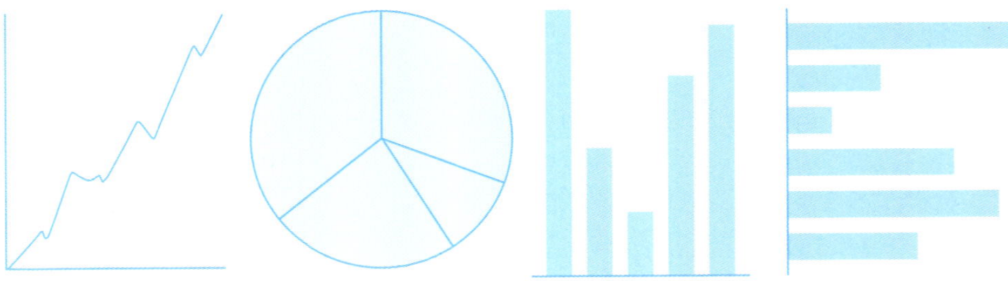

line graph, *Liniendiagramm* | pie chart, *Kreisdiagramm* | column graph, *Säulendiagramm* | bar graph, *Stabdiagramm*

Die Nummern ❶ und ❷ beziehen sich auf die Aufgabennummern oben.

❶ Um das Stabdiagramm zu beschreiben, kopieren und vervollständigen Sie den folgenden Lückentext. Versuchen Sie nicht, das Diagramm in irgendeiner Weise zu interpretieren.

The bar chart compares ____ according to ____ of their users as a ____ of respondents between ____ % and ____ %. The survey was carried out by ____. The ____ compared in the ____ are, in alphabetical order, ____, ____, ____, ____, ____, ____, ____, ____, ____, and, finally, ____.

❷ Verwenden Sie das Material im Kasten, um das Stabdiagramm zu interpretieren.

USEFUL VOCABULARY

according to ...; about; approximately; circa; roughly at ... %; with ... %; from ... % to ... %

bar chart; perceived honesty; respondent; national/regional accent; leading accent; marked decrease/drop/fall; middle field/group

(to) find; (to) be followed by; (to) be made up of

C Arbeitsblatt

1 Describe the bar chart and say what its purpose is.

2 Interpret the information in the bar chart.

12 Karikaturen interpretieren

A Karikatur und Aufgaben

Je nach Quelle gibt es zurzeit zwischen sieben und zwölf Millionen illegale mexikanische Immigranten in den USA, hauptsächlich in Kalifornien und Arizona. Die große Mehrheit der „*illegals*" überquert die US-mexikanische Grenze zu Fuß oder wird in Lastwagen gegen Bezahlung hineingeschmuggelt.
Die Lösung des Problems der vielen illegalen Immigranten ist äußerst umstritten. Eine Meinung besagt, dass sie einfach zusammengetrieben und abgeschoben werden sollten, obwohl dies eine logistische und vor allem menschenrechtliche Katastrophe wäre. Am anderen Ende der Meinungsskala steht der Ruf nach einer allgemeinen Amnestie.

© Steve Kelley

(to) reclaim = zurückerobern

ASSIGNMENTS

1. Describe the cartoon.
2. Explain the message of the cartoon.

B Praktische Hilfe und Arbeitsschritte

Wir sprechen von humorvollen und politischen Karikaturen *(comic/humorous cartoons, political cartoons)*. Der erste Typ dient der Unterhaltung, der zweite – wie hier – ist eine Art politischer Kommentar.

Methode: Beschreibung

Schritt 1: Zuerst sollten Sie sich die Zeit nehmen, die Karikatur sorgfältig zu studieren und alle Einzelheiten zu erkennen. Vergessen Sie nicht, dass in politischen Karikaturen nichts zufällig oder ohne Bedeutung ist.

Schritt 2: Im zweiten Schritt beschreiben Sie die Karikatur, ohne zu versuchen, sie zu interpretieren.

Beachten Sie dabei:
Bei **Bildbeschreibungen** verwenden wir grundsätzlich eine Form des Präsens, und zwar:

- Für die **Ortsbeschreibung** *(setting)* benutzen wir das *simple present*, oft mit *there is/there are* (es gibt):

EXAMPLE

There is an immigrant family of three on the left.

- Wenn wir sagen wollen, **was in einem Bild zurzeit passiert**, benutzen wir das *present progressive*:

EXAMPLE

A white American **is pointing** his finger at the immigrants.

- Wenn wir verdeutlichen wollen, was gerade *(just)* oder neulich *(recently)* passiert ist, verwenden wir das *present perfect*:

EXAMPLE

The immigrants **have entered** the United States illegally.

USEFUL VOCABULARY	Beschreibung der Karikatur
on the right/on the left	
in the middle	
speech bubble	
white American	
Native American	
Mexican family	

Methode: Deutung

Schritt 1: Zunächst geht es darum, die Botschaft *(message)* des Karikaturisten zu identifizieren und zu erklären. Hier ist es natürlich sinnvoll, mit den sinntragenden Wörtern *(key words)* in den Sprechblasen – also *reclaim*, *illegal immigrants*, *pack* – zu arbeiten.

Schritt 2: In diesem zweiten Schritt sollten Sie versuchen, die wahrscheinliche Position des Karikaturisten zu deuten. In politischen Karikaturen können Sie davon ausgehen, dass der Karikaturist eine ablehnende bzw. kritische Haltung zum Thema hat.

USEFUL VOCABULARY	Deutung der Karikatur
(to) be the real victim *(Opfer)*	
(to) be a hypocrite *(Heuchler)*/hypocritical *(heuchlerisch)*	
(to) pick on an easy target	
(to) ridicule/hold sb up to ridicule *(Spott)*	
(to) poke fun at sb/sth	
(to) ignore the consequences of what one does	
(to) reject a policy as inhumane/antisocial	
(to) try to illuminate a situation	
(to) show a situation in a new light	

C Arbeitsblatt

1 Describe the cartoon.

2 Explain the message of the cartoon.

13 Persönliche Stellungnahme

A Text und Aufgaben

Dieser Artikel über die Risiken des menschlichen Klonens *(human cloning, the cloning of humans)* stammt von *Bionet*, einer europäischen Website, die sich naturwissenschaftlichen Themen widmet.
Der Autor ist der Meinung, dass, während die Stammzellenforschung im Interesse der Krankheitsbekämpfung in Ordnung ist, das menschliche Klonen abzulehnen ist.

Human cloning – the risks
The aim of research into human cloning has never been to clone people, or to make babies for spare parts [1]. The research aims to obtain stem cells [2] to cure disease. However, results of research into animal and human cloning for stem cells have been published and, like all scientific findings, these are available world-wide. It was inevitable [3] that one day this knowledge would be abused [4]. Now a handful of people across the world have announced that they have already cloned a baby. However, the world is still waiting for proof that a cloned baby exists. These individuals don't work for any university, hospital or other government-regulated institution. On the whole, the scientific community throughout the world has consistently [5] opposed any suggestions of cloning a baby. "The majority of published research shows that death or mutilation [6] of the clone are the most likely outcomes of mammalian cloning [7]," said John Kilner, president of the Centre for Bioethics and Human Dignity [8] in the United States.
No one is sure how far human cloning has actually gone. By April 2003 Clonaid, a company created by the Raelian sect [9], said they had already created five human baby clones. The first, Eve, was allegedly [10] born in America. A United States court has ordered Clonaid to reveal [11] the whereabouts of the American mother and cloned baby, but neither have come forward. Of the five allegedly cloned babies, none have been DNA tested to see if they really are clones of existing people.
Others around the world – for example the Italian scientist Dr. Severino Antinori – are actively trying to clone a human child. Most scientists strongly disapprove [12] of this work. He has claimed there are mothers pregnant with cloned babies, but again, no evidence has been forthcoming.
Doctors consider the risks of human cloning to be very great.
"To subject [13] human beings to cloning is not taking an unknown risk, it's knowingly harming people," Kilner said.
Most scientists agree with this. The vast majority of attempts at cloning an animal have led to deformed embryos or miscarriages [14] once implanted [15]. Most scientists argue that the few cloned animals which are born suffer from deformities which are undetectable [16] by scans and tests in the womb [17], for example defects [18] to the lining of the lungs.

In 1996, Dolly the sheep was born. She was the first animal cloned from the DNA derived from an adult sheep rather than using DNA from an embryo.
Although Dolly seems healthy enough, there were questions over whether she would age more quickly than a normal sheep. She died in February 2003 having been diagnosed with a progressive lung disease.
Dolly was the only sheep out of 277 attempts that made it to a live birth. Who would accept those odds when experimenting with human babies?
However, there are people who agree with cloning to have a child. Some may be parents who have lost a baby and want to replace[19] it, others may be people who want children of their own but can't have them in the traditional way. For example, where a man cannot produce sperm he could get his own DNA inserted into his partner's egg - creating a clone of himself.
If cloning was your only possible chance to have a child, would you use it? And who would you want to know? Could you spot a cloned child?

558 words

1 spare part = Ersatzteil, 2 stem cell = Stammzelle, 3 inevitable = zwangsläufig, 4 (to) abuse = missbrauchen, 5 consistently = konsequenterweise, 6 mutilation = Verstümmelung, 7 mammalian cloning = Klonen von Säugetieren, 8 dignity = Würde, 9 Raelian sect = extreme religiöse Sekte in den USA, 10 allegedly = angeblich, 11 (to) reveal = aufdecken, 12 (to) disapprove = missbilligen, 13 (to) subject = unterwerfen, 14 miscarriage = Fehlgeburt, 15 (to) implant = einpflanzen, 16 undetectable = unfeststellbar, 17 womb = Gebärmutter, 18 defect = (hier) Fehlbildung, 19 (to) replace = ersetzen

ASSIGNMENTS

1. Explain the author's reasons for writing and publishing the article.
2. Summarise the risks attached to the cloning of humans.
3. Give your own opinion of human cloning, explaining your reasons.

B Praktische Hilfe und Arbeitsschritte

Der abschließende Teil einer Oberstufenklausur verlangt immer eine persönliche Stellungnahme zu dem im Text behandelten Thema. Dies kann - wie hier - in Form eines Kommentars *(comment)* oder eines Lesebriefes *(letter to the editor)* sein.

Besonders bei komplexeren Themen kann sich der Prüfer auch nur auf einen Teilaspekt der Problematik beziehen. In solchen Fällen ist es äußerst wichtig, dass Sie diesen Aspekt richtig erkennen und abgrenzen und dass Sie sich ausschließlich darauf konzentrieren.

Schreiben Sie nur nicht einfach drauflos in der Hoffnung, dass Sie „irgendwo und irgendwie“ die vom Prüfer erwünschte Antwort „mit erwischen“. Die Verwendung von überflüssigem und irrelevantem Material ist vielleicht die häufigste Schwäche bei der Bearbeitung solcher Aufgaben.

Methode

Sollen Sie Ihre Meinung als Leserbrief zum Ausdruck bringen, dann beachten Sie diese Formalitäten:

- Anrede: *Sir or Madam – Further to your report on human cloning ...*
- Schlussformel: *Anna Schmidt, Düsseldorf*
- im heutigen Sprachgebrauch: kein *Dear* vor *Sir or Madam*, kein *Yours faithfully* vor Ihrem Namen.

Schritt 1: Lesen Sie sich die Fragestellung genau durch. Handelt es sich um eine breit angelegte, allgemeine Frage zum Inhalt, oder geht es nur um einen Teilaspekt?

Schritt 2: Wie stehen Sie persönlich zu dem angesprochenen Thema? Auf einem Konzeptblatt formulieren Sie eine vorläufige Aussage.

Schritt 3: Sammeln Sie Belegmaterial aus dem Text und aus anderen Quellen, die Sie vielleicht zu demselben Thema im Unterricht bearbeitet haben.

Schritt 4: Auf das Konzeptblatt schreiben Sie jetzt einen zusammenhängenden Text unter Verwendung des gesammelten Materials. Bleiben Sie dabei streng beim Thema und präsentieren Sie Ihre Argumentation nach folgendem Muster:

1. **Introduction:** Präsentation der eigenen Meinung in Form einer knappen, direkten Aussage
2. **Development:** Begründung Ihrer Meinung anhand des gesammelten Beweismaterials
3. **Conclusion:** Wiederholung der einleitenden Aussage und (sehr knappe) Zusammenfassung der wichtigsten Argumente

Achtung! Viele Schüler(innen) lassen den Schlussteil weitgehend oder gänzlich weg. Das Fehlen dieses Teils erzeugt beim Leser nicht nur den Eindruck, dass der Verfasser „mittendrin“ abgebrochen hat, sondern auch, dass er selbst von seinen eigenen Argumenten nicht besonders überzeugt ist.

Schritt 5: Überprüfen Sie sorgfältig die sprachliche Richtigkeit Ihres Textentwurfs, indem Sie ihn Satz für Satz bewusst durchlesen. Beachten Sie dabei besonders die folgenden grammatischen Punkte (sie sind die Hauptfehlerquellen):

GOOD TO KNOW – Überarbeitung des Textentwurfs

1. **Zeit:** Haben Sie das Präsens konsequent und durchgängig verwendet? Vergessen Sie dabei nicht, dass das *present perfect* ebenfalls eine Zeitform des Präsens ist. Falls Sie indirekte Rede und *if*-Sätze verwendet haben, prüfen Sie, ob Sie die richtigen Zeitformen eingesetzt haben.
2. **Wortstellung:** Die Grundstellung im Englischen ist immer S-P-O (Subjekt-Prädikat-Objekt), auch nach einem einleitenden Adverb. Überprüfen Sie insbesondere, ob die Stellung der Adverbien (*always, sometimes, never* usw.) richtig ist.
3. **Anwendung des bestimmten Artikels:** Generell wird der bestimmte Artikel im Englischen viel weniger als im Deutschen verwendet. Der klassische Fehler ist also die unnötige Verwendung des Artikels. Deshalb: *When in doubt, leave it out.*
4. **Gerundium oder Infinitiv?** Vergessen Sie nicht, dass auf bestimmte Verben je nach Bedeutung das Gerundium oder der Infinitiv folgt. Andere Verben stehen immer entweder mit dem Gerundium oder dem Infinitiv.

Schritt 6: Wenn Sie mit Ihrem Entwurf zufrieden sind, fertigen Sie die Reinschrift an. (Lassen Sie ein Drittel des Blattes als Korrekturspalte frei!)

USEFUL EXPRESSIONS – Die persönliche Meinung äußern

I am	of the opinion certain convinced		that ...					
I	believe think							
I	agree disagree	with	the author the writer *(Name)*	when	he/ she	argues asserts claims	that ...	
						expresses the	opinion view	that ...
						tries to persuade us writes	that ...	
(Name)	asserts reasons suggests		that ..., but in my		experience opinion view	he she	forgets ...	

on the one hand ..., but on the other we	may not must not should not	forget ...
my reasons are firstly ..., secondly ... and finally ...		

Einschränkende sprachliche Mittel:

as far as I	am aware, ... can see, ... have heard, ... know, ...			
broadly speaking, generally speaking, on the whole,	it is	perhaps possibly	reasonable	to say ...
the evidence seems to suggest ..., but we should consider ...				
I get the impression that ...				
I think it is safe to claim that ...				
It is often argued that ..., but we could equally well claim ...				

USEFUL VOCABULARY

The author's motive for ... is ...
Stem cell research should not be confused with ...
Mainline scientists reject the idea of ...
With research results in the public domain, maverick scientists such as ... are bound to ...
... points out that the cloning of mammals has not been easy/successful ...
The author/... gives/offers/presents the following evidence to back up/ support his opinion/view that ...

Firstly he points out that ... Secondly implanted embryos often/sometimes ... Thirdly ...

In my opinion/view, human cloning is never/sometimes acceptable/right/to be welcomed because ... I feel/think that ...

One circumstance in which human cloning could/might be acceptable is to increase the birthrate/...

C Arbeitsblatt

1 Explain the author's reasons for writing and publishing the article.

2 Summarise the risks attached to the cloning of humans.

3 Give your own opinion of human cloning, explaining your reasons.

1 Inhaltsfragen beantworten

Seite 12/13

1. **Describe the reaction of drug campaigners to the new addiction figures.**
   The reaction of drug campaigners can be described as one of shock. This is because the new statistics on drug use among the homeless are very much worse than earlier thought.

2. **Explain how the homeless react to their sense of hopelessness.**
   Homeless people attempt to overcome their feelings of hopelessness by using drugs like cocaine, ecstasy, tranquillisers and, of course, alcohol.

3. **Point out the reasons why the homeless often reject the help available to them.**
   The homeless do not use night shelters and hostels because of the disorder, violence and drug abuse they find there.

4. **Analyse the connection between the research findings and the opinion of Louise Casey, the 'Homelessness Tsar'.**
   Louise Casey told people not to give money to the homeless because they often just used it to buy drugs or alcohol instead of food. The new data seems to support her opinion.

5. **Give the opinion of many drug activists on possible government action in view of the new situation.**
   Drug campaigners would like the authorities to spend much more money on helping homeless addicts. For example, only one in seven alcoholics had had any help in the four weeks before they were interviewed by researchers.

6. **Comment on Shaks Ghosh's attitude to the fight against drugs.**
   In my opinion, Shaks Ghosh's thinking on the fight against drug abuse is illuminating. Clearly, it is essential that addicts accept that they have a problem and recognise that they must do all they can to break their habit and get off drugs. I quite agree with Ghosh, too, that it is a terrible setback when such people are then denied the help they need. Without this essential support, they soon lose heart and give in to their addiction again.

3 Struktur von fiktionalen Texten

Seite 22

1. **Describe the setting of the story.**
   The setting of the story is a shop with a flat/with living accommodation above it. The house is full of valuable antiques/objects/things, and is well protected by means of shutters on the windows and locks on the doors. The only inhabitant of the house is an old antique dealer called Mr Price. It is a foggy Saturday evening, and Mr Price has got a large sum of money hidden in the wardrobe in his bedroom.

2. **Describe Mr Price's feelings. When does the writer make use of explicit characterisation and when does he use implicit characterisation?**
   The writer tells us about Mr Price's state of mind by both explicit and implicit characterisation. We hear that Mr Price "had shutters fitted to the ground floor windows and strong locks put on all the doors" (ll. 4–5) and that he had "a cupboard, which he had had specially made" (ll. 5–6) in which he kept valuable articles. Later in the story, we read how Mr Price hides the day's money/takings in an overcoat pocket, locks the coat in a wardrobe and then hides the key under his pillow. We understand from this implicitly that Mr Price is a rather nervous, fearful man. This makes him careful, perhaps over-careful, and leads him to always expect or fear the worst.
   The writer, as omniscient narrator, says Mr Price was, for example, "always afraid" (l. 2), that the money made him "feel very nervous" (l. 11), that he "could not help thinking of a story he had heard ..." (ll. 20–21) and, finally, that he "called out in a nervous voice" (ll. 26/27). The explicit information about the old antique dealer confirms and intensifies our impression of his feelings and character.

3. **From whose point of view is the incident described? Who tells the reader the story?**
   The story is told entirely from Mr Price's point of view/through Mr Price's eyes. The policeman would certainly tell the incident at the window quite differently. We are not told the story by Mr Price himself, but by a fictional character, the omniscient narrator, who obviously knows Mr Price and his situation very well. In this case the narrator and the author, i.e. the person who actually wrote the story down, may be regarded as being one and the same, but this is not always so.

4. By using the line numbers, try and find the structure of the story: exposition – rising action – climax/turning point – falling action.

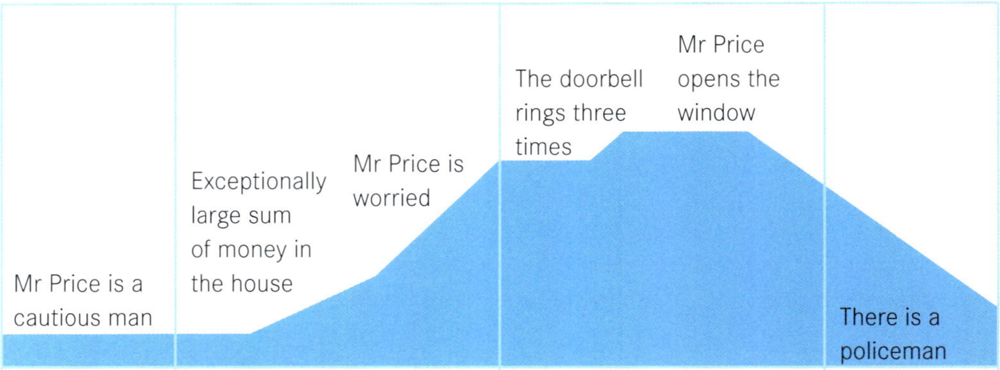

exposition	*rising action*	*climax*	*falling action*
line 1 to 8	line 9 to 17	line 17 to 28	line 28 to 29

4 Atmosphäre in fiktionalen Texten

Seite 31/32

1. **Describe what happens in the extract.**
   Joe Lampton – 'I' in the extract – has gone out for a walk by himself. Soon, he begins to enjoy himself. He has not had a walk around Warley by himself in the rain for a long time. After about half an hour, Joe finds himself watching the river as it flows under the bridge in Snow Park. He looks over the railing at the swollen river, and imagines it breaking its banks and flooding the town. Although this is in fact impossible, Joe finds the thought satisfying.
   Joe continues to stare down at the river in the rain. Some trick of light makes the surface of the river look silver, not black. The river is flowing away, away from Warley. The wind becomes stronger, and Joe catches the sour smell of the river. It is like a mastiff, coming out of the darkness.

2. **Read the description of a) Snow Park and b) the river. Give your own impression of these places.**
   Snow Park: Snow Park is in Warley. A river, crossed by a bridge with an iron guard rail, flows through the park. The park has a lot of trees in it. There is a gas lamp at the entrance to the bridge. To the left of where Joe is standing is Warley Forest; to the right a line of trees hides the bandstand and the tennis courts.

   The river: The river is swollen because of rain, and the water is cold. It flows between the trees in the park. The river is so full that another day of rain could make it break its banks. But Warley itself lies high above the river, so that it cannot be flooded. The water looks black, but a trick of light makes it look silver. The water smells sour, like (the wet fur of) a dog.

   Personal impression: At one level, the reader gets a rather negative impression of both the park and the river. Everything is dark, cold and wet. Places like the bandstand and the tennis courts, which promise joy and entertainment, are hidden. The water smells sour, like a powerful and aggressive fighting dog. The river looks as if it could break its banks and flood the park. At a deeper level we get a more positive impression of the river. Suddenly it no longer looks black, the colour of death, but silver, the colour of light. The water cannot reach the town, but it is escaping from it. It is flowing away to wherever rivers flow to.

3. **Looking at both the introduction to the text and the extract from the novel, describe Joe Lampton's appearance and mood.**
We know from the introduction that Joe has a wealthy wife, which enables him to have a high standard of living. He has a good job at his father-in-law's firm and a son, who despises him. Joe himself comes from a simple working-class background. He is not happy. He feels isolated and excluded from the middle-class circles in the town.
We can assume that Joe is in his thirties. In the extract, we hear that he is wearing a hat, which he has pulled down over his eyes because of the rain. Although he is enjoying his walk, Joe's mood is thoughtful and rather depressed. He thinks of the river bursting its banks and flooding the town. He hates and resents Warley so much that he wishes this would happen, but he knows it is impossible. The river cannot reach or harm the town, because the town is high above it. He envies the freedom of the fast-flowing water, as it flows away from the town to some unknown place.

4. **Point out how the author establishes a unity of place and person. Support your opinion by quoting from the text.**
The setting of the park and the river can be said to reflect Joe's underlying mood. The author has established a unity of place and person. The place is dark, cold, wet, even threatening: "(the river) was swollen with the last two days of heavy rain; another day like today, ... and it would burst its banks"; "the black cold water ...", "..., the iron cold under my hands". Joe's mood is thoughtful, dissatisfied and resentful. He seems to want to take revenge upon Warley: "... something profoundly satisfying about the idea of a flood, ... engulfing ... the town". But Joe knows that this can never happen, for the town is high above the river, out of reach of the water: "it couldn't happen because the town was too high above the river, but it ought to happen". Just as the water cannot reach the town, so Joe cannot reach his wife's family and social class. They are high above him, unattainable.
At the end of the extract, Joe becomes more optimistic. He seems to identify with the river as it flows away from Warley towards some unknown place (ll. 17/18), smelling like a mastiff, a strong and powerful fighting dog (l. 19).

5 Analyse von Gedichten

Seite 38/39

1. **Describe the scene portrayed in the poem.**
   A boat is sailing across a lake at night. It is foggy, and the boat sounds its whistle/foghorn all the time. The crew is trying to find the entrance to the harbor.

2. **Analyse Sandburg's use of imagery, e.g. the boat and the harbor.**
   The poet compares the boat to a lost child, and the harbor to a mother.
   The "harbor's breast" means the entrance to the harbor, and the "harbor's eyes" stand for the lights that show where the entrance to the harbor is.

3. **The poem falls into three parts. Use line numbers to identify each part and explain its function**
   The first part of the poem goes from line 1 to line 5. This introductory part sets the scene. The second part is made up of lines 6 and 7. The function of this part is to suggest the poem's deeper meaning by comparing the boat to a lost child. The last two lines, lines 8 and 9, comprise the final part in which the characteristics that are common to both the boat searching for the safety of the harbor and of the lost child looking for its mother are explained.

4. **Sandburg uses the stylistic devices *simile, alliteration* and *personification* to express his vision. Find an example of each.**
   There is a simile in line 6 "Like some lost child". There are three examples of alliteration in the poem, for example "Calls and cries unendingly" (l. 5) and "In tears and trouble" (l. 7). The whole poem is built on personification as the boat is compared to a child, and the harbor to a mother.

6 Autorenabsicht I: *narrative texts*

Seite 44/45

1. **Describe the sequence of events leading up to Kamel Bourgass's arrest in Manchester.**
   Manchester anti-terrorist police went to a flat in Crumpsall. They were looking for Al Qaeda suspects. After they had left the flat, they realised that there could be a connection between the occupants *(Bewohner)* of the flat and the ricin poison that police had found in London the week before. Five special branch officers then went back to the flat to search it. They were unarmed and they did not handcuff the occupants during the search. Suddenly one of the occupants, Kamel Bourgass, seemed to go mad. He grabbed a knife and killed one of the officers, Stephen Oake, and tried to kill the four others. This led to his arrest and court appearance.

2. **Pick out concrete details from the text. Why may the reporter have included these? What effect do they have on the reader's understanding of the event?**
   This press report contains a lot of concrete details about time, place and people. Examples of such details of time are "four days earlier" (l. 4), "yesterday" (l. 11), "more than an hour after … " (l. 24) and "last week" (l. 26). Similar exact details of place are "in the dock" (l. 1), "in a flat" (l. 5) and "at Belmarsh in South London" (ll. 8/9). There are many details of the people involved both in the event itself – the court appearance of a murder suspect – and the events leading up to it – the discovery of ricin poison in a London flat and the consequent *(sich daraus ergebend)* police search of a flat in Manchester. Examples of such personal details are "terrorist suspect Kamel Bourgass" (ll. 1/2), "the 27-year-old Algerian" (l. 8), "… with a pouting lip and staring eyes …" (l. 4) and "… the 40-year-old, who was married with three children, …" (l. 20). The reporter includes these details to give his report plausibility *(Glaubwürdigkeit)*. Such concrete details satisfy readers' curiosity *(Neugier)* and convince *(überzeugen)* them that they are getting the full facts about a real event.

3. **Analyse how the reporter's use of language makes it clear to the reader that this is a neutral account of a real event.**
   The reporter mainly achieves *(erreichen)* objectivity and neutrality by using the passive. This focuses on what happened, i. e. events, rather than on the people involved in them. Examples of such use of the passive are "was handcuffed" (l. 2), "was alleged to" (l. 5), "is accused of" (l. 17) and "was charged with" (l. 19). However, throughout the report the writer makes use of neutral language and generally avoids sensational *(reißerisch)* words. For example, in the sentence "He was a short, not particularly aggressive looking man and his bowed head gave him an almost apologetic air" (ll. 11–13), the adjectives give the reader objective or factual information about a person accused of having murdered a police officer. The objectivity of the report also depends on the reporter's use of factual detail and the avoidance of giving any kind of personal opinion about the murder suspect.

7 Autorenabsicht II: *persuasive texts*

Seite 50/51

1. **Why is it possible to say that this advertisement is a good example of the use of the AIDA formula?**

The four letters AIDA stand for attention, interest, desire and action. In this ad, attention is attracted by the big photo of a beautiful modern cruise ship on a smooth sea. The colour of the ship, white, suggests purity and freedom from care *(Kummer)*. Interest is mainly aroused by the offer of a 30 % price reduction for early bookings. Desire to go on a cruise with the Adonia is created by the fact that there are no children on board, important to often older cruise passengers, and by strong words and expressions like "stunning" (l. 1), "unforgettable holiday" (ll. 8/9), "the best in live music" (l. 9) and "superb superliner" (ll. 15/16). Finally, the phone number, website address and coupon make it easy to take action and turn desire into reality.

2. **Using two colours, underline those parts of the advertisement that are mainly informative, and those that are intended to persuade. Is it always possible to separate these two functions?**

Informative: name of ship – latest addition to P&O fleet – departures from Southampton – 30 % off some bookings – no children – first season – brochure request line – bars, lounges, four pools – live music – cruises to the Mediterranean, the Baltic, the Fjords – how to get more information – address of company – disclaimer

Persuasive: stunning addition – inaugural season – Britain's latest superliner – ready to take you on an unforgettable holiday – enjoy the best in ... – be one of the first to experience ... – superb superliner – take in the best of ... – Life doesn't get much better than this.

Often it is not possible to separate the two functions. Even in those parts of the ad that are mainly informative, the use of positive adjectives like "stunning" and "the best in", and verbs like "enjoy" and "relax" try to create a highly favourable impression or image of the Adonia in the reader's mind.

3. **Some of the informative elements you have underlined are instructive, i.e. they tell the reader what to do. Show this by looking at the language.**

The informative elements in the ad are partly instructive. These instructive elements use the imperative in two ways, firstly, to tell the reader what to do and, secondly, to make recommendations. Examples of the former are "call our brochure line ..." (ll. 18/19), "clip the coupon" (l. 20) and "post to ..." (l. 21). Examples of the imperative used to make recommendations, i.e. to express 'should', are "enjoy the best in ..." (l. 9) and "swim in one of the Adonia's four pools" (ll. 12/13). This use of the imperative is very characteristic of persuasive texts like ads.

4. **How would you characterise the language of the more persuasive elements in the ad, for example "A stunning addition to our fleet" (l. 1)?**

In addition to the use of the imperative, other language characteristics of advertisements of this type are, firstly, the use of strong adjectives and evocative verbs to arouse desire in the reader, secondly, the use of the modal verb "can" to encourage the reader to take action, thirdly, the use of enumeration for emphasis and, finally, the use of the infinitive to give instructions.

Further examples of strong adjectives are "unforgettable" (l. 8), "the best in ..." (l. 9) and "superb" (l. 15), while examples of evocative verbs are "enjoy" (l. 9) and "relax" (l. 10). In line 14 "can" is used to encourage action in "You can be one of the first to ...". One example among others of enumeration is "... the best of the Mediterranean, the Baltic and the Fjords" (ll. 16–18). An example of the infinitive used to give instructions is "To find out more ..." (l. 18).

8 Autorenabsicht III: *informative texts*

Seite 56

1. **Say how British people's perception of 'Received Pronunciation' (RP) has changed, and what effect this has had.**
   In the past 'Received Pronunciation' or 'RP' was a kind of badge. It told others that its user was not only well-educated, but also quite high up the social scale. In short, RP was essential to getting on in business and society. Nowadays that has all changed. RP is now seen as snobbish and old-fashioned. According to the text, it now attracts "contempt rather than respect" (l. 5), while in Hollywood films it is seen as "a cliché for brutality, arrogance and stupidity" (ll. 7/8). The effect of this shift in public perception is that broadcasters and call centres now prefer regional dialects to RP as the latter is no longer a sign of "trustworthiness and authority" (ll. 8/9).

2. **Why are the British, particularly men in the IT industry, becoming increasingly interested in taking elocution lessons?**
   The problem with regional dialects is that other people, particularly non-native speakers who use English as a second language and learnt RP at school, find them difficult to understand. This is obviously a big disadvantage in meetings and when giving talks or making presentations. For this reason, British speakers of regional dialects are taking elocution lessons, which teach them how to speak clearly and understandably.
   Men in the IT industry are particularly interested in taking elocution lessons because many of them have moved up the career ladder. Now they no longer work in isolation with things such as computers, where a strong regional accent does not matter, but work with people in management.

3. **What use does the writer make of linguists and speech trainers? Why do you think he or she does this?**
   The writer often quotes or refers to the opinions of linguists like Peter Trudgill, a sociolinguist, and David Crystal, an authority on the English language, and speech trainers like Ann Jones of the Society of Teachers of Speech and Drama and Sarah Mann, director of the London Language and Drama School. The writer thus makes sure that the reader is aware of these experts' experience and qualifications. He or she quotes them so often to lend the report weight and authority.

9 Autorenabsicht IV: *instructive texts*

Seite 60/61

1. **Looking at the language, show that this is an instructive text.**
   It is clear that this in an instructive text firstly by the writer's use of structures such as the imperative – for example, "Hook up your DVD player, ..." (l. 1), "look on the back of your DVD player, ..." (l. 2) and "See *page 14* for more details ..." (l. 8) – and participle structures like "Before hooking up your speakers ..." (l. 12) and "While pressing down the speaker tab ..." (ll. 17/18). In addition, the writer makes use of printing, layout and graphical techniques that are typical of such texts. The main aim is absolute clarity without risk of misunderstanding. Thus he makes use of blown-up drawings or 'magnifiers' and printing techniques such as bold and italic print.

2. **A friend has lost the operating instructions for his or her DVD receiver. Write down what you would say to your friend when telling him or her how to connect up the equipment. Then compare the language you have used with that of the written operating instructions.**
   "Well, first of all you have to look at the back of the player to see if it has an optical output. That's just a socket marked Digital Out, okay? Now, if your player has an optical output, plug the receiver cable into it, right? If it has an ordinary analog terminal, then connect the receiver to that, of course. Okay so far? Fine. Well, now you just hook up the speakers to the tab connections. They're on the right-hand side of the back of the receiver. You can't really make any mistakes because all the tabs are clearly marked. Now, you can use the player with just two speakers, front left and front right, but five speakers are better if you want really good surround sound, okay? Oh, and please don't forget to put colour coded stickers on the speaker wires, will you? Otherwise, if you're like me, you'll forget which wire goes to which speaker."

   Differences:
   1. Use of friendly, non-technical language like *first of all you have to look at ...* instead of the imperative.
   2. Use of softeners like *Well, ..., Now, ...* and *Anyhow, ...*
   3. Use of checkers like ..., *okay?, ..., okay so far?* and ..., *right?*
   4. Use of short forms *(that's, they're)*
   5. Use of question tags *(..., will you?)*

10 Autorenabsicht V: *argumentative texts*

Seite 67/68

1. **According to Glen Owen, what does Dr Mercer find worrying about the present situation, and what does he think should be done about it?**

   Glen Owen says that Dr Mercer thinks that the triviality of mass entertainment – most particularly "mindless" TV and an obsession with top-ten lists of unrelated facts – is producing politically ignorant and inactive school-leavers. These young people do not know how to make use of their democratic rights and seem to show little interest in social issues. The result is that schools have to "work overtime" to correct this deficit.

   Dr Mercer wants the BBC and TV production companies like Celador to produce current events programmes for teenagers of the same quality as natural history programmes like the BBC's *The Life of Mammals*.

2. **Examine how Dr Mercer's use of language expresses the aim of the speech he intends to give before other head teachers.**

   Dr Mercer, a speaker at the coming Catholic Independent Schools Conference, wants to persuade his listeners of the truth of his opinion that mass entertainment, particularly TV, is "damaging pupils and threatening the stability of society".

   With this aim in view, both Glen Owen, the reporter, and Dr Mercer make use of language very typical of argumentative texts. To begin with, especially Dr Mercer's choice of words is highly emotive in expressions like "forced to work overtime" (ll. 4/5), "undo the damage" (l. 5), "mindless television" (l. 5) and "list mania" (l. 10), and amounts to hyperbole or intentional exaggeration. Such language transmits the force of Dr Mercer's convictions to his audience.

   Dr Mercer's use of stylistic devices is also intended to emphasise his argument, for example enumeration in "top tens, rich lists, poor lists, what's in, what's out, even a list of so-called Greatest Britons, ..." (ll. 10–11). Similarly, the device of repetition is used for the same reason, for example "voter apathy, especially among the young ..." (l. 33) and "The failure to educate the young to think well for themselves ..." (l. 34). Such repetition is sometimes linked to a further important stylistic device, contrast, as in the sentence "Many young people no longer believe in rebellion, but don't believe in conforming either. They don't believe in the protest culture, but don't really want meaningless pop either" (ll. 36–38).

   Certain grammatical structures are also characteristic of argumentative texts. For example, 'will' is used to forecast a future development in "Our schools will have to work increasingly hard to compensate for this vacuum ..." (l. 19) and 'should' is used to make an urgent recommendation in "... broadcasters should engage the interest of teenagers ..." (l. 23).

   Finally, in the concluding part of his report, Glen Owen quotes John Dunford of the Secondary Heads Association and some recent survey findings to support Dr Mercer's main argument.

11 Grafiken beschreiben und deuten

Seite 71/72

1. **Describe the bar chart and say what its purpose is.**
   The bar chart compares ten accents according to the perceived honesty of their users as a percentage of respondents between 0 % and 30 %. The survey was carried out by the Aziz Corporation. The ten accents compared in the chart are, in alphabetical order, American, Birmingham/West Midlands, Cockney, Continental European, Liverpool, Newcastle, Scottish, South East England (RP), Welsh and, finally, West Country.

2. **Interpret the information in the bar chart.**
   According to the bar chart, about 28 % of respondents found Scottish to be the most honest accent of the ten, followed by the West Country at 25 %.
   The middle group is made up of six accents from Welsh and Newcastle with around 21 %, South East England or RP 19 %, American 18 %, Continental European 17 % and Birmingham/West Midlands 15 %. There is then a marked drop in perceived honesty to Liverpool at 11 % and, finally, Cockney at approximately 9 %.
   The drop from the most honest accent, Scottish, to the least honest, Cockney, is hence nearly 20%. The drop between the two leading accents to the middle group, and from the middle group to the least honest two accents is around 4 % in each case.

12 Karikaturen interpretieren

Seite 76

1. **Describe the cartoon.**
   In the middle of the cartoon, there is a fat white businessman. He is wearing a dark business suit and a tie. The businessman is pointing his finger accusingly at an immigrant family of three. We can assume that they are Mexican immigrants as the father is wearing a typical Mexican hat and he has a dark moustache. On the right, there is a Native American. He also has the typical hairstyle and appears to be wearing soft leather trousers and moccasins.
   The left hand speech bubble expresses what the businessman says when he sees the Mexicans, i.e. that it's time to reclaim America from illegal immigrants. When he hears this, the Native American says to the businessman, "I'll help you pack."

2. **Explain the message of the cartoon.**
   The businessman speaks to the reader about the Mexicans; the Native American speaks personally to the businessman. He does not deny that the Mexicans are, or at least could be, illegal immigrants. However, from his point of view this definitely applies to white Europeans who entered his country illegally and took it over. The businessman does not seem to be aware of this irony.

13 Persönliche Stellungnahme

Seite 82/83

1. **Explain the author's reasons for writing and publishing the article.**
   Firstly, the author wishes to correct a common misunderstanding. The aim of human cloning has never been to produce either a perfect copy of a living human or babies as a source of spare body parts. Its purpose has always been to produce stem cells to cure diseases. Secondly, the author wishes to condemn the abuse of human cloning by some maverick scientists and to expressly warn against it as harmful.

2. **Summarise the risks attached to the cloning of humans.**
   Respectable scientific opinion is firmly against human cloning because it frequently results in miscarriages during pregnancy, deformities, weak health and early death. It is hence unacceptably risky. Furthermore, many such conditions cannot be observed and treated in the womb.

3. **Give your own opinion of human cloning, explaining your reasons.**
   Pro: I am against irresponsible human cloning for trivial reasons such as simply to produce people with beautiful bodies. I am also very much against using cloning to produce a 'governing elite' to run ordinary people's lives.
   However, in my opinion, human cloning could be acceptable in certain circumstances. The most obvious of these is the cloning of a dead child or the cloning of donors of kidneys and bone marrow *(Knochenmark)*. Both these can be extracted to save human life without endangering the life of the cloned donor. I also think that cloning could be used as just one technique in enabling people unable to give birth to children naturally to have a family.

   Contra: I can accept the cloning of cells for medical purposes, but that is as far as I am willing to go. I reject the cloning of humans completely. I cannot accept it in any circumstances. I say this although I know that a kind of cloning occurs in nature when a fertilised female egg splits to produce identical twins. However, this happens spontaneously, which means that it cannot be planned, and hence abused.
   The reason for my rejection of human cloning has nothing to do with religious ideas such as the belief that 'creation belongs to God'. I am quite simply convinced that if human cloning is allowed by the United Nations, we can be absolutely sure of one thing: some individuals, groups or even countries will certainly abuse it to produce 'tailor-made superhumans' to oppress the rest of us.

Seite 8 f.: **Homeless in drugs epidemic**, Ben Summerskill und Dino Mahtani, The Observer, London, 14. Juli 2002

Seite 17: **The Antique Dealer**, zur Verfügung gestellt von Karl Hartmann, München 1990, Autor unbekannt

Seite 23: **Life at the Top**, John Braine, Eyre & Spottiswoode, London 1962

Seite 33: **Lost**, aus: Chicago Poems, Carl Sandburg, Copyright 1916 von Holt, Rinehart and Winston, erneuert 1944 von Carl Sandburg, Nachdruck mit Genehmigung von Houghton
Mifflin Harcourt Publishing Company

Seite 34: **Night Train**, W. H. Auden, Zit. nach Commentary for a G. P. O. Film, Juli 1935

Seite 40 f.: **As seven armoured officers guarded him, he was calm and still**, Paul Harris, Daily Mail, London, 18. Januar 2003

Seite 46 f.: **P&O Cruises**, Anzeige in Daily Mail, London, 18. Januar 2003

Seite 52 f.: **We want to talk proper**, The Economist, London, 5. Dezember 2002

Seite 57 f.: **Quick Start Guide, Operating Instructions**, Audio/Video Multi-Channel Receiver VSX-C3000, VSX-C300-S, Pioneer Corp., Tokio 2002

Seite 62 f.: **TV trivia is our weakest link, says head**, Glen Owen, TimesOnline, London, www.timesonline.co.uk, 17. Januar 2003

Seite 69: **Stabdiagramm**: Speak up, The Aziz Corporation, erschienen in: The Economist, London, 5. Dezember 2002

Seite 73: **Cartoon**: Steve Kelley

Seite 77 f.: **Human cloning – the risks**, Bionet, http://www.bionetonline.org/English/Content/sc_cont5.htm (letzter Zugriff am 23. Januar 2012)

Klausurtraining Textarbeit

Inhaltsverzeichnis

Vorwort

Der zweite Teil dieses Buches – *Klausurtraining Textarbeit* – zeigt Ihnen, wie Sie Ihre Leistungen im Fach Englisch in der Oberstufe optimieren können. Das Klausurtraining kann nicht – dafür ist es auch nicht konzipiert – den Unterricht ersetzen. Vielmehr ist es eine für das Selbststudium geeignete Ergänzung zum Unterricht.

Aufbau und Inhalt des zweiten Teils
Der zweite Teil gliedert sich in drei Bereiche:
1. Einführungskurs (Lerntipps und besonders relevante Fertigkeiten)
2. Arbeitsteil (Units 1–12)
3. Anhang (Lösungen, Glossar literarischer Fachbegriffe)

Im **Einführungskurs** werden sieben grundlegende Fertigkeiten eingeführt und geübt, die für alle Textformen oder Aufgaben der Oberstufe gleichermaßen wichtig und geeignet sind. Hier sind vor allem die Informationen und das Sprachangebot zu den Operatoren (*operative verbs*) von zentraler Bedeutung (siehe S. 13–15).

Die **Units 1–6** befassen sich mit Sachtexten; die **Units 7–12** mit fünf literarischen Texten und einem Cartoon. Die sechs Themenbereiche – jeweils in Form eines Sach- und eines literarischen Textes umgesetzt – sind zentrale Themen im Oberstufenunterricht der meisten Bundesländer. Die Aufgabenstellungen richten sich durchweg nach den Einheitlichen Prüfungsanforderungen (EPA), die für alle Bundesländer gelten.

Alle Units sind identisch sowie benutzerfreundlich aufgebaut und wie folgt unterteilt:

Titel der Unit und Benennung des Übungsschwerpunktes

A Text und Aufgaben
- ▷ Einleitung zum Text
- ▷ Text mit Zeilenzähler und Wortzahl
- ▷ einsprachige Worterklärungen
- ▷ (ggf.) weitere nicht lexikalische Erklärungen
- ▷ Aufgaben mit Angabe des Anforderungsbereiches (I: Textverständnis, II: Analyse, III: Beurteilung). Die Aufgaben, die schwerpunktmäßig behandelt werden, sind fett hervorgehoben.

B Praktische Hilfe und Arbeitsschritte
- ▷ Informationen und Erklärungen zu den Schwerpunktaufgaben
- ▷ Arbeitsschritte und Sprachmittel zu den Schwerpunktaufgaben

Im Anhang finden Sie die **Lösungen** zu den Aufgaben: Die dort enthaltenen Lösungsvorschläge halten sich eng an die Arbeitsschritte und die angegebenen Sprachmittel. Sie sind allerdings nicht die „einzig richtigen Antworten“, sondern eher Formulierungshilfen.

Im **Glossar** wird u. a. die in den Units verwendeten literarurwissenschaftlichen Fachbegriffe alphabetisch aufgelistet und erklärt. Verweise auf Einträge im Glossar sind mit einem Pfeil (→) gekennzeichnet.

Praktische Tipps

Da die Units nicht aufeinander aufbauen, können sie – abgesehen vom Einführungskurs – in beliebiger Reihenfolge bearbeitet werden. Die relevanten Informationen und Anregungen stehen meist bei den Aufgaben und Texten.

Schritt 1: Zuerst sollten Sie den **Einführungskurs** durcharbeiten. Die grundlegenden Fertigkeiten, die dort geübt werden, werden bei den Units als bekannt vorausgesetzt und nicht mehr wiederholt.

Schritt 2: Die Grundlage der Arbeit ist immer ein Text. Ein **intensives Lesen des Textes** ist deshalb unumgänglich; es wird jedoch durch die Vokabelerklärungen erleichtert.

Schritt 3: Wenn Sie den Text weitgehend verstanden haben, **lesen Sie alle Aufgabenstellungen** durch.

Schritt 4: Die untergeordneten Aufgaben (Normaldruck) dienen vor allem dem **Leseverständnis**. Deswegen ist es meist sinnvoll, zunächst diese Fragen zu bearbeiten, bevor Sie sich den Schwerpunktaufgaben zuwenden. Um den Arbeitsweg zu verkürzen, können Sie auch die Lösungen zu den untergeordneten Aufgaben sofort ansehen.

Schritt 5: Jetzt sollten Sie die **Schwerpunktaufgaben** (Fettdruck) lösen. Lesen Sie zuerst gründlich die einleitenden Hinweise. (Übersetzungen literaturtheoretischer Begriffe stehen in Klammern und können im Glossar nachgeschlagen werden.) Anschließend arbeiten Sie die Schritte unter Anwendung des angegebenen Sprachmaterials systematisch durch.

Schritt 6: Wenn Sie mit Ihrer Antwort zufrieden sind, vergleichen Sie diese mit den **Lösungsvorschlägen**.

Bevor es nun gleich mit dem Klausurtraining losgeht, lohnt es sich, sich noch mal die zehn goldenen Regeln der Textarbeit in Erinnerung zu rufen.

REMEMBER **Die zehn goldenen Regeln zur Textarbeit in der Klausur**

Regel 1: Lesen Sie zuerst den ganzen Text, um den Sinn zu erfassen. Achten Sie beim zweiten Lesen auf Ihnen unbekannte und unverständliche Wörter.

Regel 2: Es ist selten notwendig, alle unbekannten Wörter nachzuschlagen. Beachten Sie zuerst die sinntragenden Wörter. Diese sinntragenden Wörter sind in der Regel Substantive (Nomen) und Verben (Tätigkeitswörter), die häufig mit Adjektiven bzw. Adverbien (Eigenschafts- bzw. Umstandswörter) näher beschrieben werden. Die anderen Ihnen unbekannten Wörter können Sie zunächst ignorieren.

Regel 3: Verschwenden Sie keine Zeit mit unnötigem Nachschlagen im Wörterbuch. Oft kann die Bedeutung von Wörtern durch ihre Ähnlichkeit mit dem Deutschen, durch die Wortbildungslehre oder aus dem Kontext leicht erschlossen werden.

Regel 4: Schreiben Sie nie „einfach los“! Lesen Sie alle Aufgabenstellungen in Ruhe genau durch. Sonst kann es leicht passieren, dass Sie entweder zwei Aufgaben in einer Antwort bearbeiten oder dass zwei Antworten weitgehend identisch sind. Beim Lesen der Aufgaben fragen Sie sich immer wieder: „Was will der Prüfer von mir wissen?“

Regel 5: Beachten Sie, dass Informationen zu einem Aspekt nicht nur in einem Abschnitt, sondern im gesamten Text verstreut vorkommen können. Deswegen ist es unerlässlich, den Text immer als Ganzes zu betrachten!

Regel 6: Inhaltsfragen beziehen sich ausschließlich auf den Text. Arbeiten Sie nur die im Text vorkommenden, faktischen Informationen heraus und interpretieren Sie diese nicht.

Regel 7: Schreiben Sie den Text nicht einfach ab! Arbeiten Sie Inhalte zu einer bestimmten Fragestellung heraus und fassen Sie diese zunächst in Stichwörtern oder Stichpunkten zusammen.

Regel 8: Zitieren Sie knapp und präzise. Längere Zitate werden oft über ihre Funktion als Beleg hinaus missbraucht, z. B. um Sprachfehler zu vermeiden oder um eine Antwort „aufzublähen“.

Regel 9: In Ihrer persönlichen Stellungnahme sollten Sie nicht nur die im Text enthaltenen Informationen und Wertungen erarbeiten, sondern auch die Erkenntnisse berücksichtigen, die Sie in diesem Kursabschnitt gewonnen haben.

Regel 10: Verhalten Sie sich dem Prüfer gegenüber fair und korrekt, indem Sie ...

- ▷ deutlich lesbar schreiben,
- ▷ Worttrennungen vermeiden (im Englischen selten nötig),
- ▷ bei Korrekturen das ganze Wort bzw. den ganzen Textabschnitt durchstreichen und neu schreiben (vermeiden Sie Pfeile, Ziffern und Randkorrekturen),
- ▷ eine großzügige Korrekturspalte freilassen,
- ▷ die Wörter zählen und deren Zahl akkurat angeben,
- ▷ Wiederholungen vermeiden, mit denen nur die Wortzahl erhöht werden soll,
- ▷ Ihre Antworten eindeutig und richtig nummerieren,
- ▷ nicht mogeln und andere dabei auch nicht unterstützen.

Viel Spaß und Erfolg beim Arbeiten mit **Besser in Englisch!**
Der Autor

A Mit unbekannten Wörtern umgehen

Da in der Oberstufe nur Originaltexte eingesetzt werden, werden Sie viele Wörter nicht kennen. Selten jedoch ist es notwendig, alle unbekannten Wörter nachzuschlagen. Der Gebrauch eines Wörterbuches ist zeitintensiv – die Erklärungen enthalten oft weitere unbekannte Wörter – und kann auch recht frustrierend sein. Versuchen Sie daher zunächst, die Bedeutung eines unbekannten Wortes folgendermaßen zu erschließen:

▷ **Internationale Wörter:**
Viele englische Wörter, insbesondere im Bereich der Wirtschaft und Industrie, der Medien, der Jugendkultur, des Transportwesens und des Sports, sind „international" geworden. Diese Wörter – z. B. manager, advertising spot, jeans, car, biker, camera, video, camping, tourist, stewardess und golf – kommen fast identisch in vielen Sprachen vor.

▷ **Ähnlichkeit mit dem Deutschen:**
Viele englische Wörter des alltäglichen Lebens – z. B. bread, bring, come, family, field, fish, garden, house, make, sing, street usw. – haben sich aus einer frühen Form der deutschen Sprache entwickelt. Obgleich diese Wörter anders als im Deutschen geschrieben und gesprochen werden, sind sie für Deutschsprachige leicht zu erkennen.
Genauso wichtig wie diese Wörter sind auch Fremdwörter, wie z. B. „aggressiv", „Demokratie", „Diplomatie", „Politik", „Sozialismus", „telefonieren" usw., die im Deutschen verwendet werden. Diese Wörter basieren vorwiegend auf einem lateinischen bzw. altgriechischen Wortstamm und kommen – ebenfalls mit kleinen Änderungen – auch im Englischen vor, also im Falle der o. g. Beispiele aggressive, democracy, diplomacy, politics, socialism, (to) telephone usw.

1 Read the sentences and translate the highlighted parts into German.

1. Trade unions are based on the basic idea of solidarity.

2. Many Muslims reject the West for cultural and religious reasons.

3. The British established massive tea plantations in northern India.

4. The EU states hope to hinder immigration by cooperating more closely.

5. The UN has declared slavery illegal throughout the world, but it still exists in some regions.

6. Some conservative American politicians want the government to stop drug smuggling by using the army as well as the police.

7. The cabinet discussed a resolution about the import of toxic materials into Britain.

8. Many sociologists have found that Britain is still a country divided by class privilege.

9. One historian thought European integration would take several generations.

10. Many smaller companies have gone bankrupt because of the credit crisis.

▷ **Wortbildung:**
Anhand der Wortbildungslehre können Sie viele zusammengesetzte Wörter zumindest sinngemäß ohne Schwierigkeit verstehen.

Wörter werden gebildet durch:
– Änderung der Wortbedeutung durch Vorsilben.

EXAMPLES

probable → **im**probable; understand → **mis**understand; discovery → **re**discovery

- Änderung der Wortart durch Nachsilben.

EXAMPLES

express (Verb) → expression (Substantiv); care (Substantiv) → careful (Adjektiv); careless (Adjektiv) → carelessly (Adverb)

- Zusammensetzung von Substantiven.

EXAMPLES

postman, postbox, post office usw.

2 **Read this extract from a text about Birmingham more than once if necessary. Then – without using a dictionary – give the meaning of the highlighted words and expressions in German. Many of them are probably new to you in this form, but think about German!**

Now one of the most modern commercial and technological centres [1] in Europe, just a generation ago [2] Birmingham's future looked hopeless [3].
Once a small agricultural town [4], Birmingham owed its importance to the industrialisation of the economy [5]. Concentrating on metal products [6], during the 19th century Birmingham became Britain's biggest centre for the production of industrial machinery [7] and exported its products [8] all over the world. In those days, the city was proud to call itself the 'Workshop of the World' [9].
But like many other old industrial towns [10] in Britain, the industrialisation of the USA [11] and large parts of northern Europe, the loss of markets [12] in the old Empire and its geographical position [13] meant the end for Birmingham.
In the 1950s and 60s, investors [14] were anything but optimistic [15] about the city's future, and who could blame them? Birmingham seemed to be a wasteland [16] made up of the ruins of factories and warehouses [17] and unused canals and goods yards [18].

1.
2.
3.
4.
5.
6.
7.
8.

9.
10.
11.
12.
13.
14.
15.
16.
17.
18.

B Schlüsselwörter bzw. -ausdrücke erkennen

Schlüsselwörter und Schlüsselausdrücke, meist Subjekte und/oder Objekte eines Satzes, sind für die Aussage des Satzes maßgeblich. Durch Adjektive oder Adverbien können diese genauer beschrieben sein.

EXAMPLES **Die „Kernaussage“ des Satzes**

I would like to disagree most strongly with the one-sided publicity that you have given to animal rights in recent months.

→ In diesem Satz sind sind die Schlüsselwörter bzw. Schlüsselausdrücke: disagree, one-sided publicity und animal rights. Andere Ausdrücke – z. B. I would like to ..., most strongly und in recent months – gehören nicht zur „Kernaussage“ des Satzes.

Auch in Aufgabenstellungen sind die Wörter bzw. Ausdrücke nicht gleich wichtig, zum Beispiel in der folgenden Aufforderung (aus einer Klausurarbeit).

Show what effect the problem of double identity has on many American Jews.

→ Die Wörter show, effect, double identity und American Jews drücken die „Kernaussage“ des Satzes aus.

3 **Read the question and underline the three key words. Then underline the related key words and phrases in the text.**

What influence do genes have on intelligence?

"When we look at good adoptive families, we know that the children of more intelligent natural parents will tend to be more intelligent than the children of less intelligent natural parents. This suggests that genes are the decisive factor in intelligence," says Sandra Carr, professor of psychology at Yale University.

On the other hand, she agrees with Richard Snow, professor of education and psychology at Stanford University, that an unhappy home life with little intellectual stimulation can keep a child from ever using the intelligence he/she carries in his/her genes. "But such extreme cases are rare," said Professor Carr. "The fact is that when we compare children in any given family environment - good or bad - the children of more intelligent biological parents always perform relatively better than the children of less intelligent biological parents."

C Textinhalte stichpunktartig notieren

Notieren Sie Sätze oder Abschnitte auf einem Konzeptpapier, wobei Sie zuerst alle nicht sinntragenden Wörter weglassen. Letztere sind Strukturwörter, also Artikel, Präpositionen, Hilfsverben usw., die vorwiegend grammatische Funktion haben, sowie Pronomen, Adverbien und Adjektive.

Berücksichtigen Sie auch keine „Floskeln", Höflichkeitsformen, Frageanhängsel und andere rhetorische Stilmittel.

EXAMPLE **Sinntragende Wörter notieren**

Nehmen wir als Beispiel diesen Satz aus einem Artikel über afrikanische Amerikaner:
A middle-class Afro-American engineer at a party suddenly says that he is worried about his teenage daughter. She goes to a local integrated school and perhaps she will "lose touch with her Afro-Caribbean heritage".

Lassen wir die Strukturwörter, Pronomen usw. weg, bleibt eine Kette von Substantiven und Verben, die den „Kernsinn" des Satzes ausdrückt:
Afro-American, engineer, worried, daughter, goes, integrated, school, lose, touch, Afro-Caribbean heritage.

4 **Here are further sentences from the same article. Make notes by crossing out the structural words and less important qualifiers.**

1. The author (...) was born in the late 1940s in then segregated Chicago, went to an integrated high school and university in the 1960s and early '70s and is now a professor of English at an integrated university in California.
2. Something in the lives of Afro-Americans must be different from that of other minority groups, such as the new immigrants from Asia and Latin America.
3. An Afro-American civil rights activist speaks to a white salesman in a hotel bar. He makes the salesman feel so guilty about slavery and segregation that the white man gives the elderly Afro-American barman a $ 20 tip.
4. A talented Afro-American university teacher tells the author that he is looking for the softest academic job he can find so that he has as much time as possible to go fishing.

5. Mr Steele reduces this sad catalogue to two particular problems.
6. The first is that Afro-Americans have less self-confidence than other groups and suffer from a fear of failure because of the worldwide view of them as being “intellectually inferior”.

D Der Umgang mit Anforderungsbereichen und Operatoren

▷ **Anforderungsbereiche**

In der Oberstufe werden gemäß den Einheitlichen Prüfungsanforderungen (EPA) der Länder drei Anforderungen gestellt, und zwar:

1. das Verstehen und Wiedergeben eines Textes
2. die analytisch-interpretierende Auseinandersetzung mit dem Text
3. die eigene Stellungnahme zu dem Text und die Bewertung des Textes

Diese drei Anforderungsbereiche spiegeln sich deshalb in drei unterschiedlichen Teilaufgaben wider:

1. Comprehension/orientation/context (AB I)
2. Analysis (AB II)
3. Evaluation: comment or recreation (AB III)

▷ **Operatoren** ***(operative verbs)***

Im allgemeinem Gebrauch sind Operatoren Verben, die eine Handlung, ein Ereignis oder eine Situation in Gang setzen, oft in Form einer Aufforderung bzw. Arbeitsanweisung, irgendetwas zu tun. Spezifisch auf Oberstufenenglisch übertragen sind typische Operatoren Verben wie analyse, compare, comment on, describe und point out (s. unten).

▷ **Wichtige Operatoren nach Anforderungsbereich (AB)**

Anforderungsbereich I

1. **describe** *beschreiben* – eine detaillierte und möglichst konkrete Darstellung geben
   Describe the setting of the story and its effect on the characters' state of mind.
   Describe the situation the protagonists find themselves in at the end of the story.

   auch AB II, Analyse:
   Describe how the writer creates an atmosphere of suspense.

   auch möglich in „Kombiaufgaben“, AB I/II:
   Describe and **interpret** the cartoon.

2. **outline** *umreißen* – nur die Schwerpunkte eines Themas präsentieren, ohne ins Detail zu gehen
   Outline the author's views on the effects of globalisation on the developing world.

3. **state** *darlegen* – klar und unmissverständlich sagen/schreiben
   State briefly the problems faced by ethnic minorities in the UK.

4. **present** *darstellen* – (neu-)strukturieren und niederschreiben
   Present the situation of the main character at the beginning of the story.

5. **point out** *hinweisen auf* – gewisse Aspekte eines Themas herausfiltern und erklären
   Point out the writer's attitude to artificial insemination.

6. **summarise** *zusammenfassen*; write a summary *eine Zusammenfassung schreiben* – eine kurze Darstellung der Schwerpunkte eines Textes geben
   Summarise the information on the dangers of climate change given in the text.
   Write a summary of the author's position on climate change.

Anforderungsbereich II

7. **analyse** *analysieren*; examine *untersuchen* – gewisse Aspekte und/oder Merkmale eines Textes beschreiben und erklären
   Analyse the opposing views on social class held by the two protagonists.
   Examine the author's use of language.

8. **characterise** *charakterisieren*; write a characterisation *eine Charakterisierung schreiben* – die Charaktere beschreiben und untersuchen, wie sie präsentiert werden
   Characterise the main characters in the play.
   Write a characterisation of the main protagonists in the story.

GOOD TO KNOW **Charaktermerkmale**

eher positiv:
agreeable (angenehm), cooperative, courageous, fair/fair-minded, generous, honest, loyal, nice, open, pleasant, predictable (berechenbar), reliable (zuverlässig), tolerant, trustworthy, understanding, warm-hearted, well-behaved, ...

eher negativ:
aggressive, boastful (angeberisch), brutal, cold, cynical, disagreeable (unangenehm), disloyal, greedy, mean (gemein), narrow-/small-minded (engstirnig), nasty, pompous, promiscuous (den/die Sexualpartner(in) häufig wechselnd), sly (gerissen), unfair, unpleasant, unpredictable (unberechenbar), unreliable (unzuverlässig), violent, vulgar, ...

Beachten Sie: Erfahrungsgemäß treten vor allem bei der Beschreibung negativer Merkmale Probleme und Schwächen auf!

9. **explain** *erklären* – beschreiben und im Detail definieren
   Explain the protagonist's obsession with sport.
   auch möglich in „Kombiaufgaben“:
   Explain how the pie chart and the line graph support the writer's view.

10. **illustrate** *veranschaulichen* – erklären bzw. verdeutlichen anhand von Beispielen
    Illustrate the author's use of metaphorical language.

11. **interpret** *interpretieren* – Bedeutung verdeutlichen
    Interpret the message that the author evidently wishes to convey.

12. **compare** *vergleichen* – Ähnlichkeiten und Unterschiede ermitteln und aufzeichnen
    Compare the two characters' attitude to the war.
    auch Anforderungsbereich III:
    Compare the parents' opposing views on boarding schools.

Anforderungsbereich III

13. **comment** *kommentieren* – die eigene Meinung zu dem Thema ausdrücken und begründen
    Comment on the author's claim that the lack of Afro-Americans in senior management can be traced to the view blacks have of themselves.

GOOD TO KNOW **Verfassen eines Leserbriefes**

Es kommt häufig vor, dass ein Kommentar in Form eines Leserbriefes *(letter to the editor, reader's letter)* verlangt wird.

Ihr Brief sollte **folgende Bestandteile** aufweisen:
Absender (*writer's/sender's address*), Datum (*date*), Empfänger (*addressee*), Anrede (*salutation*), Brieftext (*body text*), Schlussformel (*complimentary close*)

Achten Sie unbedingt auf die **formellen Merkmale:**
Dear Sir or Madam (kein Komma)
I refer to your leader about ... (folgende Zeile)
oder
Sir or Madam – I refer to your leader about ... (gleiche Zeile mit Gedankenstrich)

Schreiben Sie den Brief **kurz und bündig**, damit er gelesen und u. U. veröffentlicht wird. Benutzen Sie einen **formelleren Stil**.

14. **discuss** *diskutieren* – ein Thema argumentativ untersuchen
    Discuss the implications of globalisation as described in the press article.

15. **evaluate** *auswerten* – nach gründlicher Überlegung eine begründete Meinung bilden
    Evaluate the impact of illegal immigration on the Californian economy.

▷ **Die Bearbeitung von Aufgaben**
Beachten Sie: Benutzen Sie die Zeitform, die in der Aufgabenstellung verwendet wird – und bleiben Sie dabei.

EXAMPLES **Zeitformen beibehalten**

Explain why John Howard **quotes** the two scientists at such length.
→ John Howard **quotes** the two scientists at length because he **wants** to give his argument authority.

Characterise the relationship Joe **had** to his wife's family and point out how the author **makes** the nature of this relationship clear to the reader.
→ **Joe had** a bad relationship to Susan's family. **The author makes** this clear by telling us that Susan's father **gave** him a job with a "pretty title but no power" (l. 46) and "**enjoyed** ignoring him at the club" (ll. 48/49).

Um den einleitenden Satz der Antwort zu bilden, ist es meist sinnvoll, Teile der Aufgabenstellung zu übernehmen.

EXAMPLES **Antworten einleiten**

State how Norman Mailer portrays himself in the interview.
→ In the interview Norman Mailer portrays himself as …

According to the author, explain which measures the government should take in order to reduce violent crime.
→ According to the author, the government should take the following measures to reduce violent crime: …

Evaluate how Alison's dream influenced her later life.
→ Alison's dream influenced her later life in that …

5 **Use these instructions from exam papers to form the first sentence of an answer.**

1. Describe the aims of the geneticist Paul Smith as they are presented in this article.

2. According to Russell Baker, point out the most painful side of giving up a private car.

3. Explain why Esther visited Dr Gordon.

4. Outline how Mr Steele explains the paradoxical situation of Afro-Americans.

5. Describe what tricks people who want to emigrate to the USA use to get round immigration laws.

6. Summarise the immigration issues that the writer deals with in his essay.

7. Describe the sequence of events which led to Billy's decision to leave home.

8. Comment on the writer's view that the export of toxic waste to developing countries is "a kind of neo-imperialism".

E Sich in der „eigenen Sprache“ ausdrücken

Obwohl Sie sich für Ihre Arbeit an der Aufgabenstellung und natürlich auch am Text orientieren können, sollten Sie eigene Formulierungen verwenden oder zumindest merklich einbringen. Vor allem im lexikalischen Bereich gibt es fast immer Möglichkeiten, die Aussage des Originals anders zu formulieren.

EXAMPLES **Eigene Formulierungen**

Alison Fox **claims** that the **most undemocratic feature** of British life is the **awful** secrecy **engaged in** by the government.
→ Alison Fox **argues** that the **least democratic aspect** of British life is the **terrible** secrecy **practised** by the government.

Unlike in America, where **the media has** a **right to information by law**, the British government can **forbid** the publication of anything that it **thinks** is – or **could** be – **not in** the public interest.
→ **In contrast** to America, where **journalists have** a **legal right to information**, the British government can **stop** the publication of anything that it **says** is – or **might** be – **against** the public interest.

6 **Replace the highlighted words or expressions with alternatives from the list.**

answered *argument* *built* *came into* *damaged* *deal with* *excused*
hang *kill* *looking for* *parts* *purchased* *sat down* *shown to be*
take an interest in *the death penalty* *think about* *understand* *worried*

1. The government is searching ______ for ways to tackle ______ crime.
2. Joe entered ______ the room and took a seat ______.
3. When asked his opinion, he replied ______ that he didn't concern himself with ______ such things.
4. The antique dealer bought ______ a strong safe and had it cemented ______ into the wall of his office.
5. The witness was exposed for ______ the liar she was.
6. Just consider ______ the following thesis ______.
7. The fine stone of the building has already been defaced ______ by vandals.
8. The best argument for capital punishment ______ is that if you execute ______ murderers, they can at least never murder ______ again.

9. Trainees with good qualifications are exempted from ______ some sections ______ of the exam.

10. Susan just didn't comprehend ______ what her husband was so concerned ______ about.

7 **Find an alternative from the list for these adjectives.**

apparent *argumentative* *assorted* *awful* *big-hearted* *bright* *childish* *committed* *considerate* *enthusiastic* *disagreeable* *friendly* *gloomy* *hard-hearted* *interesting* *jealous* *lovely* *mean* *poisonous* *sceptical* *small-minded* *uninterested* *vivacious* *wealthy* *young*

1. affable ______
2. clever ______
3. envious ______
4. generous ______
5. indifferent ______
6. kind ______
7. morose ______
8. obvious ______
9. quarrelsome ______
10. spiteful ______
11. uncharitable ______
12. whole-hearted ______
13. zealous ______
14. beautiful ______
15. doubtful ______
16. fascinating ______
17. horrid ______
18. juvenile ______
19. lively ______
20. nasty ______
21. petty ______
22. rich ______
23. toxic ______
24. various ______
25. youthful ______

8 **Replace the highlighted words and expressions with alternatives from the list.**

awful *bought* *brought up the topic* *did not bother* *escape* *fast-moving vehicles* *having a car* *in fact* *intelligent* *jump* *look at more* *present intake* *proportion* *seen* *sterile* *supporters* *women* *wonderful gift*

1. Migrants vault ______ freeway divider walls and flee ______ through eight lanes of speeding traffic ______.
2. Proponents ______ of further ______ immigration argue that the current influx ______ is actually ______ lower than the 1900–1920 peak when considered ______ as a percentage ______ of the US population.
3. Other commentators praise the institution as a godsend ______ for wives ______ who want bright ______ and healthy children but whose husbands are infertile ______.
4. When drivers neglected ______ to complain about the unspeakable ______ costs of car ownership ______, I subtly raised the subject ______ myself by inviting them to inspect ______ the Rembrandt I had just purchased ______ with money saved by not driving.

F Richtig zitieren

EXAMPLES

❶ The author expresses her contempt for the class society by referring to the upper classes as "the idle rich" (l. 8) and as "selfish dinosaurs"(l. 17) who live a life of "privilege by an accident of birth" (ll. 18/19).

❷ I agree with the author when he rejects Professor Oscar Handlin's argument that American Jews have the same relationship to Israel as Italian and Irish Americans have to Italy and Ireland (ll. 37–41).

Tipp 1: Ein Zitat dient dazu, eine Aussage oder These (The author expresses her contempt for the class society by ...) oder eine Wertung (I agree with the author when he ...) zu belegen oder zu begründen.

Tipp 2: Wörtliche Zitate stehen immer in Anführungszeichen ("...") ❶. Zitiert man sinngemäß, werden keine Anführungszeichen gesetzt ❷. Bei längeren Zitaten ist es ratsam, sinngemäß zu zitieren.

Tipp 3: Unmittelbar nach dem Zitat – gleichgültig ob wörtlich oder sinngemäß – wird dessen Quelle – hier die Zeile – angegeben. Die Quelle, also die Originalstelle, wird in Klammern gesetzt und wie folgt geschrieben:

▷ l. 10 (= in Zeile 10)
▷ ll. 10/11 (= in Zeilen 10 und 11)
▷ ll. 10–13 (= von Zeile 10 bis Zeile 13)

Tipp 4: Wollen Sie die Quellen im Satz erwähnen, dann zitieren Sie wie folgt:

EXAMPLES

In line 8 the author refers to the upper classes as "the idle rich" and **in line 17** as "selfish dinosaurs". **In lines 18 and 19**, she points out that they live a life of "privilege by an accident of birth". **Between lines 23 and 34**, she goes on to explain how ideas of class damage society as a whole.

G Die sprachliche Richtigkeit überprüfen

Die häufigsten Fehler werden durch falsche Analogien, d. h. meist durch ähnlich klingende Wörter und durch im Deutschen und Englischen unterschiedliche Strukturen (beides Interferenz) verursacht. Die Voraussetzung für eine wirkungsvolle Überprüfung sprachlicher Richtigkeit ist, solche „Interferenzfallen" zu erkennen.

Beachten Sie: Die folgende Auswahl zeigt die wichtigsten Fehlerquellen, die in der Regel auf Interferenz zurückzuführen sind:

1. Satzstellung und Stellung von Adverbien
2. Der bestimmte Artikel
3. Das Vollverb
   - die *progressive*-Zeiten
   - das *present perfect*
   - das Futur, besonders für Pläne, Absichten, Vereinbarungen
   - die Fragestellung und Verneinung bei den *simple*-Zeiten
4. Die unvollständigen Hilfsverben und ihre Ersatzverben
5. Der *if*-Satz
6. Verb + Infinitiv, Verb + *-ing*-Form
7. Schreib- und Kommaregeln

Bei der Überprüfung eines von Ihnen verfassten Textes sollten Sie äußerst systematisch und Schritt für Schritt vorgehen. Betrachten Sie zunächst immer den gesamten Satz als sprachliche Einheit. Vom Verb ausgehend können Sie dann die verschiedenen Bestandteile des Satzes überprüfen.

Schritt 1: Überprüfen Sie das Verb im Hinblick auf **Person** und **Zeitform** und natürlich auf seine **Schreibweise.** Da das *simple present* vorwiegend für die Textarbeit verwendet wird, sollten Sie die *-s*-Endung in der 3. Person Singular und die Verneinung mit do besonders im Auge behalten.

Beachten Sie:
- die Zeitenfolge bei *if*-Sätzen. (Denken Sie daran, dass would **nie** im *if*-Teil steht.)
- die indirekte Rede. Da in der Textanalyse das einleitende Verb meist im *simple present* steht, findet in der Regel **keine Zeitverschiebung** statt!
- die Bildung des Passivs (Zeitform von be + Partizip Perfekt).

EXAMPLES

The book **was published** in 1994.
This play **has been produced** hundreds of times.

Überprüfen Sie besonders die Bildung des Passivs mit Modalverben (Modalverb + be + Partizip Perfekt).

EXAMPLES

Tickets **can be bought** at the theatre.
The concert **had to be cancelled** because of illness.

Schritt 2: **Subjekt** und ggf. **Objekt(e) des Verbs** nach **Form**, **Stellung** und **Schreibweise** überprüfen! Dies dient der Kontrolle des Gebrauchs folgender Wortarten bzw. Wörter:
- Der bestimmte Artikel (the): Deutsche Muttersprachler tendieren dazu, den Artikel zu häufig zu verwenden. Beachten Sie, dass der bestimmte Artikel bei Substantiven, die nur im Plural vorkommen, und bei abstrakten Substantiven wie life, society, politics, nature usw. **nicht** verwendet wird! Daher: When in doubt, leave it out!
- Some/any: Beachten Sie, dass some üblicherweise in positiven Aussagesätzen und any in negativen Aussagesätzen und Fragesätzen verwendet werden. Dies gilt auch für Zusammensetzungen mit some und any.

- Much/many*:* Normalerweise verwendet man much/many in negativen Aussage- und in Fragesätzen. Much/many + too kommen aber auch in positiven Aussagesätzen vor.
- A little/a few, little/few: Diese Wörter werden wie much/many verwendet. Beachten Sie, dass a little und a few „nicht viel, aber gerade genug", aber little und few – also ohne Artikel – „nicht so viel wie erwartet/erhofft/benötigt" bedeuten.
- Substantive, die nur im Singular stehen: Wörter wie advice, evidence, information, knowledge und news sind für die Textanalyse wichtig. Im Gegensatz zum Deutschen werden sie im Englischen nur im Singular verwendet. Will man diese Wörter im Plural verwenden, muss man a bit of bzw. a piece of hinzufügen.

Schritt 3: **Pronomen** nach **Form** und **Beziehung** überprüfen! „Beziehungsfehler" kommen vor, wenn die Beziehung zwischen einem Pronomen und einem Substantiv nicht eindeutig ist. Um diesen Fehler zu vermeiden, sollten Sie im Zweifelsfall das Pronomen durch das entsprechende Substantiv oder den Namen ersetzen. Achten Sie besonders auf die korrekte Anwendung und Schreibweise der *self*-Pronomen und von each other/one another!

Schritt 4: **Verb + Präposition-** bzw. **Verb + Adverb-Kombinationen** überprüfen! Eine tückische Fehlerquelle ist die falsche Verwendung von Präpositionen bzw. Adverbien mit bestimmten Verben – wie z. B. (to) apply to, (to) consist of, (to) compare with, (to) separate from – und von *phrasal verbs* wie z. B. (to) look after, (to) get on with, (to) stand up for, (to) turn into usw. Hierfür gibt es keine Regeln, dafür aber viele Abweichungen vom Deutschen! Im Zweifelsfall schlagen Sie das betreffende Verb im Wörterbuch nach.

Schritt 5: Alle **Verb + Infinitiv-** und **Verb** + ***-ing*-Form-Kombinationen** überprüfen! Wie in Schritt 4 sind auch diese Zusammensetzungen eine Fehlerquelle. Da es hier keine zuverlässige Regel gibt, sollten Sie im Zweifelsfall ein Wörterbuch verwenden. Achten Sie besonders darauf, dass nach einigen Verben – z. B. (to) like, (to) prefer, (to) stop usw. – je nach Bedeutung der Infinitiv oder die *-ing*-Form steht.

Schritt 6: **Die Stellung von Adverbien** gründlich überprüfen! Viele Fehler sind auf die falsche Stellung von Adverbien, besonders von Satzadverbien, von Adverbien der unbestimmten Zeit und von kurzen (ein Wort!) Häufigkeitsadverbien zurückzuführen.

Beachten Sie:
- **Satzadverbien**, die den Sinn des ganzen Satzes bestimmen – wie z. B. luckily, unfortunately, maybe, obviously und of course –, stehen am **Satzanfang**.
- **Adverbien der unbestimmten Zeit** – wie z. B. already, just, now, soon, still usw. – und **kurze Häufigkeitsadverbien** – wie z. B. always, never, occasionally, sometimes usw. – stehen unmittelbar vor dem Verb, das sie bestimmen, aber unmittelbar nach be.
- Alle **anderen Adverbien** stehen am Satzende. Treten mehrere Adverbien auf, gilt die Reihenfolge **Art und Weise – Ort – Zeit**.

Schritt 7: Überprüfen Sie die **Kommasetzung**! Der am häufigsten vorkommende Fehler ist der unnötige Gebrauch eines Kommas. Deswegen gilt auch hier – wie beim bestimmten Artikel – die Regel: When in doubt, leave it out!

Das Komma wird gebraucht:

- ▷ nach dem *if*-Teil eines *if*-Satzes, wenn dieser Teil an erster Stelle steht,
- ▷ nach dem einleitenden Verb in der direkten Rede,
- ▷ um einen nicht notwendigen Relativsatz von dem Hauptsatz zu trennen,
- ▷ um Hauptsätze zu verbinden, die durch and, as, but, for, or verbunden sind,
- ▷ um die Wörter in einer Aufzählung voneinander zu trennen, obwohl sie vor and und or oft weggelassen werden.

Das Komma wird nicht gebraucht:

- ▷ vor Satzgefügen, die mit that, what, where, which, who usw. beginnen,
- ▷ nach dem einleitenden Verb in der indirekten Rede,
- ▷ um einen notwendigen Relativsatz von dem Hauptsatz zu trennen.

9 **Each of the following sentences contains one mistake. Where to look is given before each section, e.g. verbs, nouns and pronouns etc. Correct the mistakes.**

Verbs

1. Most of the characters is female.
2. When we met him again, Joe Lampton was married for five years.
3. Macbeth meet the witches on a lonely heath.
4. After Antonio had asked him for money, Shylock had made fun of him.
5. Most politicians exagerate the importance of political parties.
6. The story would be more interesting if it would reflect real life.
7. If the report had concentrated on just one topic, it had been easier to understand.
8. Joe says that Susan loves her father more than she loved him.
9. The witches tell Macbeth that one day he would be king.
10. Joe is unhappy but he must not lead that kind of life.

Nouns and pronouns

11. I can't find something about this problem in the first part of the text.
12. The author says that too much videos are bad for children.
13. There are evidences for this in the final paragraph.
14. Can you give me some informations about trains to Glasgow, please?
15. The police is getting worried about drug dealers in schools.
16. Susan is the wife of Joe Lampton.
17. The front door is in fact at the house's side.
18. Philosophy is about fundamental questions of the human life.

19. He has been in the hospital for six months now.
20. The most great Scottish authors wrote in English.
21. They didn't build their house theirselves, did they?
22. Joe and Susan did not really love themselves but they still got married.

Verb + preposition and phrasal verb

23. This book consists from twelve units.
24. Compared of *King Lear, Macbeth* is an easy Shakespeare play.
25. I don't know if we'll go out tomorrow; it depends with the weather.
26. Tom has been waiting on his girlfriend outside the cinema for nearly an hour.
27. How long has Susan been married with Joe?
28. Mark's a terrible snob. He looks down people less fortunate than himself.

Verb + infinitive, verb + -ing-form

29. The government suggested to close several London hospitals.
30. Nobody dares disagreeing with Mr Davis.
31. Tom promised his doctor giving up smoking.
32. Can you imagine to work with dangerous criminals?
33. Would you prefer staying at home this evening?
34. It's hard but you can't avoid to meet your ex-girlfriend sometimes.

Position of adverbs and adverbial phrases

35. We missed the first part of the film unfortunately.
36. Wendy still is doing her homework.
37. I'm afraid Mr Allen already has left the office.
38. You can of course come with us to the party if you want.
39. We go sometimes to the theatre in York.
40. Every day Wendy has to visit her elderly parents.
41. Always Mr Scott gives us homework to do at the weekend.
42. Milk is daily delivered in Britain, even on Sundays.
43. We enjoyed the story about the two dogs particularly.

Commas

44. The girl, who was sitting next to me, gave me a big smile.
45. The moment he spoke I knew, where he came from.
46. The author claims, that human rights are impossible to enforce.
47. The man you know, the one Ann met at our party phoned her the same evening.

1 Sachtext: Class Society

Inhaltsfragen
Autorenabsicht: informative Sachtexte

A Text und Aufgaben

This feature article is from *Options*, a quality British women's magazine. In it the writer looks into the special problems of women who married outside their own social class or peer group. To do this, she uses a case study approach, allowing the women to speak largely for themselves.

Going for a bit of rough

Laura Marcus explores love and marriage between the classes

According to research, our best chance of finding lasting happiness is with someone from our own class and background. Shared childhood experiences, speaking the same language[1] and an understanding of each other's lives are absolutely vital[2] to most couples. Others enjoy a sense of adventure when they enter a different world. But while it may be an adventure at first, tolerance levels can drop after a few years. Trivialities such as calling the sitting room the lounge[3] can drive one partner crazy, as it's what this represents that can reopen the divide once so easily and lovingly bridged.

"For me, the difference really arose when it came to choosing schools," says Olivia, who has a working-class background, but whose partner, George, went to a public school[4] and wanted his sons to do the same. "There was no way I was sending my sons to boarding school[5] when they were only eight, even if we could afford it and it would give them a fantastic education." Olivia says the pressures on her were enormous. "I could see his parents thinking: 'She doesn't understand. She'll drag them down[6] to her level.' It came between us to the point where we had to have counselling[7]."

The counsellor helped Olivia and George negotiate[8] their way through the impasse[9] by suggesting they send the boys to a private day school. "I still don't like it, but it's a compromise. At least they won't be subjected to[10] that barbaric playing fields mentality[11]." Yet George was a product of exactly that kind of upbringing, and Olivia fell in love with him. Is there a contradiction[12] here, or even a little hyprocrisy[13]?

"I love George for himself, he's kind and has a wicked[14] sense of humour," says Olivia. "But if I'm honest, his background did add to his attraction - because of his confidence. A moneyed background gives you self-assurance. He made me feel secure[15] for the first time in my life but I don't think it's anything to do with his schooling. I think we can give our kids confidence too, but with loving attention as much as an expensive education."

Sometimes it's not so much a class barrier couples leap across[16] as a financial one. As Olivia says, money makes a difference, and for Ruth, also brought up in a working-class home, marrying her millionaire boss's son caused enormous problems. "My father said they'd never accept me, and he was right. Ian's mother was convinced I was a gold digger[17]. I really think that parents and friends have a vested interest[18] in keeping you where you are."

Yet despite this lack of support, Ruth and Ian were together for 15 years. Ruth says class differences undoubtedly played a part in their final split[19]. "His family never accepted me and I never felt at home with them. You can only fight this for so long, it wears you down in the end. I feel very bitter about the whole thing – they never gave us a chance. I'm sure his mother is delighted we're divorced." But do parents really have that strong an influence? Ruth says that they do. "It's not the parent without[20] but the parent within. It's a subtle conditioning, and although you might rebel[21] when you're 20, by the time you're 40 you realise you've become just like your parents. I'm sure that's what happened to Ian. It's as if he began to see me through his mother's eyes. It was awful."

But it doesn't have to be like this. If you fall for someone from a different class, there are ways of making your life easier. First, you must accept that it won't be the same as marrying within your own peer group. "Always deal with your differences," advises Olivia. "Don't let things fester[22]. If you can't stand his mother's charity balls[23] or his father's darts night, say so, and why. Chances are you feel ill at ease[24] and this needs understanding. But if you find some event tedious[25], negotiate[26] not to go, in return for something else. Remember, it's him you're married to. Not his family."

703 words

1 language = *(here)* dialect, way of speaking, 2 vital = essential, 3 lounge = middle-class word for living room, 4 public school = elite private school, 5 boarding school = school where the pupils live at school during term time, 6 (to) drag down = (to) pull down, 7 counselling = help in form of expert advice, 8 (to) negotiate = *(here)* (to) find with difficulty, 9 impasse = stalemate, 10 (to) be subjected to = (to) be forcibly exposed to, 11 playing fields mentality = idea that competitive sport is the most important element in education, 12 contradiction = opinion that does not agree with other opinions held by the same person, 13 hyprocrisy = acting against one's stated beliefs, 14 wicked = *(here)* bad in a pleasant and amusing way, 15 secure = safe, 16 (to) leap across = (to) jump over, 17 gold digger = sb who marries for money, 18 vested interest = act of keeping things as they are for selfish reasons, 19 split = separation, 20 without = *(here)* outside, 21 rebel = fight traditional ideas, 22 (to) fester = (to) become much worse because it's not talked about, 23 charity ball = formal dance to make money for a good cause, 24 ill at ease = uncomfortable, 25 tedious = boring, 26 (to) negotiate = *(here)* (to) reach agreement by discussion and compromise

ASSIGNMENTS

(Anforderungsbereich I: Textverständnis)

1. **Explain to what extent Olivia and Ruth's experiences support research findings into cross-class relationships *(Beziehungen über Klassengrenzen hinweg)*.**
2. **Point out less important examples of class-related behaviour *(durch Klassenzugehörigkeit bedingtes Verhalten)* mentioned in the text.**
3. **Describe the attitudes of the parents mentioned in the text to their child's marriage partner.**

(Anforderungsbereich II: Analyse)

4. **Compare the two women's experiences.**
5. **Characterise Laura Marcus's article with reference to her intention.**

(Anforderungsbereich III: Bewertung)

6. Comment on Laura Marcus's remark that there may be "even a little hyprocrisy" in Olivia's attitude.

B Praktische Hilfe und Arbeitsschritte

Die Nummern 1–5 beziehen sich auf die Aufgabennummern oben.

1–4 Inhaltsfragen

Aufgaben zum Textverständnis sind auch in der gymnasialen Oberstufe wichtig, wobei sie jedoch tief greifender und vielschichtiger sind als die einfachen „W-Fragen", die in der Mittelstufe gestellt werden.

Eine Analyse vieler Abiturvorschläge zeigt, dass ...

- ▷ die Antwort auf Fragen zum Textverständnis etwa vier bis fünf Sätze umfasst,
- ▷ sehr viele Fragen durch Ausdrücke wie *according to the author, in this article, to what extent* usw. eingeschränkt werden,
- ▷ der nachgefragte Inhalt selten nur anhand einer Textstelle oder eines Textabschnittes ermittelt werden kann.

Methode

Aus den o. g. Gründen empfiehlt sich bei der Bearbeitung auch von scheinbar „einfachen" Aufgaben zum Textverständnis die folgende Arbeitsweise.

Schritt 1: Lesen Sie alle Fragen durch, bevor Sie mit der Bearbeitung der ersten beginnen. Sonst kann es leicht passieren, dass Sie Textmaterial für die Antwort einer Frage verwenden, das besser zu einer der nachfolgenden Fragen passt.

Schritt 2: Manchmal werden Aufgaben nur deshalb falsch gelöst, weil die Aufgabenstellung nicht richtig, meist nicht vollständig, verstanden wurde. In solchen Fällen empfiehlt es sich, mit Schlüsselwörtern bzw. Schlüsselbegriffen zu arbeiten. Nachdem Sie die Schlüsselwörter bzw. -begriffe in der Frage gefunden haben, sollten Sie dieselben Wörter bzw. Ausdrücke im Text finden. So können Sie die für Ihre Antwort relevanten Textstellen leicht erkennen. Diese heben Sie am besten durch Unterstreichungen oder mit einem Textmarker hervor.

Schritt 3: Bei der Bearbeitung der Aufgaben sollten Sie sich von einer Frage leiten lassen: **Was will der Prüfer von mir wissen?** Ursache für inhaltliche Schwächen bei der Bearbeitung von Textfragen ist häufig, dass die Anwort Nebensächliches und/oder Ungefragtes enthält. **Bemühen Sie sich also immer, präzise und genau zu antworten.** Wenn Sie mehr als fünf oder sechs Sätze geschrieben haben, können Sie davon ausgehen, dass Sie wahrscheinlich Material verwendet haben, das für die Antwort irrelevant ist.

Schritt 4: Oft fällt es schwer, einen ansprechenden einleitenden Satz für eine Antwort zu formulieren. Die Aufgabenstellung kann hierfür hilfreich sein.

Schritt 5: Sie sollten, wann immer es Ihnen möglich ist, „Ihre eigene Sprache" verwenden. Trotz der potenziell höheren Fehlerquote schätzen es die meisten Prüfer, wenn ihre Schüler selbstständig arbeiten, statt einfach nur den Originaltext abzuschreiben.

Schritt 6: Geben Sie keine Klausur ab, ohne sie auf sprachliche Richtigkeit überprüft zu haben. Viele Fehler sind kleine Ausrutscher, die meist auf Flüchtigkeit oder Nervosität zurückzuführen sind.

USEFUL EXPRESSIONS **Inhaltsfragen**

1

(to) agree **with** research findings in that ...

(to) support ... in so far as ...

(to) experience/have marriage difficulties/problems

(to) be/come **from** a different (social) class

(to) be middle/working class

(to) have few/not have shared *(geteilt)* childhood experiences

(to) tend to do sth

(to) see life **through** different eyes/**from** a different angle *(Blickwinkel)*

(to) cause friction *(Reiberei)*

❷

(to) have to do **with** sth

(to) be concerned **with** ...

(to) be in the habit *(Gewohnheit)* **of** ...

(to) drive sb crazy/make sb angry

(to) refer **to** *(darauf hindeuten)* a particular habit/event

(to) talk **about** irritants *(Reizthema)*

(to) discuss a problem/talk a problem **over**

(to) not let sth fester *(nagen)*

❸

(to) hear about a person's attitude *(Einstellung)* **to** sth

(to) object **to** *(Einwände erheben gegen)* sth

(to) take exception **to** *(an etwas Anstoß nehmen)* an attitude/opinion/wish

(to) be (secretly) convinced **of** sth *(insgeheim davon überzeugt)*

(to) drag/pull sb down to a lower level *(Niveau)*

(to) not accept a person as an equal/as a full member of a family

(to) have a vested interest *(eigennütziges Interesse)* **in** ...

(to) keep sb in his/her place *(in seine/ihre Schranken weisen)*

(to) add to other difficulties/problems

(to) complicate a situation

(to) be/become worn down *(aufgerieben)* **by** ...

(to) point **out** changes **in** another person

(to) become/grow more like another person

(to) see life **through** another person's eyes

(to) hear about a person's attitude *(Einstellung)* **to** sth
(to) object **to** *(Einwände erheben gegen)* sth
(to) take exception **to** *(an etwas Anstoß nehmen)* an attitude/opinion/wish
(to) be (secretly) convinced **of** sth *(insgeheim davon überzeugt)*
(to) drag/pull sb down to a lower level *(Niveau)*
(to) not accept a person as an equal/as a full member of a family

❹

(to) survive *(fortbestehen)* in spite **of** difficulties/problems
(to) love a partner enough to seek a solution to a problem
(to) get outside help/expert advice
(to) be willing to compromise
(to) succeed **in** solving a problem
(to) be made worse/exacerbated *(verschärfen)* **by** ...
(to) marry sb for money
(to) end/result **in** divorce
(to) change one's personality/attitude
(to) be strong enough to stand **up to** sb *(sich jdm. entgegenstellen)*
(to) be (deeply) hurt/bitter

❺ Autorenabsicht: informative Sachtexte

Sachtexte (→ non-fictional texts) können gemäß der Autorenabsicht (→ intention) in fünf allgemeine Gruppen unterteilt werden. In der Oberstufe sind in der Regel meist nur informative *(informative)*, argumentative *(argumentative)* und – bei Sachtexten weniger häufig – erzählende *(narrative)* Texte für die Bearbeitung relevant.
Der Artikel von Laura Marcus besteht aus zwei Fallstudien (→ case study). Die Autorin lässt die beiden Frauen Olivia und Ruth über ihre Erfahrungen sprechen. Die informativen Elemente überwiegen, der Text ist nur geringfügig mit Wertungen durchsetzt. Die Aufgabenstellung erfordert, dass Sie die Textintention analysieren und Ihre Analyse anhand der verwendeten Sprachmittel begründen. Die folgende Darstellung soll Ihnen dabei helfen:

GOOD TO KNOW **Informative Sachtexte**

Die Intention informativer Sachtexte ist, ein Thema sachlich darzustellen, ohne die Meinung des Schreibenden in den Vordergrund zu stellen.

Solche Texte weisen folgende **Merkmale** auf:

- In informativen Texten verwendet man meist das *simple present*:
  Others **enjoy** a sense of adventure when they **enter** a different world.
- Am Anfang der Texte steht in aller Regel eine These, also eine klar umrissene Darstellung des Themas, meist als positive Aussage formuliert:
  ..., our best chance of finding lasting happiness is with someone from our own class and background.
- Um dem Text Glaubwürdigkeit zu verleihen, werden Betroffene erwähnt oder fachliche Autoritäten zitiert:
  Olivia says the pressures on her were enormous.
- „Objektive Beweise" wie Statistiken, Forschungsergebnisse usw. können eine These oder eine Gegenthese faktisch belegen:
  According to research, our best chance of finding lasting happiness is ...

Methode

Schritt 1: Sie haben in diesem Stadium der Textarbeit bereits Verständnisfragen beantwortet oder eine Zusammenfassung erarbeitet, sodass Sie mit dem Text vertraut sein sollten. Sollte dies nicht der Fall sein, lassen Sie sich nicht irritieren. Beginnen Sie trotzdem mit der schrittweisen Bearbeitung dieser Aufgabe. Eventuelle „Verständnislücken" schließen sich während der Textarbeit meist von selbst.

Schritt 2: Schauen Sie sich die oben genannten Merkmale eines informativen Sachtextes an. Mithilfe von Unterstreichungen bzw. eines Textmarkers suchen Sie entsprechende Beispiele im Text. Notieren Sie diese dann unter Angabe der Fundstelle auf einem Konzeptblatt.

Schritt 3: Abschließend verfassen Sie unter Verwendung dieses Sprachmaterials eine Antwort in Form eines fortlaufenden Textes. Überraschend viele Schüler/innen lassen diesen äußerst wichtigen Schritt aus. Beachten Sie jedoch, dass eine Auflistung von Beweisen – siehe Schritt 2 – nicht ausreicht, um die Aufgabenstellung zu erfüllen.

USEFUL EXPRESSIONS	Autorenabsicht (informative Sachtexte)

(to) be in the form of case studies *(Fallstudie)*
(to) present information in the form of ...
(to) have/show features *(Merkmal)* of informative texts
(to) be intended to achieve a certain aim
(to) give information **about**/clarify *(klären)* a particular topic
(to) be written in the ... tense
(to) be used to express ...
(to) be typical **of** ...
(to) begin/open **with** ...
(to) introduce a topic to the reader/the reader to a topic (l. ...)
(to) quote expert opinion
(to) refer **to** research findings
(to) make a text more credible *(glaubwürdig)* by ...
(to) allow people/protagonists to speak for themselves
(to) feel (evident) sympathy **for** ...
(to) not express one's own opinion
(to) leave the reader to reach his/her own conclusion

Schritt 4: Bevor Sie die Reinschrift anfertigen, überprüfen Sie Ihre Antwort sowohl auf inhaltliche Vollständigkeit als auch auf sprachliche Richtigkeit.

2 Sachtext: Urban Society

Zusammenfassungen

A Text und Aufgaben

This piece about the effectiveness - or otherwise - of London's congestion charge is from the *Guardian*, a British quality paper. In his report, Dan Milmo describes why London is as congested now as it was when the congestion charge was first introduced, and what can be done to solve the problem.

Transport: London still gridlocked[1] despite congestion charge[2]

The London congestion charge is losing its battle against gridlock after it was revealed that the capital's streets are as gridlocked now as they were before the levy[3] was introduced.

The £8-a-day charge was considered one of the great successes of Ken Livingstone's reign as mayor after it was introduced five years ago. However, a boom in roadworks and traffic-calming measures[4] has reduced driving space and pushed up congestion despite a drop in the number of vehicles entering central London.

Pedestrians are expected to bear the consequences of the fightback against lengthening tailbacks[5], with pedestrian schemes facing the axe[6] and experts calling for shorter crossing times at traffic lights. Boris Johnson, the new London mayor, said he would scrap[7] plans for pedestrian areas, take action against road-digging utility companies[8] and allow motorbikes in bus lanes to reverse the tide of congestion.

Transport for London (TfL) said yesterday that gridlock in the zone is the same as it was before February 2003, when the measure was introduced. There are 100,000 fewer vehicles entering central London but they are taking longer to travel through - driving 1 km takes 2.3 minutes longer than it does at quieter times of day.

The latest figures will give ample[9] ammunition to the scheme's opponents, particularly those who criticised the extension of the charging zone to west London last year as a measure driven more by revenue-raising[10] than green issues[11]. According to yesterday's TfL report there has been no easing[12] of congestion in the western zone since the charge was extended to Kensington and Notting Hill.

Johnson (...) said: "I have always thought that the congestion charge is a blunt instrument[13]. It has proved successful in cutting traffic coming into London but on its own has not solved the problem of congestion. Various roadworks and building schemes going on in the capital have also eroded[14] its impact. I am therefore introducing a more comprehensive approach to easing congestion."

The mayor said he would force utility companies to apply for permits[15] before starting roadworks and announced the scrapping of a plan to turn part of Parliament Square in Westminster into a pedestrian zone. Traffic light signals will also be left on green or red for longer periods of time in order to smooth out[16] traffic.

The scheme's backers argue that congestion would be even worse without the congestion charge, which is levied on drivers entering central London between 7am and 6pm on weekdays.

Professor Stephen Glaister, a transport specialist at Imperial College London and former TfL board member, said the figures were no surprise because congestion had been inching back[17] to 2002 levels for years. "Congestion would be a lot worse were it not for the charge," he said. Congestion levels in the first three years of the charge were up to 30% lower than 2002 results, but the start of roadworks by Thames Water and other utility firms in 2006 started to push congestion back up.

TfL said cramped[18] road space is the biggest cause of congestion. It said 70,000 fewer cars enter the original charging zone compared with 2002, with 30,000 fewer entering the western zone, but gridlock has increased because the reduction in road space has been greater. TfL said utility companies make up to 14,000 applications a month to dig up London roads.

Malcolm Murray-Clark, the TfL executive[19] who introduced the scheme, said the central zone was not under threat[20] but admitted that the western extension could be altered or dropped altogether. Edmund King, president of the AA, said: "It is disappointing that the charge is not doing what it says on the tin[21], which is to reduce congestion."

612 words

1 gridlocked = completely jammed, unable to move at all, 2 congestion charge = sum of money paid by drivers to enter a given area, here central London, 3 levy = sum of money charged to do sth, 4 traffic-calming measure = anything done to slow traffic down, 5 tailback = line of slow-moving or stationary vehicles, 6 (to) face the axe = (to) be abolished, scrapped, 7 (to) scrap = (to) do away with, (to) abolish, 8 utility company = firm that supplies gas, electricity, water etc., 9 ample = plenty of, 10 revenue-raising = money-earning, 11 green issue = anything done to protect the environment, 12 easing = making easier, 13 blunt instrument = primitive, ineffective means of doing sth, 14 eroded = worn away, 15 permit = written permission to do sth, 16 (to) smooth out = (to) make more balanced, even, 17 (to) inch back = (to) gradually return, 18 cramped = narrow, lacking in space, 19 executive = manager, 20 under threat = in danger, 21 "what it says on the tin" = "what it claims to be"

ASSIGNMENTS

(Anforderungsbereich I: Textverständnis)

❶ Point out why the congestion charge has not been as effective in solving London's traffic problems as originally hoped.

❷ Describe what effect new measures to solve London's traffic congestion are likely to have.

❸ **Summarise the text in not more than 200 words.**

B Praktische Hilfe und Arbeitsschritte

Die Nummer ❸ bezieht sich auf die Aufgabennummer oben.

❸ Zusammenfassung

Eine Zusammenfassung ist eine kurze schriftliche Darstellung eines Textes, die als zusammenhängender Text präsentiert wird. **Sie ist keine bloße Auflistung!** Anhand einer Zusammenfassung wird festgestellt, ob ein Text vollständig verstanden wurde. Der Prüfer kann die Arbeitsanweisung unterschiedlich formulieren, z. B.:

GOOD TO KNOW **Mögliche Aufgabenstellungen**

Write a summary of the text.
Summarise the text in not more than ... words/sentences.
Write a summary of the text using not more than ... words.
Reduce the text to about a quarter/a third/... of its original length.
Point out the writer's main thoughts/arguments in about ... words/sentences.
Trace the writer's train/chain of thought *(Gedankengang)* in about ... words.

Die Kürzung eines Textes erfolgt durch

- das Auslassen von Sätzen, Satzteilen, Wortgruppen und sogar ganzen Textabschnitten, die nicht unmittelbar zur Darstellung der Thesen oder wesentlichen Gedankengänge des Autors beitragen,
- die präzise Neuformulierung inhaltlich relevanter Textteile. Fassen Sie sich kurz.

Methode

Schritt 1: Lesen Sie zunächst den Text mindestens zweimal. Einmal, damit Sie den allgemeinen Sinn erfassen, und ein zweites Mal, um die Feinheiten zu verstehen.

Schritt 2: Lesen Sie jetzt den Text nochmals Satz für Satz durch. Lassen Sie sich dabei immer von der Frage leiten: **Was will der Autor mir mitteilen?** Setzen Sie Klammern um alle Sätze, Satzteile, Ausdrücke usw., die unwesentlich, also entbehrlich sind. Die Praxis hat gezeigt, dass folgende Textelemente ausgeklammert werden können:

- Statistik, Ziffern, Daten
- Einleitungen für Beispiele: *as in the case of ...; as when ...; for example; for instance*
- Einleitungen für Anekdoten, Nebensächliches: *by the way, ...; furthermore, ...; incidentally, ...; I remember when ...; moreover, ...; that reminds me of the story of ...*

- ▷ Stilmittel (→ stylistic device) wie Aufzählung (→ enumeration), Gleichnis (→ simile), Übertreibung (→ exaggeration, hyperbole), Wiederholung (→ repetition) ...
- ▷ Einleitungen für Zitate: *as ... argues/claims/points out/remarks/says ...; ... once pointed out/said/wrote that ...*
- ▷ Einleitungen für Lebensweisheiten, Redensarten: *as everybody knows, ...; as the prophet says ...; as the proverb/saying goes ...*

Schritt 3: An diesem Punkt der Textarbeit haben Sie eine Sammlung einzelner Sätze, Satzteile und Textabschnitte zusammengestellt, die nun in die Form eines zusammenhängenden Textes gebracht werden muss. Leider lassen einige Schüler/innen diesen äußerst wichtigen Schritt aus und erarbeiten keine Zusammenfassung, sondern bestenfalls eine Auflistung der wichtigsten Inhalte. Entwerfen Sie deshalb zuerst einen schlüssigen Text auf einem Konzeptblatt. Folgende Formulierungen können hierfür hilfreich sein.

USEFUL EXPRESSIONS	Zusammenfassungen
at the beginning of the article/book review ...	
in the second/third/following/final paragraph ...	
in the opening/middle/concluding part/section ...	
(to) introduce an argument	
(to) develop an argument/a train of thought	
(to) follow a train of thought	
(to) present evidence to support an argument/a claim	
(to) emphasise the most important arguments/ideas/thoughts	
(to) conclude by summarising/repeating the main arguments	
(to) be given evidence in the form of statistics	
(to) be presented **with** (further) evidence/data	
(to) be informed **of**/told **about** ...	
(to) be devoted **to** a description/an exploration of ...	
(to) be given **over to** a description (of ...)	

Schritt 4: Bevor Sie die Reinschrift anfertigen, überprüfen Sie Ihre Antwort sowohl auf inhaltliche Vollständigkeit als auch auf sprachliche Richtigkeit.

3 Sachtext: Education

Autorenabsicht: wertende Sachtexte

A Text und Aufgaben

This article comes from the opinion column of the *Daily Mirror*, a left-of-centre British tabloid. The author gives his opinion of the British school system in the light of 'wild claims' *(übertriebene Behauptungen)* from the government that exam results show that school standards are rising. The author uses what happened during a power cut in Hammersmith, London, to support his own view that such claims are far too optimistic and have little to do with the awful reality.

Educated kids? It doesn't add up [1]

I've banged on [2] more than once about the level of education among too much of the youth of this country.

Despite wild claims [3] from the government that they're better educated than ever, neither literacy [4] nor numeracy [5] is impressive. It's all very well shopkeepers having machines to work out what punters [6] have purchased and what change should be returned. They not only total everything but also register the money tendered [7] and then work out how much cash should be handed back to the customer.

You've all seen it in operation [8]. You fill a supermarket trolley with goodies [9], get given a bill for, say, £74.60 and hand over four crisp £20 notes. Kerching! [10] ... the machine tells the cashier that £5.40 has to be handed back.

All seems so easy. Well, it is until there's a problem with the electricity supply, as happened the other day in Hammersmith, West London. I don't know the dreary [11] details, but the result was that one whole area of this busy street, including coffee bars, stationery shops, travel agents, etc. had their electricity supply suddenly cut off.

The result was complete chaos. Workers in the area decided to shut up shop while the 'sparkies' [12] sorted matters out. One went over to one of the coffee shops. Begging to remain nameless [13], she told me what happened next. She and a pal [14] ordered a couple of lattes [15] and buns [16] before proffering [17] a £10 note as payment. Straightforward [18] enough, you might think. But it wasn't. The waitress took the money and then realised that she didn't have a machine to add up the cost of these four items. Oh, dear! She had to do so in the old-fashioned way. If not in her head, then by writing the amounts on a piece of paper. She couldn't, despite four attempts. In the end she just gave up, said the coffees and buns were on the house and added that when she could get rid of the customers she'd shut the place down until electricity was restored [19].

What an indictment [20]. And an answer to those who say our 'hopes of the future' [21] are passing exams better than ever before. I don't think so.

I'm not a bad adder-upper myself. As an articled clerk[22] to a firm of chartered accountants[23] many moons ago[24], (...) I had to audit[25] companies. As a lowly[26] sort of fellow, (...) it was my job to 'cast' (that means add up) endless rows of figures. This was before decimalisation[27], in the days of pounds, shillings and pence (20 shillings made up one pound, 12 pennies one shilling, so it wasn't so easy). The wimps[28] would cast the pennies first, then the shillings and finally the pounds to reach a final figure. An old boy taught me the trick of casting whole amounts in one go. He was a genius, I was just about OK.
I never regretted[29] learning to add at speed. It's always made doing 'expenses'[30] so much easier.

499 words

1 (to) add up = *(here)* (to) not agree with reality, 2 (to) bang on = (to) often complain about sth, 3 claim = statement which is not sure to be true, 4 literacy = ability to read and write, 5 numeracy = ability to do mathematical calculations, 6 punter = *(here)* shopper, 7 (to) tender = *(here)* (to) pay, 8 in operation = *(here)* as it happens, 9 goodies = food and drink, 10 Kerching! = word used by magicians when doing a trick, 11 dreary = *(here)* boring, 12 sparky = *(coll.)* electrician, 13 (to) beg to remain nameless = (to) ask not to tell the name, 14 pal = *(coll.)* friend, 15 latte = Italian coffee with milk, 16 bun = kind of dry cake, 17 (to) proffer = (to) offer, 18 straightforward = uncomplicated, 19 (to) restore = *(here)* (to) switch on again, 20 indictment = sign that a society/system is very bad/wrong, 21 'hopes of the future' = *(here)* young people, especially those at school, 22 articled clerk = person qualified to help a lawyer or accountant, 23 chartered accountant = person qualified to advise clients on their tax affairs, 24 many moons ago = a very long time ago, 25 (to) audit = (to) check that a company's accounts and taxes are correct, 26 lowly = low down in a hierarchy, junior, 27 decimalisation = introduction of decimal system, 28 wimp = weak person, 29 (to) regret = (to) feel sorry, 30 expenses = *(here) Spesen*

ASSIGNMENTS

(Anforderungsbereich I: Textverständnis)

❶ Explain why the power cut in Hammersmith called the government's 'wild claims' into question.

(Anforderungsbereich II: Analyse)

❷ **Say what the author's aim in writing this article is and analyse how it is expressed in his use of language.**

B Praktische Hilfe und Arbeitsschritte

Die Nummer ❷ bezieht sich auf die Aufgabennummer oben.

❷ Autorenabsicht: wertende Texte

Vor allem in der Presse werden wertende Texte *(evaluative texts)* (→ intention) verwendet, um die Bedeutung eines entscheidenden Ereignisses *(critical event)* darzustellen.

Texte dieser Art weisen folgende Merkmale *(characteristics)* auf:

- Sie enthalten erzählerische Elemente und wertende Elemente *(narrative/evaluative elements)* (→ intention).
- Bei den erzählerischen Elementen wird normalerweise die Vergangenheit und bei den wertenden meist die Gegenwart verwendet.
- Häufig wird **a)** der Zeitpunkt des Ereignisses durch Adverbien wie *the other day, last week, a few days ago, at the weekend* usw. und **b)** ggf. auch sein zeitlicher Ablauf durch Adverbien wie *after that, then, later on, in the end* usw. beschrieben.
- Mehr oder minder konkrete Einzelheiten über Ort (wo?) und Personen (wer?) spielen eine wichtige Rolle, um die Glaubwürdigkeit *(plausibility)* der Geschichte zu erhöhen und das Leserinteresse zu wecken *(arouse the reader's interest)*.
- Bei Boulevardzeitungen *(tabloids)* bringt der Autor seinen eigenen Standpunkt (→ point of view) zum Ausdruck, vor allem durch seine Wortwahl (→ choice of words).

Methode

Schritt 1: Vergewissern Sie sich, dass Sie den Text in allen Details wirklich verstanden haben.

Schritt 2: Markieren Sie **a)** die wertenden und **b)** die erzählerischen Elemente.
Tipp: Die beiden Elemente sind anhand der Zeitformen *(tenses)* leicht zu erkennen.

Schritt 3: Jetzt konzentrieren Sie sich auf die Absicht des Autors. Beschreiben Sie seine Intention mithilfe des Materials in der Übersicht.

USEFUL EXPRESSIONS Autorenabsicht
(to) make one's own opinion/point of view/position clear
(to) attempt/try to convince/persuade the reader that ...
(to) refer to opposing claims/views in that ...
(to) call into question/criticise the government's claim that ...
(to) make fun of/ridicule somebody else's opinion/ ...

Schritt 4: Jetzt geht es darum, die sprachliche Umsetzung der Autorenabsicht zu verdeutlichen. Zu diesem Zweck untersuchen Sie in erster Linie die Wortwahl, besonders verwendete Adjektive *(wild, dreary, ...)* und Verben *(bang on, shut up shop, ...)*.

USEFUL EXPRESSIONS | **Wortwahl und Struktur**

(to) open an article/opinion column with ...

(to) go on to say that ...

(to) point to an incident to show that ...

(to) describe what happened when there was a power cut in ...

(to) poke fun at/ridicule a waitress because she ...

(to) employ/make use of strong adjectives/verbs such as ...

(to) use repetition *(Wiederholung)*/hyperbole *(Übertreibung)* to emphasise that ...

(to) speak ironically of 'hopes for the future' to make clear how ...

Schritt 5: Auch bei solchen Aufgaben tendieren Schüler/innen dazu, eine Antwort in Form einer Auflistung von Belegstellen aus dem Text zu erarbeiten. Wie bei allen Antworten ist es aber äußerst wichtig, dass Sie versuchen, einen abgerundeten und fortlaufenden Prosatext zu verfassen.

Schritt 6: Bevor Sie die Reinschrift anfertigen, überprüfen Sie Ihre Antworten auf inhaltliche Vollständigkeit und auf sprachliche Richtigkeit.

4 Sachtext: The American Dream

Charakterisierung
Stilmittel in Sachtexten

A Text und Aufgaben

This highly autobiographical text comes from a *Newsweek* interview with the late American writer, journalist and political activist Norman Mailer († 11 October 2007). Mailer's first and probably most famous novel, *The Naked and the Dead*, was published in 1948. This World War II novel shows soldiers not as the heroic defenders of freedom so popular in Hollywood films, but as defenceless anti-heroes in a cynical power game. At the time of this interview in his 80s, Mailer's highly critical 'anti-American' opinions continued to make him a thorn in the establishment's side.

The last word

(...) Norman Mailer has written 31 books. He has won the Pulitzer Prize[1] twice. He has directed four films and written 10 screenplays. He has been married six times and has nine children. He was once arrested for stabbing[2] his second wife. He ran for[3] mayor of New York twice. He has arthritis in his knees and sometimes walks with two sticks. With his wife, the artist and novelist Norris Church Mailer, he lives (...) beside the ocean in Provincetown, Massachusetts, where he recently sat down for an interview with *Newsweek's* Malcolm Jones.
He does not like interviews. Excerpts[4]:

So what do you make of Iraq?

Leaving aside[5] all the usual explanations – the oil, the fact that if the people in power in this country win, they will then have this commanding position[6] in the Near East – forgetting all that, the fact is, that war could just go on and on and on. But I don't think that bothers[7] our leaders very much. I think they kind of like the idea that if the country gets very military, then they can stop all the 'frees' – free love, gay liberation, women's liberation – all the things they detest[8]. There's no question that the level of uncertainty, the absence[9] of absolutes, has probably never been greater. So the longer the danger goes on, the longer they have to create a new kind of society. We're in for curious[10] times.

How's your health?

My knees are no good. But I really think, the key[11] thing as you get older is that you learn to cleanse yourself[12] of self-pity. And, of course, I have certain religious beliefs that make it easier. I don't have this certainty, thank God, that once you die you die, and that's the end of it. On the contrary, I believe in a form of karma[13], I believe in reincarnation – not for everyone! I think reincarnation is a reward of a sort. Where we go is another matter. Another great thing about getting older (...) is that you get much more efficient and economical about what you want to do. You no longer want to be president of the United States or have everyone in the world say you're the greatest writer who's ever lived. You know it's nonsense now. You're in the lap of history[14]. You could easily be forgotten in 20, 30, 40 years. There's no telling[15] and it's not important, since you will not be there.

In your new book, you say that the things you've hated most in your life have all triumphed[16].

I listed plastic, superhighways, highrise architecture, which is an abomination[17] of everything. Those are the three. And the platitudes[18] of politicians have only gotten[19] worse. I've been saying for a while – and it drives most American patriots mad with rage – that the country has gotten more loutish[20]. And maybe the whole world has been getting that way, because we've been exporting that loutishness. It's one of our great cultural commodities[21]: crap[22].

Has anything gotten better?

I think journalism has gotten better – the writing has. There's no doubt in my mind that *The New York Times* is better written today than it was 40 years ago. The novel has not exactly gotten better. The novel has been dwindling[23] since the end of the 19th century, because of one inescapable fact[24], which is that it is no longer as essential to[25] people's cultural lives as it used to be. The movies replaced it, certainly, and television. Novelists have lost the sense that we make a difference.

596 words

1 Pulitzer Prize = USA's most important annual prize for writers/journalists, 2 (to) stab = (to) stick a knife into sb, 3 (to) run for = (to) be a candidate, 4 excerpt = part from a longer text, 5 leave aside = apart from, 6 commanding position = top position, 7 (to) bother = *(here)* (to) worry, 8 (to) detest = (to) hate, 9 absence = lack of, 10 curious = *(here)* strange, 11 key = *(here)* most important, 12 (to) cleanse oneself = (to) free oneself, 13 karma = Hindu and Buddhist afterlife, 14 (be) in the lap of history = (be) for history to decide, 15 (be) no telling = (be) no way of knowing, 16 (to) triumph = (to) win, 17 abomination = quality of extreme awfulness, 18 platitude = often repeated cliché, 19 gotten *(AE)* = become *(BE)*, 20 loutish = adjective of 'lout', a vulgar bully, 21 commodity = product , 22 crap = shit, 23 (to) dwindle = (to) die out, 24 inescapable fact = fact that cannot be ignored, 25 essential = absolutely necessary

ASSIGNMENTS

(Anforderungsbereich II: Analyse)

1. **Describe what picture of Norman Mailer the reader gets from the interview and explain how it is transmitted.**
2. **Analyse Mailer's use of language, particularly stylistic devices.**

B Praktische Hilfe und Arbeitsschritte

Die Nummern ❶ und ❷ beziehen sich auf die Aufgabennummern oben.

❶ Charakterisierung

Die Lebensphilosophie eines Menschen, seine sozialen, politischen und sonstigen Überzeugungen bestimmen seine Gemütslage und seine Handlungen in allen Situationen und Lebenslagen. Daher haben viele Aufgabenstellungen die treffende Schilderung des Charakters und der Persönlichkeit von Personen zum Thema. Beachten Sie, dass zwar der Charakter einer Person im Zentrum der Betrachtung steht, diese jedoch auch äußerliche Merkmale einschließt, wie z. B. physische Eigenschaften, Kleidung, Gewohnheiten, Sprache, Herkunft usw.

Wir unterscheiden zwischen direkter und indirekter Charakterisierung (direct/indirect → characterisation).
Direkte Charakterisierung ist eine konkrete Beschreibung einer Person. Indirekte Charakterisierung ist eine mittelbare Schilderung einer Person anhand ihrer Handlungen, Äußerungen, Gesten usw. Es wird dem Leser überlassen, selbst Rückschlüsse zu ziehen.
Hier sind zwei Beispiele. Das erste stammt aus *Rain* von W. Somerset Maugham. Das zweite Beispiel ist aus Dennis Kurumadas *Just Along for the Ride.* (Diese Kurzgeschichte wird in **Unit 11** ausführlich analysiert.)

COMPARE **Direkte und indirekte Charakterisierung**

▷ When he sat down under the light and took off his hat you saw that he had very red hair, and a bald patch on the crown, and the red, freckled skin which accompanies red hair; he was a man of forty, thin, with a pinched face, precise and rather pedantic; and he spoke with a Scots accent in a very low, quiet voice.

▷ "This is really crummy *(lausig)*. I think we ..."
I was cut off by Phil. "Hey, let's drive up to somebody ... some kid ... and flatten him."
"What?" I said.
"We drive up slow, then swing open the door real fast, and knock the guy on his can *(Hintern)*."
We all looked at him kinda funny.
"Well, it's something to do," Phil said.
"Aw, why not? Okay, we'll do it."
We began looking around for a victim.
"You guys are nuts *(verrückt)*," I said. "What if he calls the cops?"
"You worry too much. Whenever we wanna have some fun, you always chicken out *(kneifen)*."

Der erste Abschnitt enthält eine konkrete Personenbeschreibung. Maugham schildert dem Leser, wie der Mann aussieht, wie alt er ist, wie er spricht, woher er stammt und einige Merkmale seines Charakters, nämlich, dass er *"precise and rather pedantic"* ist. Nichts wird nur angedeutet und keine Facette der geschilderten Persönlichkeit der Vorstellung des Lesers überlassen.
Der zweite Abschnitt dagegen enthält keine eindeutig formulierten Aussagen über Phils Persönlichkeit. Der Leser erfährt nur, dass Phil zunächst einen dümmlichen Vorschlag macht, den er gegen die anderen durchsetzt. Trotzdem zeichnet dieser Vorfall ein Charakterprofil von Phil. Phil ist ein verantwortungsloser Junge, der bereit ist, andere Menschen nur zum Spaß zu gefährden. Die Befindlichkeiten seiner Opfer interessieren ihn nicht. Darüber hinaus besitzt Phil offensichtlich eine so starke Persönlichkeit, dass er sich in einer Gruppe durchsetzen kann.

Methode

Schritt 1: Vergewissern Sie sich, dass Sie den Text in allen Details verstanden haben.

Schritt 2: Unterstreichen Sie alle Sätze bzw. Satzteile, die mit Mailers Leben, Gedanken, Persönlichkeit, Motivation usw. zu tun haben.
Die Textteile, die herauszusuchen sind, sind:
- ▷ Aussagen von Mailer über sich selbst,
- ▷ Wiedergaben dessen, was andere Menschen über Mailer sagen oder denken,
- ▷ Meinungsäußerungen, Erlebnisse, Taten, Anekdoten usw., die Einblicke in Mailers Gedankenwelt geben.

Schritt 3: Schreiben Sie zuerst alles, was Sie in Schritt 2 gesammelt haben, stichpunktartig oder als kurze Notiz auf ein Konzeptblatt.

Schritt 4: Sehen Sie sich jetzt Ihre Auflistung genauer an. Teilen Sie das Material in zwei Gruppen: die direkte und die indirekte Charakterisierung.

Schritt 5: Verfassen Sie anschließend eine Charakterisierung Mailers auf einem Konzeptblatt. Bei der Erarbeitung Ihrer Antwort sollten Sie deutlich machen, ob es sich um eine direkte oder indirekte Charakterisierung handelt.

USEFUL EXPRESSIONS **Charakterisierung**

(to) characterise oneself/a person directly/indirectly

(to) be an example of direct/indirect characterisation is ...

(to) get/receive insights *(Einblicke)* into a person's personality/intellectual world *(Gedankenwelt)*
(to) begin by telling the reader that ...
the opening paragraph is devoted/given over to background biographical information about ...
(to) transmit information about ... by ...
(to) gather/understand that ... is a/an emotional/passionate/strong/... person because we hear/read that ...
(to) make one's own opinion/point of view/position clear
(to) argue that ... because ...
(to) make oneself unpopular with ... because ...
(to) believe in ...
(to) feel/think that America has become ...
(to) call into question/criticise the claim/idea/view that ...
(to) become more efficient/quieter/wiser/... as one gets older/with advancing years
(to) be in good health except for ...

Schritt 6: Bevor Sie die Reinschrift anfertigen, überprüfen Sie Ihre Antwort sowohl auf inhaltliche Vollständigkeit als auch auf sprachliche Richtigkeit.

❷ Gebrauch von Stilmitteln

Was sind Stilmittel?

Wir können unterscheiden zwischen Stilmitteln (→ stylistic device), die häufig in Sachtexten verwendet werden, und rhetorischen Stilmitteln, die vor allem in literarischen Texten zu finden sind. Rhetorische Stilmittel (wie Betonung, rhetorische Frage usw.) können natürlich auch in Sachtexten Anwendung finden.

In Sachtexten werden folgende sprachliche Stilmittel eingesetzt:

- ▷ Wortwahl (→ choice of words)
- ▷ Stilebene (→ style), z. B. formell *(formal)* oder umgangssprachlich *(colloquial)*
- ▷ Auflistung (→ enumeration)
- ▷ Wiederholung (→ repetition)

- ▷ Betonung/Hervorhebung (→ emphasis)
- ▷ rhetorische Frage (→ rhetorical question)

Was ist der Zweck von Stilmitteln?

Stilmittel werden immer verwendet, um

- ▷ einen Gedanken hervorzuheben,
- ▷ etwas anhand eines Bildes (→ imagery) oder Gleichnisses (→ comparison) zu verdeutlichen,
- ▷ eine Darstellung bzw. einen Gedankengang (→ train/chain of thought) zu komprimieren.

In Sachtexten ist die erste dieser drei Funktionen die weitaus gängigste. Hier werden Stilmittel in der Regel verwendet, um einen Gedanken zu betonen *(emphasise)* oder zu verdeutlichen *(clarify)* bzw. aufzuklären *(define)*.

Methode

Schritt 1: Zunächst geht es darum, die eingesetzten Stilmittel an Textbeispielen durch Zitate zu belegen. Obwohl viele Schüler/innen es schwierig finden, Stilmittel überhaupt zu erkennen, sind diese aufgrund eindeutiger sprachlicher Merkmale leicht zu identifizieren.

Bei dieser Aufgabe konzentrieren wir uns ausschließlich auf die Stilmittel, die Norman Mailer verwendet. Im Laufe des Interviews sind dies:

- ▷ absichtliche Wortwahl (deliberate → choice of words)
- ▷ Aufzählung (→ enumeration)
- ▷ Gesprächsmittel (→ conversational device)
- ▷ Übertreibung (→ hyperbole)
- ▷ Wiederholung (→ repetition)

Weitere Hinweise zu diesen Stilmitteln finden Sie im **Glossar literarischer Fachbegriffe**.

Lesen Sie jetzt das Interview sorgfältig durch und suchen Sie Beispiele für diese Stilmittel, die Sie dann durch Zitat belegen.

USEFUL EXPRESSIONS **Gebrauch von Stilmitteln**

(to) make use of a stylistic device
(to) employ repetition/... when speaking of ...
(to) employ/make use of hyperbole/..., as when he/Mailer points out/says ...

(to) use enumeration/..., for example when Mailer answers/replies/says in line .../lines ... and ... that ...
(to) use a/an confident/critical/confiding *(vertraulich)*/emphatic/straightforward *(freimütig)*/unapologetic/... tone
(to) use the personal pronoun ..., for example ...
(to) employ colloquialisms *(umgangssprachlicher Ausdruck)* such as ...
(to) express oneself in the language of everyday speech

Schritt 2: Im zweiten Teil der Aufgabe sollen Sie deutlich machen, warum – mit welcher Absicht und Wirkung – Mailer die o. g. Stilmittel einsetzt.
Wie viele andere Aufgaben, klingt auch diese schwieriger, als sie letztendlich ist. Insbesondere in Sachtexten können Sie davon ausgehen, dass Stilmittel häufig zur Hervorhebung *(emphasising)* bzw. zur Erläuterung *(defining)* eingesetzt werden. Der Autor vermittelt dem Leser mit diesen sprachlichen Mitteln einen anschaulichen bzw. lebendigen Eindruck dessen, was er zum Ausdruck bringen will.

USEFUL EXPRESSIONS **Funktion von Stilmitteln**

(to) emphasise a point/an argument
(to) highlight a decisive *(entscheidend)* event/incident
(to) make one's meaning clear **to** the reader
(to) create a vivid impression *(anschaulicher, lebendiger Eindruck)* by ...
(to) make use **of** ... for emphasis
(to) use ... and ... to clarify *(klären)* one's intention/meaning
(to) sound friendly/confiding *(vertraulich)* **by** using colloquial language

Schritt 3: Bevor Sie die Reinschrift anfertigen, überprüfen Sie Ihre Antwort auf inhaltliche und auf sprachliche Richtigkeit.

5 Sachtext: Politics and Society

Autorenabsicht: politische Reden

A Text und Aufgaben

Martin Luther King (born 15 January 1929, Atlanta, Georgia, died by assassination 4 April 1968, Memphis, Tennessee) was the driving force behind the fight for racial equality in the USA during the 1950s and 1960s.
In 1963, King and his staff focused on Birmingham, Alabama. Their non-violent protest marches and sit-ins infuriated city officials, who used police violence, water cannon and police dogs to disperse the marchers, who included many teenagers and children. However, the terrible worldwide publicity and complete breakdown of business finally forced the white leaders of Birmingham to give in to some of King's demands, most importantly an end to racial segregation on the city's buses and in its public parks.
With the national and international spotlight on his antisegregation campaign, King organised a massive march on Washington, DC, which took place on 28 August 1963.
On the steps of the Lincoln Memorial, King called up the name of Abraham Lincoln in his famous "I Have a Dream" speech, which is now seen as having mobilised supporters of desegregation and inspired the 1964 Civil Rights Act.
The following year, Martin Luther King was awarded the Nobel Peace Prize.

Dr. Martin Luther King, inspired by the Indian leader Mahatma Gandhi, expected from his followers to stay peaceful throughout their fight for equality. His main tactic was civil disobedience, and in so-called teach-ins, he showed his people how they could protest against laws or policies without using any violence.

Nobelstiftelsen, © The Nobel Foundation, Stockholm

GOOD TO KNOW **The Civil Rights Movement**

The Civil Rights Movement between 1954 and 1968 was directed at abolishing racial discrimination against African Americans, particularly in the southern United States.

A number of groups fought to end discrimination and inequality and to achieve full civil rights for African Americans:

- the National Association for the Advancement of Colored People (NAACP): legal defence for black Americans
- the Congress of Racial Equality (CORE): freedom rides, sit-ins
- the Southern Christian Leadership Conference (SCLC): non-violent action, "passive resistance" (protest marches, sit-ins, boycotts); Martin Luther King
- the "Black Muslims" (Nation of Islam): for African culture and against integration; Malcolm X
- the Black Panther Party: militant, "violence against violence", against integration

Martin Luther King got involved in the beginnings of the Civil Rights Movement in 1955 when Rosa Parks was arrested for refusing to give up her bus seat to a white person. King led the Montgomery Bus Boycott which lasted for more than a year and ended with the abolition of racial segregation on all Montgomery public buses.

I have a dream

Aus urheberrechtlichen Gründen können wir den Text von Martin Luther Kings „I have a dream"-Rede nicht abdrucken. Sie finden die komplette Rede im Internet auf der Seite http://www.usconstitution.net/dream.htm

Die folgenden Aufgaben bzw. ihre Beantwortung im Lösungsteil berücksichtigen insbesondere den hinteren Teil der Rede ab "I say to you today, my friends, so even though we face the difficulties of today and tomorrow, I still have a dream. (...)" bis zum Ende. Für diesen Abschnitt finden Sie unten auch einige Worterklärungen zum besseren Verständnis.
Berücksichtigen Sie bei Ihrer Analyse darüber hinaus aber auch den vorangehenden Teil der Rede, aus dem die Zitate auf den Seiten 147 und 148 stammen.

Beachten Sie: Im Lösungsteil sind bei den Zitaten keine Zeilenangaben aufgeführt. Diese müssen Sie bei Ihrer Bearbeitung ergänzen. Drucken Sie sich dazu die Rede oder den oben genannten Teil am besten aus und nummerieren Sie die Zeilen durch.

1 (to) be rooted in = (to) come or derive from, 2 creed = deep belief, 3 self-evident = so obvious as to need no proof, 4 (to) swelter = (to) feel great heat, 5 injustice = (*noun*) wrong, 6 oppression = cruel abuse, 7 (to) judge sb = (to) form an opinion of sb, 8 vicious = very cruel, 9 (to) drip = (to) fall in drops, 10 interposition = (*here*) unfair misinterpretation, 11 nullification = claiming that sth is untrue, 12 (to) exalt = (to) raise up, 13 plain = (*here*) smooth, 14 crooked = opposite of straight, 15 (to) reveal = (to) show, 16 flesh = (*here*) humankind, 17 (to) hew out = (to) cut out, usually with an axe, 18 despair = feeling of extreme hopelessness, 19 jangling discord = badly out of tune, 20 (to) struggle = (to) fight, 21 prodigious = impressive, 22 mighty = huge, 23 heightening = becoming higher and higher, 24 curvaceous = having a pleasant shape, 25 hamlet = very small village, 26 Gentile = non-Jew

ASSIGNMENTS

(Anforderungsbereich I: Textverständnis)

❶ Pick out examples of racial discrimination given in the main extract from Martin Luther King's speech and in the other quotations from the speech.

❷ Describe King's vision of a better future for American society.

(Anforderungsbereich II: Analyse)

❸ **Analyse how Martin Luther King persuades his audience to support his civil rights campaign.**

B Praktische Hilfe und Arbeitsschritte

Die Nummer ❸ bezieht sich auf die Aufgabennummer oben.

❸ Sprachliche Merkmale von politischen Reden

Der Text ist ein gutes Beispiel für eine überzeugende Rede *(persuasive speech)*. Solche Reden sind meist sehr emotional und von der Lebenserfahrung des Redners stark beeinflusst. Trotz dieser Emotionalität zeigen auch gefühlsbetonte Reden dieser Art die Grundstruktur eines typischen Kommentars (*comment*), nämlich:

▷ In der **Einleitung** *(introduction)* wird das Thema der Rede knapp dargestellt.

I am happy to join with you today in what will go down in history as the greatest demonstration for freedom in the history of our nation.

▷ Im **Mittelteil I** *(development I)* wird das Anliegen des Redners präsentiert.

Five score years ago, a great American, in whose symbolic shadow we stand today, signed the Emancipation Proclamation. (...)

But one hundred years later, the Negro still is not free. One hundred years later, the life of the Negro is still sadly crippled by the manacles of segregation and the chains of discrimination. One hundred years later, the Negro lives on a lonely island of poverty in the midst of a vast ocean of material prosperity.

▷ Im **Mittelteil II** (*development II*) wird die These mit Argumenten (Belegen) gestützt und eventuell gegen eine Antithese abgewogen.

(...) We can never be satisfied as long as the Negro is the victim of the unspeakable horrors of police brutality. We can never be satisfied as long as our bodies, heavy with the fatigue of travel, cannot gain lodging in the motels of the highways and the hotels of the cities. We cannot be satisfied as long as the Negro's basic mobility is from a smaller ghetto to a larger one. We can never be satisfied as long as our children are stripped of their selfhood and robbed of their dignity by a sign stating: „For Whites Only." We cannot be satisfied as long as a Negro in Mississippi cannot vote and a Negro in New York believes he has nothing for which to vote. (...)

▷ Im **Schlussteil** *(conclusion)* werden die wesentlichen Argumente für die eigene Position kurz zusammengefasst und daraus eine Schlussfolgerung (*consequences*) gezogen.

GOOD TO KNOW **Sprachliche Merkmale**

Überzeugende Reden zeigen eine Reihe charakteristischer sprachlicher Merkmale.

Besonders wichtig sind:

▷ Ausdrücke der persönlichen Meinung, z. B.:
I believe/think ...; in my opinion/view ...; it is (often) said that ... but (in my opinion) ...; those who think that ...

▷ Ausdrücke der Betonung (*emphasisers*, → emphasis), z. B.:
there can be no doubt that ...; it is certainly the case that ...; it is (absolutely) clear that ...

▷ rhetorische Fragen (→ rhetorical questions):
There are those who are asking the devotees of civil rights, "When will you be satisfied?"

▷ Ausdrücke der Empfehlung, z. B.:
... should/ought to ...; ... needs urgently to ...; ... is to be recommended to ...

▷ der Gebrauch von Vergleichs- (→ comparison) bzw. Kontrastmitteln (→ contrast), z. B.:
as for ..., they ...; on the one hand ..., but on the other (hand) ...; while it may be true that ...; we should not forget/should remember that ...; in any case/event, the fact is (that) ...

▷ der Gebrauch von Stilmitteln. Wichtige Stilmittel in politischen Reden sind:
Wiederholung (→ repetition)
Übertreibung (→ hyperbole, exaggeration)
Vergleich (→ simile)
Metapher (→ metaphor)
Symbolik (→ symbolism)

Methode

Schritt 1: Lesen Sie die Rede mehrmals durch, um sinntragende Wörter bzw. Ausdrücke zu klären und das Textverständnis zu sichern.

Schritt 2: In erster Linie möchte M. L. King seine These belegen, dass die schwarze Bevölkerung unter unerträglicher Diskriminierung und gar Unterdrückung leidet.
Dieses Ziel erreicht er, indem er seine Argumente - oft durch erzählende *(narrative)* (→ intention) und manchmal durch informative *(informative)* (→ intention) Abschnitte unterstützt - darstellt.
Zuerst sollten Sie diese zwei Komponenten der Rede - also 1) erzählend, 2) informativ - identifizieren und mit Zeilenangaben notieren.

Schritt 3: Erläutern Sie nun unter Verwendung des nachfolgenden Sprachmaterials die **sprachlichen** Merkmale der zwei Komponenten der Rede - erzählend und informativ (s. oben).

Beachten Sie: Viele Schüler/innen begehen hier den Fehler, nur auf der inhaltlichen und nicht auf der sprachlichen Ebene zu arbeiten. Es handelt sich hier aber nicht um das **Was?**, sondern um das **Wie?**.

USEFUL EXPRESSIONS **Politische Reden**

(to) be an example **of** a persuasive/argumentative speech

(to) want/wish to prove *(beweisen)* the theory/thesis that ...

(to) support *(unterstützen)* an argument **by** ...

(to) give/present evidence/factual information, as when ...

(to) not be (purely) factual, but (partly) evaluative *(wertend)*

(to) give/imply one's (own) opinion

(to) contain informative/narrative components

(to) show (some) typical features **of** narrative texts such as ...

(to) discover/find (a number of) features characteristic/typical **of** argumentative or evaluative texts

(to) find opinion-giving expressions/means of emphasis/expressions used **for** recommending such as ...

(to) make use **of** *will* for forecasting *(voraussagen)*/passive forms, for example, ...

(to) employ/use (several/some) comparative and superlative forms to highlight *(betonen)* one's opinion

(to) use contrast, as when ... **for** persuasion

Gebrauch von Stilmitteln

(to) be in addition **to** textual characteristics

(to) make use **of** (certain/specific) stylistic devices such as ... and ...

(to) often crop up *(auftauchen)* in speeches of this kind

Schritt 4: Verfahren Sie nun in der bekannten Weise: Entwerfen Sie eine vorläufige Antwort auf einem Konzeptblatt und überprüfen Sie diese vor der Anfertigung Ihrer Reinschrift sowohl auf inhaltliche Vollständigkeit als auch auf sprachliche Richtigkeit.

6 Sachtext: Economy and Ecology

Allgemein verständliche wissenschaftliche Texte
Persönliche Stellungnahme

A Text und Aufgaben

This comment column is by Paul Collier, who directs the Centre for the Study of African Economies at Oxford University. In his piece, Collier argues that the banning of genetically-modified (GM) crops by the European Union has had and is having a very negative effect on both research into genetic modification and, as a consequence of this, on Africa's chances of producing enough food to feed its fast-growing urban population.

To take on global hunger, genetic modification is crucial [1]

The origin of the ban on GM crops in Europe was the BSE scare [2], whose real cause was the capture [3] of health and food regulation (in the UK) by the farming interest. Across Europe, agricultural protectionism disguised as consumer protection led to a ban on British beef. BSE had nothing to do with GM, but it set a precedent [4]: soon "genetically-modified food" became "Frankenfood [5]", an experiment on consumers. To cap it all [6], GM came from research by US corporations and so provoked [7] hostility from the left. (...) The result was a winning coalition: agricultural protectionism plus anti-Americanism and the paranoia [8] of health-conscious consumers.

The GM ban has three adverse [9] effects. It has retarded [10] productivity in European agriculture; grain production could be increased by about 15% were the ban lifted. More subtly [11], because Europe is out of the market for GM technology, the pace [12] of research has slowed. GM research takes a long time to bear fruit, and its core [13] benefit - the permanent reduction of global food prices - cannot be fully achieved by private enterprise alone. European governments should be funding this research. Private money for research depends on the prospect [14] of sales, so the ban has not only blocked public research - it has reduced private research as well.

However, the worst consequence [15] of the European ban is that it has frightened African governments - with the exception of South Africa - into banning genetic modification, too. They fear that growing modified crops would shut them out of European markets. (...)

But Africa cannot afford the GM ban. Its cities, fed by imports, need global prices to be low. Without cheap food the children of the urban poor will be malnourished [16]. Africa's farmers, broadly self-sufficient [17], need higher productivity. Productivity per acre has stagnated, so rising production has depended on expanding [18] the area under cultivation. But with population growth this option is running out.

On the horizon is climatic deterioration [19] due to global warming. The semi-arid [20] parts will get drier, and rainfall variability will mean more droughts [21]. In southern Africa, the staple [22] food – maize – is likely to become unviable [23]. Whereas for other regions the challenge of climate change is to reduce carbon emissions, in Africa it is primarily about agricultural adaptation[24]. (...) This is what GM offers, if only sufficient money is put into research. There has as yet been no work on the crops specific to the region, such as cassava[25] and yams[26].

We are still on the first GM generation: single-gene transfer – in which a gene that gives one crop an advantage is isolated and added to another to give it the same advantage. But even this stage offers the credible[27] prospect of important gains[28]. Maize can be made more resistant to drought, buying Africa time in the struggle[29] against climatic deterioration. Grain can be made resistant to fungi[30], reducing the need for chemicals and cutting storage losses (which currently waste about a quarter of the crop). GM is not the only answer, but without it the task of keeping Africa's food production abreast[31] of its population growth is daunting[32].

Europe can afford to be romantic about organic food, but the African poor cannot. The return to organic peasant agriculture is an appealing fantasy with disturbing consequences. The GM ban has already persisted[33] for 12 years: how much more hunger must be endured[34] before it is faced down[35]?

574 words

1 crucial = of central importance, 2 BSE scare = fear of "mad cow disease", 3 capture = (*here*) taking control of, 4 precedent = model, example, 5 "Frankenfood" = short for "Frankenstein food", 6 "to cap it all" = "on top of everything else", most importantly, 7 (to) provoke = (to) give rise to, 8 paranoia = (*here*) unreasonable obsession, 9 adverse = negative, 10 (to) retard = (to) hinder, 11 more subtly = in a less obvious way, 12 pace = speed, 13 core = most important, 14 prospect = hope, 15 consequence = result, 16 malnourished = not having enough food, 17 self-sufficient = able to feed oneself and one's family, 18 expanding = increasing, 19 climatic deterioration = worsening of the climate, 20 semi-arid = very dry, 21 drought = long period without rain, 22 staple = primary, main, 23 unviable = too expensive to do, 24 adaptation = change, 25 cassava = *Maniokstrauch*, 26 yam = *Süßkartoffel*, 27 credible = plausible, 28 gain = (*here*) plus point, 29 struggle = fight, 30 fungi = *Pilze*, 31 abreast = (*adv.*) keep up with, 32 daunting = (*adj.*) causing feelings of hopelessness, 33 (to) persist = (to) not stop or change, 34 (to) endure = (to) put up with sth, 35 (to) face down = (to) beat, defeat

ASSIGNMENTS

(Anforderungsbereich I: Textverständnis)

❶ Give reasons why European public opinion is largely against the use of GM crops.

❷ Summarise the author's reaons for supporting genetic manipulation in agriculture.

(Anforderungsbereich II: Analyse)

❸ **Analyse the characteristics of a popular scientific text as demonstrated in this comment on the use of GM crops.**

(Anforderungsbereich III: Beurteilung)

❹ **Write a comment on the pros and cons of the widespread use of GM crops in agriculture. Give your own opinion.**

B Praktische Hilfe und Arbeitsschritte

Die Nummern ❸ und ❹ beziehen sich auf die Aufgabennummern oben.

❸ Allgemein verständliche wissenschaftliche Texte

Ein allgemein verständlicher wissenschaftlicher Text (→ popular scientific text) ist ein sachlicher, informativer Text *(informative text)* (→ intention) mit spezifischen Merkmalen. Ein solcher Text vermittelt komplizierte wissenschaftliche Informationen auf verständliche, für Laien nachvollziehbare Weise, ohne jedoch dabei Daten, Ergebnisse usw. so zu vereinfachen, dass sie faktisch nicht mehr stimmig sind.

GOOD TO KNOW **Sprachliche Merkmale**

Die typischen sprachlichen Merkmale eines allgemein verständlichen wissenschaftlichen Textes sind:

- ▷ Häufige Verwendung des Präsens, besonders für naturwissenschaftliche Tatsachen:
  GM research **takes** a long time to bear fruit, and its core benefit – the permanent reduction of global food prices – **cannot be** fully achieved by private enterprise alone.
- ▷ Verwendung des *will*-Futurs für Erwartungen und Voraussagen:
  Without cheap food the children of the urban poor **will be** malnourished.
  The semi-arid parts **will get** drier, and rainfall variability **will mean** more droughts.
- ▷ Verwendung des Passivs, um einen Vorgang objektiv zu beschreiben:
  How much more hunger **must be endured** before it **is faced down**?

- Verwendung von einschränkenden Ausdrücken *(qualifiers)*, z. B.:
  as yet, broadly, primarily, usually, possible, similar
- Zitieren anerkannter Experten und Forscher, häufig mit akademischem Titel
- Verwendung von wissenschaftlichen Daten und Statistiken
- Ersatz der wissenschaftlichen Terminologie durch allgemein verständliche Ausdrücke, ohne den Sinn der Aussage zu beeinträchtigen:
  can be made statt can be rendered, resistant to drought statt impervious to drought, reducing the need for statt minimising the application of chemicals, cutting storage losses statt diminishing storage losses, waste statt deplete

Methode

Schritt 1: Da diese Aufgabe erst nach der Überprüfung des Textverständnisses gestellt wird, wird davon ausgegangen, dass der Text bekannt ist. Sollte dennoch etwas unklar sein, dann klären Sie dies jetzt.

Schritt 2: Jetzt suchen Sie Beispiele für die spezifischen Merkmale, die für einen populärwissenschaftlichen Text gelten, heraus. Belegen Sie diese durch Zitate oder Zeilenangaben.

Tipps:

1. Beginnen Sie mit den offensichtlichen Merkmalen und gehen Sie dann die schwierigeren an (s. „Suchreihenfolge“ unten).
2. Verlieren Sie keine Zeit und Mühe mit der Suche nach Merkmalen, die gar nicht vorkommen. Es ist oft der Fall, dass nicht alle Merkmale in einem Text enthalten sind. Wenn Sie eins oder mehrere Merkmale nicht finden, dann lassen Sie sich deswegen nicht irritieren. Arbeiten Sie einfach weiter.

GOOD TO KNOW Die „Suchreihenfolge“

Diese „Suchreihenfolge“ wird Ihnen helfen, so schnell und effektiv wie möglich zu arbeiten:

1. Namen und Zitate von Experten
2. Statistiken und Daten
3. allgemein verständliche Ausdrücke anstelle wissenschaftlicher Terminologie
4. einschränkende Adjektive und Adverbien
5. Gebrauch des Präsens *(simple present, present progressive, present perfect)*
6. das *will*-Futur
7. das Passiv
8. „mäßigende Sprache“, die Behauptungen weniger dogmatisch klingen lässt.

B Praktische Hilfe und Arbeitsschritte

Schritt 3: Nach dieser Sammelphase sollten Sie mithilfe des unten aufgeführten Sprachmaterials einen fortlaufenden Prosatext schreiben können. Viele Schüler/innen scheuen sich vor diesem Schritt. Stattdessen erstellen sie nur eine Auflistung von Merkmalen und Fundstellen. Dies ist aber nicht das Ziel der Aufgabe und kann zu erheblichem Punktverlust führen.

USEFUL EXPRESSIONS	Allgemein verständliche wissenschaftliche Texte
(to) have (many/several) features of ... texts	
(to) be a particular/specific kind of informative text	
(to) quote recognised/accepted authorities/experts	
(to) give (an argument) added authority	
(to) increase the acceptance of an argument/idea	
(to) begin/open **by** ...	
(to) go on to say that ...	
(to) devote the first/middle/last part of the report/text to ...	
(to) conclude **by** ...	
(to) summarise the whole text **by** making use of a final quotation	
(to) avoid making unsubstantiated claims *(unbegründete Behauptungen)*	
(to) provide data/evidence to support an argument	
(to) avoid specialist terminology	
(to) be replaced **with** easily understood terms	
(to) put sth into perspective	
(to) avoid exaggeration *(Übertreibung)*/sounding too definite	
(to) use/make use **of** a particular tense	
(to) use the passive to describe a process *(Vorgang)*	
(to) make use of the passive to express an idea impersonally	
(to) use moderating language **for** balance/lack of bias	

Schritt 4: Bevor Sie die Reinschrift anfertigen, überprüfen Sie Ihre Antwort sowohl auf inhaltliche Vollständigkeit als auch auf sprachliche Richtigkeit.

4 Persönliche Stellungnahme

Die letzte Aufgabe in der Abiturprüfung im Fach Englisch verlangt oft Ihre persönliche Stellungnahme zu dem betreffenden Thema. **Beachten Sie unbedingt**, dass die Aufgabenstellung alle Texte einschließt, die während des Kursabschnittes zu diesem Thema behandelt wurden.
Insbesondere bei komplexeren Themen kann der Prüfer nur einen Aspekt ansprechen. In diesen Fällen ist es wichtig, dass Sie den relevanten Aspekt richtig erkennen und sich auf diesen konzentrieren. Bei der Beantwortung solcher Aufgaben wird jedoch häufig auch Überflüssiges und Irrelevantes verarbeitet.

Methode

Schritt 1: Lesen Sie die Aufgabenstellung genau durch. Handelt es sich um eine breit angelegte, allgemein gefasste Frage oder wird nur nach einem Aspekt gefragt?

Schritt 2: Welche Meinung haben Sie zu diesem Thema? Formulieren Sie auf einem Konzeptblatt eine vorläufige Aussage. Sie sollte möglichst knapp und eindeutig sein.

EXAMPLE

The problem is that consumers do not know what the long term results of GM crops will be.

Schritt 3: Stellen Sie auf einem Konzeptblatt Argumente **für und gegen** Ihre Position zusammen. Nutzen Sie den Text als Basis für Ihre Zusammenstellung, vergessen Sie jedoch nicht, auch andere Quellen einzubeziehen, die Sie zu diesem Thema im Unterricht behandelt haben. Selbstverständlich können Sie auch Wissen verwenden, das Sie sich in anderen Fächern oder außerhalb der Schule angeeignet haben.

USEFUL EXPRESSIONS	**Persönliche Stellungnahme**
(to) think/believe/suppose/claim *(behaupten)* ...	
(to) be **of** the opinion that ...	
(to) be convinced *(überzeugt)* that ...	
(to) think **on** the one hand that ..., but **on** the other hand ...	
(to) think on the whole *(im Großen und Ganzen)* that ..., but in this particular case ...	

(to) consider *(meinen)* that ... is perfectly obvious/self-evident *(offenkundig)*
(to) agree **with** an argument/an opinion/a point of view
(to) agree **with** *(Name einer Person)* when he/she claims/says (that) ...
(to) support the idea **of** ...
(to) admit **to** *(zugeben)* sth
(to) accept an argument/a claim
(to) be strongly **against** an argument/an idea/a suggestion
(to) reject *(ablehnen)* an argument/idea
(to) disagree **with** the idea that .../of ...

Schritt 4: Entwerfen Sie mit dem in Schritt 3 gesammelten Material und dem Sprachmaterial einen zusammenhängenden Text auf einem Konzeptblatt. Bleiben Sie streng beim Thema und stellen Sie Ihre Argumentation nach folgendem Muster dar:

- **Einleitung**
  Darstellung der eigenen Meinung in Form einer knappen, eindeutigen Aussage.
- **Mittelteil**
  Zunächst eine möglichst wertfreie Darstellung der Argumente für und gegen Ihre Position.
  Begründung der eigenen Meinung und begründete Ablehnung der gegenteiligen Position.
- **Schlussteil**
  Wiederholung der einleitenden Aussage und knappe Zusammenfassung der wichtigsten Argumente für Ihre Position.

Beachten Sie, dass es sich in Schritt 4 um einen Entwurf handelt. In erster Linie geht es um die inhaltliche und strukturelle Gestaltung Ihres Textes. Obwohl Sie versuchen sollten, sprachlich möglichst fehlerfrei zu argumentieren, steht die sprachliche Korrektheit hier noch nicht im Vordergrund.

Schritt 5: Überprüfen Sie jetzt sorgfältig Ihren Entwurf auf Fehler, indem Sie ihn Satz für Satz bewusst durchlesen. Wenn Sie der Meinung sind, dass Ihr Text keine Fehler mehr enthält, fertigen Sie eine gut lesbare Fassung in Reinschrift an.

Atmosphäre in literarischen Texten

A Text und Aufgaben

In this extract from John Wain's novel *Hurry on down*, the hero, Charles Lumley, has just graduated from university. Instead of going into a middle-class profession, Charles has decided to drop out of his family and class background and become 'classless', supporting himself by doing odd jobs. After a quarrel with his middle-class girlfriend's family about his plans, Charles goes to a working-class pub to get drunk.

Hurry on down

In Charles's breast pocket was a paper packet containing his last cigarette. He took it out carefully, but it had somehow been bent, and the paper was broken in the middle. He began to smoke it, holding it so that one finger exactly covered the torn spot, inhaling deeply. The hot storm centre of alcohol in his stomach rose to meet the smouldering [1] pool of nicotine in his lungs, and, the burden of guilt [2] and fatigue [3] slipping from his shoulders, he breathed a silent prayer of gratitude [4] to the twin deities [5] of his world.

Then, as his mind cleared momentarily, he became aware of the stout-laden [6] east wind of hostility [7] that blew around him. Embarrassed and scared, he jumped up from his seat and went over to join the dense [8] crowd round the bar. The landlord [9] and his two daughters were working hard filling glasses and taking money, but he never seemed to get any nearer to being served. Several times he edged his way [10] to the bar, waiting until all those before him had been attended to [11], but always he was curtly [12] thrust aside [13] just as he opened his mouth to give his order. After twenty minutes all the ebullience [14] he had derived from [15] the whisky and the cigarette had been drained away [16], and all he felt was the fatigue of standing for so long after a day without proper food. Determinedly he held his glass out and rapped [17] it on the counter. "Gin, please," he shrilled [18]. "Four bitters, a Guinness, three rolls, and Martha says have you got 'ny Weights [19]?" rapped out [20] a stocky [21] man at his side. Charles turned on him fiercely. "Just a minute," he snapped [22], "I was here long before you." The man looked at him coldly for an instant [23], but before he could reply, his order, complete with a packet of cigarettes, was handed to him on a tray, and he rapidly counted out the required money and departed.

Charles sank to the bottom of an Atlantic of frustration. It was obvious, even to a mind dulled [24], like his, by exhaustion [25] and disappointment, why he was getting nowhere. This establishment, or at any rate this particular room of it, was predominantly [26] working class in atmosphere; consequently [27] it was peopled by raw [28], angular [29] personalities who had been encouraged by life to develop their sharp edges. His sharp edges, on the other hand, had been systematically blunted [30] by his upbringing and education. From the nursery onwards, he had been taught to modulate the natural loudness of his voice, to efface himself[31] in every possible way, to defer to[32] others. And this was the result! He had been equipped with an upbringing devised to meet the needs of a more fortunate age, and then thrust into the jungle of the nineteen-fifties. The hive[33] was full of wasps[34], all workers and all identical; but he, who differed from the others in nothing else, had been deprived of his sting. "Now then, move away from the bar when you've been served," shouted the landlord, leaning across the bar in his bullying[35] way. "I haven't been served! I want a gin and a glass of stout!" Charles shrieked[36] with sudden violence. A silence fell and everyone turned to look at him for an instant; then, indifferent[37], they turned back to their own conversations. In this way they succeeded in conveying[38], once more, the all-important fact – that he was imprisoned in his class, not one of them, condemned[39] to solitary confinement[40] if once he strayed from[41] his own kind. And yet he hated his own kind.

601 words

1 smouldering = *(adj.)* burning without a flame, 2 guilt = feeling of having done wrong, 3 fatigue = tiredness, 4 gratitude = thanks, 5 deity = god, 6 stout-laden = smelling of stout, i.e. black beer like Guinness, 7 hostility = unfriendliness, 8 dense = thick, 9 landlord = *(here)* owner of pub, 10 (to) edge one's way = (to) move bit by bit, 11 (to) be attended to = (to) be served, 12 curtly = rudely, showing no respect, 13 (to) thrust aside = (to) push aside, 14 ebullience = feeling of happiness, 15 (to) derive from = (to) get from, 16 (to) drain away = (to) run away as of water, 17 (to) rap = (to) hit sharply, 18 (to) shrill = (to) shout in a high voice, 19 Weights = brand name of cigarette once popular among the working-class, 20 (to) rap out = (to) say sharply and with confidence, 21 stocky = short and muscular, 22 (to) snap = (to) speak to sb shortly, rudely, 23 for an instant = for a second, 24 dulled = made slow, unreceptive, 25 exhaustion = extreme tiredness, 26 predominantly = mainly, 27 consequently = because of this, 28 raw = unpolished, in original state, 29 angular = with sharp edges, 30 (to) blunt = (to) make less sharp, 31 (to) efface oneself = (to) not express oneself as an independent personality, 32 (to) defer to = (to) assume that others have more rights than oneself, 33 hive = small house used to keep bees, 34 wasp = bee-like insect with poison sting, 35 bullying = *(adj.)* treating people weaker than oneself badly, 36 (to) shriek = (to) shout loudly, sharply, 37 indifferent = without interest, 38 (to) convey = (to) express, 39 condemn = *(here)* as if punished by a court of law, 40 solitary confinement = held in a cell by oneself, 41 (to) stray from = (to) move away from path, road

ASSIGNMENTS

(Anforderungsbereich I: Textverständnis)

❶ Explain "the twin deities of the world" and how they help Charles.

❷ Point out what made Charles get up and go to the bar.

(Anforderungsbereich II: Analyse)

❸ **Describe the atmosphere of the extract by referring to the setting and Charles's state of mind.**

B Praktische Hilfe und Arbeitsschritte

Die Nummer ❸ bezieht sich auf die Aufgabennummer oben.

❸ Atmosphäre in literarischen Texten

In literarischen Texten ist oft auch der Schauplatz (Handlungsort) (→ setting) für die Interpretation der Hauptperson(en) (major → character) bedeutsam. Der Autor kann im szenischen Ambiente die seelische Verfassung bzw. die Stimmung (→ mood), also den Gemütszustand (→ state of mind) der Person(en) spiegeln. Das Wechselspiel zwischen Schauplatz und Person(en) bestimmt dann weitgehend die Atmosphäre (→ atmosphere) eines Textes.

Diese Beispielaufgaben dienen der Bestimmung der Atmosphäre in literarischen Texten:

EXAMPLES **Aufgaben zur Bestimmung der Atmosphäre**

Read the descriptions of the park and the river. What impression do you get of these places?

Describe the mother's appearance and mood and show what effect these have on the atmosphere of the story.

To what extent has the author established a unity of place and person?

What role does the weather play in our understanding of this story?

Describe the atmosphere of the extract by showing the interplay between setting and character.

Methode

Schritt 1: Vergegenwärtigen Sie sich zuerst den Schauplatz. Beachten Sie, dass dieser mehr als nur den faktischen „Ort“ umfasst. Aspekte wie Uhr- und Jahreszeit, Wetter, Beschaffenheit der Örtlichkeit bzw. der Landschaft, andere anwesende Personen und sogar Tiere gehören dazu. Die folgenden Leitfragen helfen Ihnen dabei, den Handlungsort interpretatorisch einzugrenzen:

- ▷ Where does the action *(Handlung)* take place? Indoors, in a limited area *(in einem begrenzten Raum)*? Outdoors, what is the landscape *(Landschaft)* like?
- ▷ When does the action take place? At what time of year and day *(Jahres- und Uhrzeit)*? Does it take place during the day or at night?
- ▷ What is the weather like? The light conditions *(Lichtverhältnisse)*? The temperature?
- ▷ What minor characters *(Nebenfiguren)* or extras *(Statisten)* are present? What is their mood or state of mind?

Schritt 2: Betrachten Sie jetzt die Hauptperson(en) genauer. Machen Sie sich Notizen.

▷ What is his or her outer appearance *(äußere Erscheinung)* like? What about facial expression *(Gesichtsausdruck)*, posture *(Körperhaltung)* and clothing?
▷ How would you describe the main character's state of mind or mood? Happy and carefree *(fröhlich)*? Ill-tempered *(verstimmt)*? Thoughtful *(nachdenklich)*?

Schritt 3: Im nächsten Schritt betrachten Sie – vergleichend und analysierend – den Schauplatz und die seelische Verfassung der Person(en). Arbeiten Sie die Gemeinsamkeiten und die Gegensätze anschaulich heraus.

Vergleichen Sie zunächst die für die Beschreibung der Person(en) sowie des Ortes verwendeten sprachlichen Mittel, die Sie in **Schritt 1 und 2** erarbeitet haben. Wie werden sinnverwandte Wörter und Ausdrücke (Synonyme) (→ synonym) eingesetzt? Gibt es auch Wörter und Ausdrücke mit gegensätzlicher Bedeutung (Antonyme) (→ antonym)?

Schritt 4: Nach diesem vorbereitenden Schritt sind Sie jetzt in der Lage, die Atmosphäre des Textes – das Wechselspiel zwischen Ort und Romanfigur – näher zu bestimmen.

USEFUL EXPRESSIONS	Atmosphäre in literarischen Texten

(to) be determined *(bestimmt)* **by** the interplay *(Wechselspiel)* **between** ... **and** ...
(to) take place in ...
(to) last about .../not last more than about ...
(to) be limited in space and time
(to) not receive/be given (any/much) information **about** ... except (perhaps) that ...
(to) be ignored/taken no notice **of**
(to) become aggressive
(to) have no effect **on** a situation/**on** a person's behaviour
(to) be emphasised/highlighted **by** ...
(to) get rid **of** one's guilt feelings *(Schuldgefühl)*/fatigue **by** .../with the help **of** ...
(to) become aware **of** an atmosphere/mood
(to) feel embarrassed/frightened/unsure **of** oneself

(to) be pushed aside/overlooked
(to) feel isolated
(to) have no sense **of** belonging
(to) lose one's sense **of** well-being *(Gefühl der Behaglichkeit)*
(to) be highlighted **by** the reaction of ... **to** ...
(to) be met **with** indifference *(Gleichgültigkeit)*
(to) be created by ... **on** the one hand and ... **on** the other (hand)

Schritt 5: Bevor Sie die Reinschrift anfertigen, überprüfen Sie Ihren Entwurf auf dem Konzeptblatt sowohl auf inhaltliche Vollständigkeit als auch auf sprachliche Richtigkeit.

8 Literarischer Text: Urban Society

Interpretation eines Gedichts

A Text und Aufgaben

The American poet Carl Sandburg (1878–1967) was the son of poor Swedish immigrants and was largely self-taught. His collection of poems about Chicago, his native city, called simply *Chicago Poems*, appeared in 1916 when he was thirty-eight, and made him famous overnight. The following poem was written in 1914 and gave the collection its name. It is probably Sandburg's most famous, if not his best, work.

Chicago

Hog[1] butcher for the World,
Tool Maker, Stacker[2] of Wheat,
Player with Railroads and the Nation's Freight Handler[3];
Stormy, husky[4], brawling[5],
City of the Big Shoulders:
They tell me you are wicked[6] and I believe them, for I have seen your
painted women[7] under the gas lamps luring[8] the farm boys.
And they tell me you are crooked[9] and I answer: Yes, it is true I
have seen the gunman kill and go free to kill again.
And they tell me you are brutal and my reply is: On the faces of
women and children I have seen the marks of wanton hunger[10].
And having answered so I turn once more to those who sneer at[11]
this my city, and give them back the sneer and say to them:
Come and show me another city with lifted head and singing so proud
to be alive and coarse[12] and strong and cunning[13].
Flinging magnetic curses[14] amid[15] the toil[16] of piling job on job, here
is a tall bold slugger[17] set vivid[18] against the little soft cities;
Fierce[19] as a dog with tongue lapping[20] for action, cunning as a
savage[21] pitted against[22] the wilderness,
Bareheaded,
Shoveling[23],
Wrecking,
Planning,
Building, breaking, rebuilding,
Under the smoke, dust all over his mouth, laughing with white teeth,
Under the terrible burden[24] of destiny[25] laughing as a young man laughs,
Laughing even as an ignorant fighter laughs who has never lost a battle,
Bragging[26] and laughing that under his wrist is the pulse, and under his ribs
the heart of the people,
Laughing!

Laughing the stormy, husky, brawling laughter of Youth, half-naked, sweating,
proud to be Hog Butcher, Tool Maker, Stacker of Wheat, Player with Railroads
and Freight Handler of the Nation.

287 words

1 hog = pig, 2 stacker = workman who piles things up, here wheat, 3 freight handler = worker employed by a transport company to load, unload goods, 4 husky = strong, 5 brawling = fighting, 6 wicked = very immoral, 7 painted woman = prostitute, 8 (to) lure = (to) try and persuade sb to do sth he or she would not normally do, 9 crooked = dishonest, criminal, 10 wanton hunger = hunger caused by exploitation, bad treatment, 11 (to) sneer at = (to) say sth that shows contempt, rejection, 12 coarse = opposite of fine, delicate, 13 cunning = clever in a foxy way, 14 curse = violent language, 15 amid = in the middle of, 16 toil = hard physical work, 17 slugger = rather brutal and violent but fearless man, 18 vivid = bright, lively, 19 fierce = wild, eager to attack, 20 (to) lap = *(here)* (to) hang out (of a dog's mouth), 21 savage = person of different culture thought to be uncivilised, 22 (to) pit against = (to) compete against, 23 (to) shovel = (to) lift and move earth, stones etc., 24 burden = heavy weight, 25 destiny = how life turns out whatever one does, 26 (to) brag = (to) boast, point out one's strengths to others

Chicago The opening up of the west during the 19th century made Chicago one of the richest cities in America. Its position on the Great Lakes and on the border between the industrial north-east of the USA and the west meant that it became the country's most important transshipment centre *(Umschlagplatz)* for manufactured goods from the east and cattle and grain *(Getreide)* from the west. By the late 19th and early 20th century Chicago was the fastest-growing city in the USA and was on the way to replacing New York as the capital of American industry and business.
But Chicago also had a darker side. Very fast population growth, weak government and freemarket attitudes combined to produce terrible poverty among the working classes, mainly poor immigrants from Poland and Russia. The conditions in the city's slaughterhouses, sweatshops *(ausbeuterischer Kleinbetrieb)* and tenements *(Mietskasernen)* gave Chicago a very mixed reputation, but while many saw it as a vulgar, violent and immoral place, its defenders – like Carl Sandburg – were quick to point out its great vitality and enterprise *(Unternehmungsgeist)*.

ASSIGNMENTS

(Anforderungsbereich I: Textverständnis)

1. **Pick out factual information about Chicago given in the poem.**

(Anforderungsbereich II: Analyse)

2. **State who Sandburg is addressing and explain what he wants to achieve.**
3. **Find examples of Sandburg's use of imagery and say what effect it has on our understanding of the poem.**

(Anforderungsbereich III: Beurteilung)

4. Describe your own impression of Chicago at this time in its history and say whether you can imagine living in such a place.

B Praktische Hilfe

Die Nummern ❶–❸ beziehen sich auf die Aufgabennummern oben.

❶–❸ Typische Merkmale eines Gedichts

Ein Gedicht ist Dichtung in einer bestimmten Form mit besonderem Rhythmus. Äußerlich meist kurz gehalten, bietet es komplexe Inhalte in konzentrierter Form dar. Gedichte sind häufig der direkte, empfindsam-subjektive Ausdruck der Wahrnehmung (→ perception) eines Dichters. Lyrik dient in der Regel dem Ausdruck von unmittelbarer Empfindung *(sensory perception)*, Gemüt und Gefühl *(feelings/emotions)*, also des individuellen Erlebnisses, der Verinnerlichung einer Stimmung.

Wie alle Dichtung wird auch ein Gedicht in Form, äußere Gestalt *(exterior meaning)* und Inhalt, Sinn und Bedeutung (→ level of meaning) unterteilt. Sowohl die Form als auch der Inhalt sind für eine Interpretation relevant. Der Inhalt lässt sich weiter in eine Oberflächenstruktur, sachlich-faktische Bedeutungsebene, und eine Tiefenstruktur, symbolische Bedeutungsebene, gliedern. Die Sinnverdichtung und Bedeutungsintensität der zweiten Ebene wird unter anderem durch die Verwendung von Metaphern (→ imagery) oder Symbolen (→ symbolism) erzielt.

Die äußere Gestalt, die Form eines Gedichts wird in der Regel durch Reim (→ rhyme scheme), Rhythmus *(rhythm)* und Metrum *(metre)* sowie die Unterteilung in Strophen (→ stanza/verse) bestimmt. Dem entspricht innerlich die sprachliche Konzentration, also die sprachliche Verdichtung und Ökonomie, die vor allem durch Wiederholungen ein Gewebe von gedichtimmanenten Verweisen herstellt.

Allgemeine Interpretationshilfen

In der Regel werden Sie zuerst aufgefordert, die äußere Form eines Gedichts zu beschreiben. Hier einige Beispiele solcher Aufgabenstellungen:

EXAMPLES **Aufgaben zur äußeren Form**

What is the poem apparently about?

What is the explicit topic of the poem?

Describe the scene portrayed in the poem.

What information does the poet give us about ...?

Summarise the content of the poem in not more than ... sentences.

With reference to the content, show why the poet chose this title for his poem.

Danach wird der Prüfer Sie sicherlich gezielt nach dem Inhalt des Gedichts fragen. Auch hier einige Beispiele entsprechender Aufgabenstellungen:

EXAMPLES Aufgaben zum Inhalt

What do you understand by "..." (l. ...) and "..." (l. ...)?

What does the poet compare ... and ... with?

What does the poet want to express by his comparison of ... with ...?

The poet compares ... to .../contrasts ... with ... What does he hope to achieve by this comparison/contrast?

Examine the poet's use of imagery/symbolism and say what effect it has on our understanding.

Die verschiedenen inhaltlichen Bedeutungsebenen (→ level(s) of meaning) eines Gedichts können unter anderem durch Symbole und Metaphern veranschaulicht und verdeutlicht werden. Sollen Ähnlichkeiten *(similarity)*, also inhaltliche oder sprachliche Analogien, dargestellt werden, handelt es sich um einen Vergleich (→ comparison). Sandburg vergleicht beispielsweise in seinem Gedicht *Chicago* die Stadt mit einem jungen Mann. Stehen die Unterschiede *(difference)* im Vordergrund, handelt es sich um einen Kontrast (→ contrast).

Als Nächstes untersuchen Sie die Verwendung der Stilmittel (→ stylistic device). Hierfür müssen Sie diese zuerst kennzeichnen, dann deren Verwendung im Gedicht analysieren und interpretieren. Stilmittel werden zur Verdeutlichung, Veranschaulichung, Verlebendigung und Ausschmückung einer sprachlichen Aussage eingesetzt.

Abschließend werden Sie oft aufgefordert, Ihre Meinung zu einem Aspekt des Gedichts zu äußern. Meist wird erwartet, dass Sie den Inhalt des Gedichts mit anderen Texten, die Sie während des Kursabschnittes kennengelernt haben, vergleichen und in Beziehung setzen.

1 Oberflächenstruktur

Bei der Bearbeitung dieser Inhaltsfrage kennzeichnen Sie mithilfe eines Textmarkers oder durch Unterstreichungen die sachlichen Informationen, die in dem Gedicht über Chicago enthalten sind. Gehen Sie dabei rein faktisch vor, d. h., Sie werten weder die Informationen noch analysieren Sie die Symbole.

USEFUL EXPRESSIONS | **Ebene der Oberflächenstruktur**

(to) open **by** ...

(to) go on to describe ...

(to) close **by** ...

(to) repeat a claim *(Behauptung)*

(to) be given further/more information **about** ...

(to) describe ... 's negative features/side

(to) admit *(zugeben)* sth is obvious/undeniable *(unumstritten)*

(to) be characterised/marked **by** ...

(to) draw/paint a negative picture

(to) draw attention **to**/describe (more) positive traits *(Merkmal)*

(to) give a favourable impression **of** ...

❷ Adressat und Wirkung

Zunächst geht es darum, das *you/your* des ersten Teils des Gedichts (bis Zeile 13) und das *them* des letzten Teils (ab Zeile 14), zu identifizieren. Danach verdeutlichen Sie anhand Ihrer Analyse, was Sandburg mit seinem Gedicht beabsichtigt.

USEFUL EXPRESSIONS | **Adressat und Wirkung**

(to) use pronoun ... /possessive adjective ... **for** a place

(to) refer **to** a place as a person

(to) address ... as if it were a ...

(to) appear to be acting as a prosecutor *(Staatsanwalt)*

(to) change one's perspective *(Blickwinkel)*

(to) address/speak **to** the reader directly

(to) answer critics

(to) point out ... **with** energy/conviction

(to) sing the praises **of** ...

(to) set **up** a contrast **between** ... and ...

3 Tiefenstruktur

Diese Aufgabe hat die Tiefenstruktur zum Thema, also beispielsweise die Analyse der Symbole und deren Verwendung im Gedicht.

Auffällig ist, dass die Stadt Chicago wie eine Person angesprochen und geschildert wird. Diese Art, leblose Dinge als Person darzustellen – eine in der Dichtung häufig gebrauchte Form –, nennt man Personifikation (→ personification). Suchen Sie zuerst einige Beispiele dazu heraus. Analysieren Sie, inwiefern der Dichter hier Vergleiche oder Kontraste einsetzt.

Beschreiben Sie nun die Person „Chicago" näher. Die folgenden Leitfragen – die für solche Aufgaben immer hilfreich sind – werden Ihnen dabei helfen:

- Do we have to do with a male or a female (person)?
- Is the person young or old? Strong or weak? Healthy or ill? Rich or poor? Handsome *(gut aussehend)* or plain *(wenig attraktiv)*?
- Do we get any information about the person's social or occupational position or status?
- How could you characterise the person? Lively or rather sluggish? Good or evil *(böse)*? Pleasant or repulsive *(abstoßend)*? Boastful *(prahlerisch)* and arrogant or modest *(bescheiden)* and retiring *(zurückhaltend)*? Aggressive and violent or gentle *(sanft)* and peaceful? Stable or erratic *(unberechenbar)*?
- Is the person's character simple or is it complex?

Abschließend untersuchen Sie die Wirkung der Symbolik. Denken Sie daran, dass die Symbole einerseits immer für etwas anderes stehen und andererseits sich hinter diesen häufig die Intention des Dichters verbirgt.

USEFUL EXPRESSIONS Ebene der Tiefenstruktur

(to) be built **on** ... and ...

(to) be personified as ...

(to) be (further) characterised/described as ...

(to) describe **in** (solely) physical terms

(to) come across **as** ... without ... qualities

(to) deepen an image *(Bild)* **by** means of similes

(to) compare ... to ...

(to) make use **of** (strong) contrast (in order) to do sth

(to) emphasise/highlight *(unterstreichen)* the depth/sincerity *(Aufrichtigkeit)* of one's feelings

(to) achieve an effect **by** ...

(to) make use **of** repetition *(Wiederholung)*/enumeration *(Auflistung)*/alliteration *(Stabreim)*

(to) employ (very) robust/emotive language

brutal, coarse, emotional, healthy, intellectual, moral, rough, simple, straightforward, strong, uneducated, vulgar, young, ...

character, character traits, cunning, energy, ferocity, humour, personality, vitality, ...

9 Literarischer Text: Education

Form einer Kurzgeschichte
Nebenhandlungen

A Text und Aufgaben

This short story by the American science-fiction writer Isaac Asimov is set in the year 2155. In the story Asimov compares the schools in 2155, when children are taught at home by teaching machines linked to a screen, with the schools in 'the old days', when children all went to a special building and were taught by people using books.

The fun they had

Margie even wrote about it that night in her diary. On the page headed 17 May 2155, she wrote: "Today Tommy found a real book!" It was a very old book. Margie's grandfather once said that when he was a little boy his grandfather told him that there was a time when all stories were printed on paper.

They turned the pages which were yellow and crinkly [1], and it was awfully funny to read words that stood still instead of moving the way they were supposed to – on the screen, you know. And then, when they turned back to the page before, it had the same words on it that it had had when they read it the first time. "Gee," said Tommy, "what a waste. When you're through with the book, you just throw it away, I guess. Our television screen must have had a million books on it and it's good for plenty more, I wouldn't throw it away." "Same with mine," said Margie. She was eleven and hadn't seen as many telebooks as Tommy had. He was thirteen.

She said: "Where did you find it?"

"In my house." He pointed without looking, because he was busy reading. "In the attic [2]."

"What's it about?"

"School."

Margie was scornful [3]. "School? What's there to write about school? I hate school." Margie always hated school, but now she hated it more than ever. The mechanical teacher had been giving her test after test in geography and she had been doing worse and worse until her mother had shaken her head sorrowfully and sent for the County Inspector [4].

He was a round little man with a red face and a whole box of tools with dials and wires. He smiled at her and gave her an apple, then took the teacher apart. Margie had hoped that he wouldn't know how to put it together again, but he knew how all right and after an hour or so there it was again, large and black and ugly with a big screen on which all the lessons were shown and the questions were asked. That wasn't so bad. The part she hated most was the slot [5] where she had to put her homework and test papers. She always had to write them out in a punch code [6] they made her learn when she was six years old, and the mechanical teacher calculated the mark in no time. The Inspector had smiled after he was finished and patted[7] her head. He said to her mother: "It's not the little girl's fault, Mrs Jones. I think the geography sector was geared a little too quick. Those things happen sometimes. I've slowed it up to an average ten-year level. Actually, the overall pattern of her progress is quite satisfactory." And he had patted Margie's head again. Margie was disappointed. She had been hoping they would take the teacher away altogether. They had once taken Tommy's teacher away for nearly a month because the history sector had blanked out completely.

So she said to Tommy: "Why would anyone write about school?" Tommy looked at her with very superior[8] eyes. "Because it's not our kind of school, stupid. This is the old kind of school that they had hundreds and hundreds of years ago." He added loftily[9], pronouncing the word carefully: "Centuries ago." Margie was hurt.

"Well, I don't know what kind of school they had all that time ago." She read the book over his shoulder for a while, then said: "Anyway, they had a teacher."

"Sure they had a teacher, but it wasn't a regular[10] teacher. It was a man."

"A man? How could a man be a teacher?"

"Well, he just taught the boys and girls things and gave them homework and asked them questions."

"A man isn't smart enough."

"Sure he is. My father knows as much as a teacher."

"He can't. A man can't know as much as a teacher."

"He knows almost as much I betcha[11]."

Margie wasn't prepared to dispute[12] that. She said:

"I wouldn't want a strange man in my house to teach me."

Tommy screamed with laughter. "You don't know much, Margie. The teachers don't live in the house. They had a special building and all the kids went there."

"And all the kids learned the same thing?"

"Sure, if they were the same age."

"But my mother says a teacher has to be adjusted to fit the mind of each boy and girl he teaches and that each kid has to be taught differently."

"Just the same, they didn't do it that way then. If you don't like it, you don't have to read the book."

"I didn't say I didn't like it," Margie said quickly. She wanted to read about those funny schools.

They weren't even half finished when Margie's mother called: "Margie! School!"

Margie looked up. "Not yet, Mamma."

"Now," said Mrs Jones. "And it's probably time for Tommy, too."

Margie said to Tommy: "Can I read the book some more with you after school?"

"Maybe," he said nonchalantly[13]. He walked away whistling, the dusty old book tucked beneath[14] his arm.

Margie went into the schoolroom. It was right next to her bedroom, and the mechanical teacher was on and waiting for her. It was always on at the same time every day except Saturday and Sunday, because her mother said that little girls learned better if they learned at regular hours. The screen was lit up, and it said: "Today's arithmetic lesson is on the addition of proper fractions[15]. Please insert yesterday's homework in the proper slot." Margie did so with a sigh. She was thinking about the old schools they had when her grandfather was a little boy. All the kids from the neighborhood came, laughing and shouting in the schoolyard, sitting together in the schoolroom, going home together at the end of the day.

They learned the same things so they could help one another with the homework and talk about it. And the teachers were people ...

The mechanical teacher was flashing on the screen: "When we add the fractions 1/2 and 1/4 ..." Margie was thinking about how the kids must have loved it in the old days. She was thinking about the fun they had.

1043 words

1 crinkly = *(adj.)* not smooth and flat, 2 attic = room under the roof of a house, 3 scornful = *(adj.)* showing no respect, 4 County Inspector = *(here)* technician who looks after mechanical teachers, 5 slot = narrow opening, 6 punch code = code made up of holes cut in a card, 7 (to) pat = (to) touch lightly on the head, 8 superior = *(adj.)* showing to be better, 9 loftily = *(adv.)* feel cleverer, 10 regular = *(here)* normal, 11 I betcha = I bet you, 12 (to) dispute = (to) argue about, 13 nonchalantly = *(adv.)* apparently without care, interest, 14 (to) tuck beneath = (to) put under, 15 proper fraction = fraction where top number is smaller than bottom one, e.g. 1/4, 2/3, 4/5 etc.

ASSIGNMENTS

(Anforderungsbereich I: Textverständnis)

1. Compare schools in 2155 and "the old kind of school that they had hundreds and hundreds of years ago".
2. Find evidence in the text to show Margie's attitude to school.
3. Characterise the relationship between Margie and Tommy.

(Anforderungsbereich II: Analyse)

4. **Present evidence from the text to show that this is a short story.**
5. **Explain the function of the sub-plot *(Nebenhandlung)*.**

B Praktische Hilfe und Arbeitsschritte

Die Nummern ❹ und ❺ beziehen sich auf die Aufgabennummern oben.

❹ Merkmale einer Kurzgeschichte

H. H. Munro (1870–1916) – selbst ein hervorragender Autor von Kurzgeschichten – sagte einmal: *The only sensible thing I can say about short stories is that they are short.* Was wollte Munro mit dieser auf den ersten Blick banal wirkenden Bemerkung sagen? Vielleicht, dass ...

- ▷ ... eine Kurzgeschichte eine gedrängte, bündige sprachliche Komposition von geringem Umfang ist.
- ▷ ... eine Kurzgeschichte sich auf das Besondere eines Ereignisses und die Charakterisierung von Personen, Zeit und Lokalkolorit konzentriert.
- ▷ ... eine Kurzgeschichte selten mehr als zwei Hauptfiguren (major → character) enthält. Häufig steht nur eine Figur und deren Realitätswahrnehmung (→ perception; → short story) im Zentrum der Geschichte.
- ▷ ... eine Kurzgeschichte nur wenige Nebenfiguren (minor → character) enthält. Die Nebenfiguren haben häufig die Funktion, dass sie als Folie dienen, vor der die Hauptfiguren agieren und in der sie sich widerspiegeln.
- ▷ ... die Zeit der Handlung in der Regel auf einige Stunden oder wenige Tage begrenzt ist.
- ▷ ... die Handlung räumlich begrenzt ist und oft in einem Zimmer stattfindet.
- ▷ ... ein Szenen-/Ortswechsel *(change of scene)* (→ short story) selten stattfindet. Sollte ein solcher dennoch vorkommen, wird dieser oft in einer Nebenhandlung (→ subplot) – also einer „Geschichte innerhalb einer Geschichte“ – realisiert.
- ▷ ... eine Kurzgeschichte eine unerwartete Wendung (→ turning point) inmitten alltäglicher Begebenheiten – sozusagen eine Konfliktsituation *(conflict situation)* (→ conflict) – enthält, die auf den Lebenszusammenhang der Hauptperson(en) verweist.

Methode

Schritt 1: Lesen Sie den Text mehrmals und klären Sie unbekannte Vokabeln. Sollte es dann noch Textstellen geben, die Sie nicht verstehen, klammern Sie diese zunächst aus, vorausgesetzt, dass Sie die Geschichte trotzdem sinngemäß erfassen und verstehen können. Ist dies nicht der Fall, sind diese Textstellen für das Verständnis der Kurzgeschichte relevant.

Die folgenden Leitfragen könnten Ihnen weiterhelfen:

- ▷ Have the difficult passages *(schwierige Stellen)* got to do with the main character(s)?
- ▷ Do they seem to suggest *(andeuten)* a conflict either between two characters or an inner conflict between a character and his or her inner world *(„Innenwelt“)*, social environment *(soziale Umwelt)* or past?

▷ Does a difficult passage seem to have to do with some kind of turning point or change, i.e. are things somehow different than they were before? Can you characterise this change in some way? Is it for the better or for the worse?

Beantworten Sie diese Fragen so gut wie möglich und arbeiten Sie dann schrittweise weiter. In der Regel klären sich die letzten Ungereimtheiten während der Arbeit.

Schritt 2: Beschreiben Sie zunächst den Handlungsrahmen *(framework)* der Kurzgeschichte. Die oben angeführten Fragen können dabei hilfreich sein. Klären Sie außerdem: Wo findet die Handlung statt? Wie lange dauert die Handlung an? Wie viele Haupt- und Nebenfiguren sind involviert? Verwenden Sie für Ihren Text das *simple present*!

USEFUL EXPRESSIONS **Der Rahmen einer Kurzgeschichte**

(to) have many/some/a number of features/characteristics **of** a literary form

(to) limit a plot **in** space/time

(to) take place **in** ...

(to) last a certain time/a short time

(to) involve/make use **of** ... main/minor characters

(to) be **of** short duration

Schritt 3: Nachdem Sie den Handlungsrahmen dargestellt haben, wenden Sie sich der Oberflächenstruktur (exterior → level of meaning) der Kurzgeschichte zu. Halten Sie, ohne zu werten oder zu interpretieren, genau fest, was passiert. Verwenden Sie weiterhin das *simple present*!

USEFUL EXPRESSIONS **Ebene der Oberflächenstruktur**

(to) be simple/straightforward *(schlicht)*/easy to understand/follow

(to) hear/read/be told that ...

(to) be **under** the impression that ...

(to) not understand how sb could do sth

(to) become more interested in sth

(to) compare sth **with** sth	
(to) call **for** assistance/help	
(to) find/correct a fault	
(to) adjust/reprogram a machine/computer	
(to) feel disappointment **at** sth	

Schritt 4: Jetzt geht es darum, die Handlung wiederzugeben. Vielen Schülern fällt dies zunächst schwer. Denken Sie bei diesem Schritt daran, dass Literatur sich immer mit einem Konflikt und dessen Lösung beschäftigt. Finden Sie den Konflikt in der Geschichte und analysieren Sie diesen.

Beachten Sie, dass ein literarischer „Konflikt" nicht mit einem Konflikt im herkömmlichen Sinne gleichzusetzen ist. Es handelt sich vielmehr um einen Zwiespalt, ein Missverständnis, einen Streit, auch inneren Widerstreit von Motiven, Wünschen usw., oder eine enttäuschte Hoffnung bzw. Erwartung.

Die Konfliktsituation können Sie meist mit folgendem Schema leicht herausfinden: Setzen Sie inhaltliche Positionen mit positiven (+) und negativen (–) Polen gleich.

COMPARE **Positiver und negativer Pol**

Vergleichen Sie die beiden Situationen:

- Alison had been looking forward to seeing Steve again all week. When she came into the pub he was standing at the bar. He saw her and said something to his friends. He turned away from the bar and came over to her. Alison had the exciting feeling that he had been waiting for her.
- Alison had been looking forward to seeing Steve again all week. When she came into the pub he was standing at the bar. He saw her and said something to his friends. They glanced over at her and laughed loudly the way young men do. "My round, I think," said Steve.

Die erste Darstellung enthält keinen negativen Pol. Alisons Gefühle und Erwartungen werden von Steve geteilt und erfüllt. In der zweiten Darstellung gibt es dagegen einen negativen Pol: Steve reagiert anders, als Alison es erhofft hatte. Er will seine Zeit offensichtlich mit seinen Freunden verbringen. Die Spannung – also der Konflikt – entsteht durch die Diskrepanz zwischen Alisons Hoffnung und Erwartung (+) und Steves Reaktion (–).

USEFUL EXPRESSIONS **Ebene der Tiefenstruktur**

(to) be **at** a deeper level of meaning

(to) be concerned **with** a conflict situation

(to) be represented/symbolised **by** ...

(to) find oneself subordinated **to** others

(to) place demands **on** sb

(to) dictate the rhythm of sb's life

(to) be mirrored *(widerspiegeln)* **by**/reflected **in** ...

(to) consider sb stupid/naive

(to) make one's attitude/opinion clear **to** sb

(to) be in a position of authority **over** sb

(to) impose *(auferlegen)* a strict routine **on** sb

(to) give expression **to** a relationship/hierarchy

Schritt 5: Haben Sie den Konflikt bzw. die Konflikte gefunden, können Sie die Entwicklung der Kurzgeschichte analysieren. Ähnlich wie im Drama folgt auf die Einleitung (→ exposition) eine Phase der ansteigenden Spannung (→ rising action), die im Wendepunkt (→ turning point), dem Höhepunkt (→ climax) der Geschichte gipfelt. Danach folgt zum Ende hin eine kurze Phase der fallenden Spannung (→ falling action).

USEFUL EXPRESSIONS	Darstellung des Wendepunktes

- (to) place/set sth **in** contrast **to** sth
- (to) refer **to** *(hinweisen auf)* a situation/person in positive/negative terms
- (to) think sth wonderful/fascinating
- (to) realise/understand the nature of one's social relationships
- (to) gain insights **into**/an understanding of a situation/position
- (to) compare one's own life **with** that of others
- (to) escape from the reality of one's life **by** daydreaming

Schritt 6: Denken Sie daran, Ihren Entwurf auf inhaltliche Vollständigkeit und auf sprachliche Richtigkeit zu überprüfen, bevor Sie die Reinschrift anfertigen.

❺ Nebenhandlung

Schritt 1: Zunächst gilt es, die Nebenhandlung (→ sub-plot) von der Haupthandlung *(main plot)* (→ plot) abzugrenzen. Dieser Schritt ist einfach, da

▷ es sich meist um einen Ortswechsel handelt, d. h., die Nebenhandlung findet nicht am gleichen Ort wie die Haupthandlung statt. In Hemingways *A Day's Wait* zum Beispiel findet die Nebenhandlung draußen in einer Winterlandschaft und die Haupthandlung drinnen auf begrenztem Raum statt.

▷ die Nebenhandlung – wie in *The fun they had* – in einer Rückblende (→ flashback) stattfindet, d. h., der Zeitverlauf wird durch Hereinnahme vorausliegender Ereignisse unterbrochen. Dies bedingt einen Zeitenwechsel. In *The fun they had* steht die Rückblende im *past perfect*, da die Haupthandlung im *simple past* abläuft.

▷ die Nebenhandlung aus der Geschichte entfernt werden kann, ohne dass die Haupthandlung dadurch wesentlich beeinträchtigt wird.

Schritt 2: Betrachten Sie nun die Nebenhandlung. Schildern Sie zuerst die Oberflächenstruktur der Handlung, ohne dabei deren Tiefenstruktur in Betracht zu ziehen (s. Aufgabe 4, Schritte 2 und 3, Seite 174).

Schritt 3: Hier geht es nun um die Analyse der Nebenhandlung. Beachten Sie, dass Nebenhandlungen auch dazu dienen, den Charakter einer Hauptperson zu differenzieren. Wir erhalten durch die Nebenhandlung Informationen und Einblicke, die uns in die Lage versetzen, die Haupthandlung besser zu verstehen.

Die folgenden Leitfragen werden Ihnen helfen, die Nebenhandlung von *The fun they had* zu erläutern:

- ▷ Which main character is featured *(spielt eine bedeutende Rolle)* in the sub-plot?
- ▷ Are there any other characters that appear in both the main plot and the sub-plot?
- ▷ Are there any characters that appear only in the sub-plot?
- ▷ What additional information does the sub-plot give us?
- ▷ Does the sub-plot give us more insight *(Einblick)* into a particular character's behaviour and attitudes?
- ▷ What similarities *(Ähnlichkeiten)* and/or differences can you find between the characters in the main plot and in the sub-plot?
- ▷ Can you find anything in the sub-plot that has an obvious parallel in the main plot?
- ▷ Does the sub-plot seem to reinforce *(verstärken)* the meaning of the main plot, or does it seem to qualify *(einschränken)* it in some way?

USEFUL EXPRESSIONS	Nebenhandlungen
(to) be devoted *(gewidmet)* **to** ...	
(to) hear/read/be told **about** ...	
(to) supply the reader **with** essential information about ...	
(to) be difficult to appreciate/understand	
(to) be hardly credible *(kaum glaubwürdig)*	
(to) be informed/told that ...	
(to) show no/little interest **in** sb	
(to) be expected to do sth	

Schritt 4: Entwerfen Sie Ihre Antwort auf einem Konzeptblatt und vergessen Sie nicht, diese sowohl auf inhaltliche Vollständigkeit als auch auf sprachliche Richtigkeit zu überprüfen.

10 Literarischer Text: The American Dream

Drama als literarische Gattung
Stilmittel in literarischen Texten

A Text und Aufgaben

In this extract from Arthur Miller's full-length play *Death of a Salesman*, the hero, Willy Loman, is talking to his employer, Howard. Willy has worked for the firm for many years as a travelling salesman, but with increasing age and changing times he has become less successful. As Willy is paid only a commission on sales, his income has fallen so much that he no longer has enough to live off. Now Willy asks Howard if he can become an inside salesman on a fixed salary.

Death of a Salesman

Willy *(with increasing anger)* Howard, all I need to set my table[1] is fifty dollars a week.

Howard But where am I going to put you, kid[2]?

Willy Look, it isn't a question of whether I can sell merchandise[3], is it?

Howard No, but it's business, kid, and everybody's got to pull his own weight.

Willy *(desperately)* Just let me tell you a story, Howard –

Howard 'Cause[4] you've got to admit, business is business.

Willy *(angrily)* Business is definitely business, but just listen for a minute. You don't understand this. When I was a boy – eighteen, nineteen – I was already on the road. And there was a question in my mind as to whether selling had a future for me. Because in those days I had a yearning[5] to go to Alaska. See, there were three gold strikes[6] in one month in Alaska, and I felt like going out. Just for the ride, you might say.

Howard *(barely interested)* Don't say.

Willy Oh, yeah, my father lived many years in Alaska. He was an adventurous man. We've got quite a little streak[7] of self-reliance in our family. I thought I'd go out with my older brother and try to locate[8] him, and maybe settle in the North with the old man. And I was almost decided to go, when I met a salesman in the Parker House[9]. His name was Dave Singleman. And he was eighty-four years old, and he'd drummed[10] merchandise in thirty-one states. And old Dave, he'd go up to his room, y'understand[11], put on his green velvet slippers[12] – I'll never forget – and pick up his phone and call the buyers, and without ever leaving his room, at the age of eighty-four, he made his living[13]. And when I saw that, I realized that selling was the greatest career a man could want. 'Cause what could be more satisfying than to be able to go, at the age of eighty-four, into twenty or thirty different cities, and pick up a phone, and be remembered and loved and helped by so many different people? Do you know? When he died – and by the way he died the death of a salesman, in his green velvet slippers in the smoker[14] of the New York, New Haven, and Hartford[15], going into Boston – when he died, hundreds of salesmen and buyers were at his funeral. Things were sad on a lotta[16] trains for months after that. *(He stands up. Howard has not looked at him.)* In those days there was personality in it, Howard. There was respect, and comradeship, and gratitude[17], in it. Today, it's all cut and dried[18] and there's no chance for bringing friendship to bear[19] – or personality. You see what I mean? They don't know me any more.

Howard *(moving away, toward the right)* That's just the thing, Willy.

Willy If I had forty dollars a week – that's all I'd need. Forty dollars, Howard.

Howard Kid, I can't take blood from a stone, I ...

Willy *(desperation is on him now)* Howard, the year Al Smith was nominated[20], your father came to me and ...

Howard *(starting to go off)* I've got to see some people, kid.

Willy *(stopping him)* I'm talking about your father! There were promises made across this desk! You mustn't tell me you've got people to see – I put thirty-four years into this firm, Howard, and now I can't pay my insurance! You can't eat the orange and throw the peel away – a man is not a piece of fruit! *(After a pause)* Now pay attention. Your father – in 1928 I had a big year. I averaged a hundred and seventy dollars a week in commissions.

Howard *(impatiently)* Now, Willy, you never averaged –

Willy *(banging his hand on the desk)* I averaged a hundred and seventy dollars a week in 1928! And your father came to me – or rather, I was in the office here – it was right over this desk – and he put his hand on my shoulder –

Howard *(getting up)* You'll have to excuse me, Willy, I gotta[21] see some people. Pull yourself together[22]. *(Going out)* I'll be back in a little while.

693 words

1 (to) set one's table = (to) feed one's family, 2 kid = *(here) „alter Junge"*, 3 merchandise = goods for sale, 4 'cause = because, 5 yearning = great desire, 6 gold strike = discovery of gold, 7 streak = *(here)* element in a person's character, 8 (to) locate = (to) find, 9 Parker House = name of hotel used by travelling salesmen, 10 drum = sell, 11 y'understand = you understand, 12 velvet slippers = indoor shoes made of soft cloth, 13 (to) make one's living = (to) earn enough to live off, 14 smoker = train compartment where smoking is allowed, 15 New York, New Haven, and Hartford = railway company in New England (now part of Amtrak network), 16 a lotta = a lot of, 17 gratitude = deep feeling of thanks, 18 cut and dried = *(adj.)* everything decided in advance, 19 (to) bring sth to bear = (to) use sth to make things different, 20 (to) nominate = (to) choose somebody as a candidate for an official function, e.g. president, 21 gotta = got to, 22 (to) pull oneself together = (to) get control of oneself

ASSIGNMENTS

(Anforderungsbereich I: Textverständnis)

1. Say in not more than six sentences what the extract is about.

(Anforderungsbereich II: Analyse)

2. Explain why Willy tells the story of Dave Singleman at such length.
3. **Describe the elements of drama that Miller makes use of in this extract.**
4. **Analyse Miller's use of stylistic devices and say what effect they have on our understanding of Willy's situation.**

B Praktische Hilfe und Arbeitsschritte

Die Nummern ❸ und ❹ beziehen sich auf die Aufgabennummern oben.

❸ Merkmale des Dramas

Wie unterscheidet sich das Drama von erzählerischer Prosa, z. B. von einem Roman? Eine leicht zu beantwortende Frage, wenn man sich vor Augen führt, wie diese unterschiedlichen Textgattungen mit ihrem Adressaten, dem Leser sowie dem Theaterbesucher, kommunizieren.

In erzählerischer Prosa wird dem Leser die fiktionale Welt, meist das Schicksal eines Einzelnen oder einer Gruppe von Menschen, in einem fortlaufenden Text geschildert. Diese literarische Gattung ist nur in gedruckter Form zugänglich.

Im Drama wird die Handlung durch die beteiligten Personen in Dialogen oder Monologen (elements of → drama) – in geschriebener Form oder als Sprechtheater – dargestellt. Im Theater werden die Informationen in Form von gesprochenem Dialog oder Monolog (spoken → dialogue/ → monologue), durch Bewegung, also durch Mimik und Gestik, durch das Bühnenbild und über die direkte wie auch indirekte Charakterisierung (→ characterisation) der Figur vermittelt.

Methode

Schritt 1: Betrachten Sie zunächst den Raum, also den Schauplatz (→ setting) der Handlung und die Bewegung der Figuren in diesem. Beachten Sie, dass Raum- und Zeitstruktur im Drama eng miteinander verwoben sind. (Hier ist der Ort Howards Büro und die Zeit vormittags, aber wir erhalten trotzdem weitere Informationen zum „Schauplatz" in dem Textauszug.)

Der Dramatiker *(playwright)* hält seine auf der Bühne zu realisierenden Vorstellungen von Raum und Bewegung in den Inszenierungsanweisungen *(stage directions)* fest. Diese werden üblicherweise in Klammern gesetzt.

USEFUL EXPRESSIONS „Schauplatz" und Bewegung
(to) be the main setting
(to) be (apparently) morning/before midday
(to) be furnished **with** chairs/a table
(to) have a door/an exit on the right
(to) indicate movement
(to) make use **of**/use stage directions to ...
(to) emphasize a point **by** standing up
(to) make one's way towards the exit
(to) (try/attempt to) stop sb **from** doing sth

Schritt 2: Untersuchen Sie jetzt, wodurch die Figuren charakterisiert werden. Beachten Sie dabei den Unterschied zwischen direkter und indirekter Charakterisierung (direct/indirect → characterisation).

Die Charakterisierung von Willy und Howard erfolgt in diesem Auszug zwar aus einer momentanen Stimmung (→ mood) der Gestalten heraus. Diese wird auch in den Inszenierungsanweisungen realisiert, veranschaulicht zugleich jedoch das Charakterprofil der beiden. Diese Form der Charakterisierung, weitere Beispiele können rasch im Text gefunden werden, ist eine indirekte. Leicht feststellbar haben Willy und Howard nicht den gleichen Realitätsbezug *(perception of reality)* (→ perception; → short story) und nicht die gleiche Lebensphilosophie *(philosophy of life)*. Willy vermittelt seine Position in einer längeren Rede, die - auch aufgrund von Howards Teilnahmslosigkeit - fast ein Monolog (→ monologue) zu sein scheint. Diese Rede ist eine Rückblende (→ flashback) und gleichzeitig eine indirekte Charakterisierung von Willy, der Dave Singleman kontrastiv als Gegenpol zu Howard aufbaut und somit seine Werte und Weltanschauung kundtut.

USEFUL EXPRESSIONS Charakterisierung

(to) employ/use stage directions to characterise ...

(to) indicate/show sb's (present) state of mind

(to) react to sth **in** a certain way

(to) show indifference *(Teilnahmslosigkeit)* **to**/no interest **in** what sb says

(to) challenge a/an (inaccurate/foolish/exaggerated) claim *(Behauptung)* about sth

(to) be (in the form of) an oral negotiation *(mündliche Verhandlung)* **between** two people

(to) be unwilling to agree **to** a request *(Bitte)*/proposal *(Vorschlag)*

(to) be in dialogue form

(to) be (in effect/virtually) a monologue

(to) use a device to communicate directly **with** the audience *(Zuschauer)*

(to) use dialogue to characterise sb more deeply

(to) be concerned **with** (contrasting/opposing) perceptions of reality/philosophies

(to) achieve an aim **by** means of a monologue/a monologue-like speech

(to) be in the form of a flashback

(to) use sb as a symbol **for/of** sth

(to) contrast ... **with** .../set up a contrast **between** two ideas/...

(to) be expressed **by** one's attitude **to** sth/sb

(to) become impatient/embarrassed

(to) give direct insights **into** one's (business) philosophy

(to) see (business) **in** a modern/contemporary *(aktuell)* sense

(to) not accept that sth has a social dimension/component

(to) express a basic/fundamental disagreement/difference of view

Schritt 3: Verfassen Sie Ihre Antwort in Form eines zusammenhängenden Textes. Überprüfen Sie sie auf inhaltliche Vollständigkeit und auf sprachliche Richtigkeit.

4 Verwendung und Funktion von Stilmitteln

Für eine ausführlichere Behandlung der Anwendung von Stilmitteln in Sachtexten im Vergleich zu literarischen Texten sehen Sie die Anmerkungen in Unit 4, Aufgabe 2, Seite 142. Stilmittel (→ literary device) wie z. B. Gleichnis (→ simile), Metapher (→ metaphor), Personifikation (→ personification) usw. kommen häufig in literarischen Texten vor. Sie werden zur Verdeutlichung und Veranschaulichung einer Idee eingesetzt.

Methode

Schritt 1: Zuerst soll Millers Gebrauch von Stilmitteln festgestellt werden. Lesen Sie den Auszug nochmals und suchen Sie Beispiele für die folgenden Stilmittel:

- ▷ repetition
- ▷ enumeration
- ▷ personification
- ▷ full metaphor
- ▷ other metaphorical language
- ▷ contrast
- ▷ exaggeration

Achten Sie darauf, den Gebrauch der Mittel durch präzises Zitieren zu belegen und die Fundstellen durch Zeilenangaben zu benennen.

USEFUL EXPRESSIONS **Stilmittel beschreiben**

(to) employ/make use **of**/use repetition/personification as, for example, when Willy/ ... says/ ...

(to) occur in line(s) ... where ... says ...

(to) assume *(annehmen)* a remark/statement is ...

(to) appear to be intentional exaggeration as when Howard ... /points out ...

(to) to be able to find ... examples of personification

(to) employ a full metaphor

(to) represent/symbolize

(to) find other instances *(Fall)* of metaphorical language as in the sentence/ remark/utterance ...

Schritt 2: Wie in dem Mailer-Interview (Aufgabe 2, Schritt 2, Seite 144) sollten Sie jetzt die Funktion der Stilmittel erläutern.

Diese Leitfragen helfen Ihnen dabei:

▷ We are presented with two contrasting positions. Which position does Miller himself seem to support, Willy's or Howard's? How do you know?

▷ Which position does Miller apparently expect the spectator *(Zuschauer)* to support? What means does he use to ensure this?

▷ How does Willy portray himself? How does Howard portray him? How does Miller express these opposing views?

▷ Apart from the contrast between Willy and Howard, what other contrasts does Miller make use of (Willy/Dave Singleman, Dave/Howard, Howard/his father)?

USEFUL EXPRESSIONS **Funktion von Stilmitteln**

(to) emphasize *(betonen)*/highlight *(unterstreichen)* an attitude/opinion

(to) impress *(deutlich machen)* sb's position/situation **on** sb

(to) make a remark/statement vivid *(lebhaft)*/unforgettable

(to) make sth clear/understandable **to** the audience

(to) arouse/awaken understanding/sympathy/pity for sb's situation

Schritt 3: Bevor Sie die Reinschrift anfertigen, überprüfen Sie Ihre Antwort sowohl auf inhaltliche Vollständigkeit als auch auf sprachliche Richtigkeit.

11 Literarischer Text: Politics and Society

Struktur einer Kurzgeschichte
Erzählperspektive

A Text und Aufgaben

This story was written by Dennis Kurumada when he was still at high school. The hero of the story – the first person narrator "I" – is a teenager out with his four friends Dick, Steve, Phil and Reid. Dick has just got his driving licence and the boys are driving aimlessly round town. Even though that is better than sitting at home, they are bored and looking for a bit of excitement. Then Phil makes a horrifying suggestion which the others agree to.

Just along for the ride

I leaned back on the seat and watched the back of Dick's head as he steered. The '55 DeSoto [1] rumbled [2] down the rain-soaked street.

This evening's gonna [3] be a total loss, I thought. Things have gotta [4] be pretty dull [5] when all you've gotta do is drive around with a friend who just got his license [6]. But it beats [7] sitting home. So there we were, the five of us. Dick and Phil were in front. Reid, Steve, and I were in the back. We were all cold, damp, and bored. Man, we needed something to do!

"This is real crummy [8]. I think we ..."

I was cut off by Phil. "Hey, let's drive up to somebody ... some kid ... and flatten him."

"What?" I said.

"We drive up slow, then swing open the door real fast, and knock the guy on his can [9]."

We all looked at him kinda [10] funny.

"Well, it's something to do," Phil said.

"Aw, why not? Okay, we'll do it."

We began looking around for a victim.

"You guys are nuts [11]," I said. "What if he calls the cops?"

"You worry too much. Whenever we wanna [12] have some fun, you always chicken out [13]."

"There's one!"

It was raining hard, but we could see the blurred [14] figure of some guy under a streetlight on the corner. Steve laughed.

"Oh wow! This is gonna be funny."

A couple of us started laughing.

"Will you guys shut up?" said Dick. I guess it made him nervous.

The kid was about half a block away. The street wasn't too busy. Only a few cars were around.

Dick started weaving [15] across the road.

"Stop fooling around!" I said.

Steve got on the door, ready to open it. Then everything started happening too fast. The guy at the corner stepped out into the street. The car swerved[16]. The door swung open, and Steve started falling out. He grabbed[17] my arm, and we both fell back on the seat. Dick got scared and threw the car away from the kid. The head-lights flashed on a frozen figure. I could see his face, eyes wide, mouth open. There was a squeal[18] of tires[19] on the slick[20] street and a hollow thud as the figure was hurled[21], rolling across the roof. I got all mixed up[22].

"Ken Benjamin!" I said. "I think it was Ken Benjamin!"

Dick slowed down. Then he suddenly started speeding down the street.

"Dick! Stop! I know that guy! Dick, will ya[23] stop?" He didn't hear me. "Stop the car! He's my friend!"

I hit him on the shoulder and grabbed his shirt. He turned around. Tears were blob-bing up[24] in his eyes.

"Shut up, you jerk[25]! You want us to get nailed[26] for manslaughter[27]?" He hit my arm.

What a stupid thing to do! I got so scared that I started shivering like crazy. I just couldn't believe it. I felt sick.

"Hey!"

I looked up. It was Dick. He was looking in the rearview mirror[28]. There was a car behind us.

"Is he following us?" I asked.

"Well, I'll lose him," said Dick.

The car lunged[29] forward as it picked up[30] speed. I looked back. The headlights shone through the rain, about two or three hundred yards away. Dick hung a sharp right[31] up a narrow street.

Hardly anyone ever comes up this way, I thought. If he follows us up here, he's really following us. I looked back. The headlights were even closer.

We started up a winding[32] road. I looked back and could see the brown Volvo as it cut through the street ponds. Yeah, I thought, a good guy would drive one of those Volvos. What if he catches us? Ken was my friend. *Hit and run*[33], *hit and run* kept going through my head. I kinda hoped that guy would catch us.

We were out in the sticks[34] by now. The road was winding a lot. The Volvo was making his move and he was closing[35] fast. But as he rounded a curve, he turned too sharply and his car slid off the road. He couldn't have been hurt. Everyone was relieved. After that, Dick drove us all home.

It was 12.30 when I got home. Nobody was awake. I started pacing[36] around the kit-chen. I was so scared. I didn't know if we had killed him or not. I turned on the radio and listened to some music. But when the news came on, I turned it off.

You idiot, I thought. Ken was your friend. Go to his mom or something. Well, I didn't hit him! It's not my fault! Those other guys ... it wasn't my idea ... no! You were in the car. You're responsible, too. *Hit and run, hit and run.*

I got in my car and drove for a while. Then I started remembering things Ken used to say.

"I don't know what to do!" I was shouting as I drove. No answer. My mind burned.

"Go see Mrs Benjamin, you coward [37]!"

But I couldn't. I just couldn't. When I got home, the lights were on. My mother was in her robe [38].

"Your friends are here," she said. "I don't think two o'clock in the morning is the right time to ..."

I didn't listen. I just went into the front room. Dick walked up to me and said real low, "I heard on the radio that he's not dead. He isn't even hurt bad."

I didn't say anything. I just looked at him.

"No one knows," he went on. "So maybe we can get away with it."

He could see I was getting mad [39]. I could have killed him.

The others stood up and came over. I didn't say a thing. I just walked out the door, got in the car, and left.

It took me a while to find Ken's house. It was gray [40] brick, and the lights were on. Maybe it wasn't gray. I don't know. Everything looked gray. I walked up and rang the doorbell.

999 words

1 DeSoto = car once made by General Motors but no longer produced, 2 (to) rumble = (to) move with a deep sound, 3 gonna = going to, 4 gotta = got to, 5 dull = boring, 6 license *(AE)* = licence *(BE)*, 7 it beats = it's better than, 8 crummy = awful, 9 can *(AE)* = *Hintern,* 10 kinda = kind of, 11 nuts = crazy, 12 wanna = want to, 13 (to) chicken out = (to) not join in because one is afraid, 14 blurred = unclear, out of focus, 15 (to) weave = *(here)* opposite of drive straight, 16 (to) swerve = (to) move sharply to the left or right, 17 (to) grab = (to) take hold of quickly, 18 squeal = high, sharp noise, 19 tire *(AE)* = tyre *(BE)*, 20 slick = wet and slippery, 21 (to) hurl = (to) throw violently, 22 (to) get mixed up = (to) become confused, unable to think clearly, 23 ya = you, 24 (to) blob up = (to) form drops, 25 jerk = weak and foolish person, 26 (to) get nailed = (to) be arrested, 27 manslaughter = accidental killing, 28 rearview mirror = mirror to look backwards, 29 (to) lunge = (to) move quickly and violently, 30 (to) pick up = *(here)* (to) increase, 31 (to) hang a sharp right = (to) turn suddenly to the right, 32 winding = opposite of straight, 33 hit and run = *Fahrerflucht* 34 out in the sticks = in the country, 35 (to) close = *(here)* (to) catch up, 36 (to) pace = (to) walk back and forth, 37 coward = weak person unable to overcome fear, 38 robe *(AE)* = dressing gown *(BE)*, 39 mad *(AE)* = angry *(BE)*, 40 gray *(AE)* = grey *(BE)*

ASSIGNMENTS

(Anforderungsbereich I: Textverständnis)
❶ Summarise the story in not more than 400 words.

(Anforderungsbereich II: Analyse)
❷ **Describe the structure of the story.**
❸ **State from whose point of view the incident is described and say what effect this has on our understanding.**

B Praktische Hilfe und Arbeitsschritte

Die Nummern ❷ und ❸ beziehen sich auf die Aufgabennummern oben.

❷ Struktur

Der Aufbau von Kurzgeschichten lässt sich in vier Abschnitte gliedern:

Einleitung (→ exposition)

▷ In der knappen Einleitung werden der Handlungsrahmen (→ setting) (Ort, Zeit, Wetter usw.) der Geschichte und in der Regel die Hauptperson(en) (major → character) vorgestellt.

Steigende Spannung (→ rising action)

▷ Auf die Einleitung folgt ein zusammenraffendes, meist spannungssteigerndes Hinführen zum Höhe- und Wendepunkt.

▷ Der Autor beschreibt eine Schlüsselsituation bzw. ein Schlüsselereignis *(key situation/ event)* im Leben der Hauptperson(en). Gegenüber dem eher ausschweifenden Erzählen in anderen epischen Formen, z. B. einem Roman, ist die Kurzgeschichte durch stärkere Gespanntheit, rasche Steigerung und dadurch bedingten raschen Zeitlauf gekennzeichnet.

▷ Der Autor stellt in einer Kurzgeschichte kein ausschweifendes, breites Figuren-/ Milieuspektrum dar. Statt eines großen menschlichen Gemäldes gleicht die Kurzgeschichte eher einem szenischen Ausschnitt, dessen Schauplätze keine umfassenden Milieustudien erlauben, da sie häufig bühnenbildartig angelegt sind. Wie in der amerikanischen *short story* ist die Handlung der Kurzgeschichte vom ersten Satz an auf das „Unausweichliche“ hin angelegt.

Höhepunkt (→ climax)

▷ Die Geschichte gipfelt im „Unausweichlichen“: der Gestaltung eines Vorfalls, der häufig ein Wendepunkt (→ turning point) ist. Durch ihn wird das Leben der Figuren beleuchtet und die Geschichte für den Leser bedeutsam gemacht.

Abnehmende Spannung (→ falling action)

- ▷ Wie im Drama nimmt nach dem Höhe-/Wendepunkt die Spannung – manchmal sogar abrupt – ab. Die Geschichte wird ihrem Ende zugeführt, was oftmals zügig in wenigen Sätzen geschieht (→ short story).

Methode

Schritt 1: Fragen zur Form und Struktur einer Geschichte folgen immer auf die Fragen zum Inhalt. Deshalb wird dieser nun als bekannt vorausgesetzt. Sollten trotzdem noch inhaltliche Unklarheiten bestehen, klären Sie diese, bevor Sie weiterarbeiten.

Schritt 2: Die vier Teile einer Geschichte sind immer durch Richtungswechsel (→ change of direction) gekennzeichnet. Diese Wechsel, zum Beispiel nach der Einleitung zur spannungssteigernden Hinführung auf den Höhepunkt und danach spannungsabfallend zum Ende der Geschichte, können unterschiedlich gestaltet sein.

Hier folgen einige Hinweise, die Sie solche Übergänge (→ transition) rasch erkennen lassen.

Die **Einleitung** weist folgende Merkmale auf:

- ▷ Sie liefert einleitende Informationen, ohne die Fortentwicklung der Handlung direkt zu beeinflussen.
- ▷ Sie ist verhältnismäßig kurz, umfasst manchmal nur ein paar Zeilen.
- ▷ Sie ist fast immer durch einen Absatzwechsel von dem nächstfolgenden Teil getrennt.
- ▷ Manchmal ist sie durch einen Zeitenwechsel *(change of tense)* gekennzeichnet. Der Anfang der **steigenden Spannung** wird oft gekennzeichnet durch
  - einen neuen Absatz,
  - ein Adverb (*one day; a few weeks later; so it was that* ... usw.),
  - indirekte Rede,
  - eine inhaltliche Wendung.

Beachten Sie, dass die Spannung nicht immer gleichmäßig, sondern häufig „gestuft" ansteigt. Dies ist auch der Fall in *Just Along for the Ride*, wo sie in drei „Stufen" *(levels of tension)* ansteigt. Die Übergänge markieren eine bedeutsame Reaktion oder Handlung einer Hauptfigur.

Der **Höhepunkt und** die nachfolgende **abfallende Spannung** werden nur inhaltlich verständlich gemacht. Denken Sie daran, dass der Höhepunkt immer auch ein Wendepunkt ist! Die Phase der abnehmenden Spannung ist oft extrem kurz, manchmal gar nur auf einen Satz beschränkt, z. B. *She looked at him and left the room, never to return.* Es ist sinnvoll, sich die Struktur einer Geschichte zunächst anhand einer Skizze vor Augen zu führen (s. Lösungen, Seite 224).

Schritt 3: Beschreiben Sie anhand Ihrer Skizze die Struktur der Geschichte. Achten Sie darauf, immer Zeitformen des Präsens zu verwenden:

EXAMPLE

In the exposition Kurumada **sets** the scene and **introduces** the two main characters, the narrator and Dick. This section **goes** from line 1 to line 7.

Obwohl das *simple present* am häufigsten verwendet wird, können Sie auch die anderen Formen des Präsens, also das *present progressive* und das *present perfect*, verwenden:

EXAMPLE

In the exposition Dick **is driving** his friends around in his car. He **has just passed** his driving test. The boys **are feeling** bored and **are looking for** some excitement.

USEFUL EXPRESSIONS **Aufbau und Textstruktur**

Einleitung

(to) begin a text **with** ...

(to) call a section ...

(to) go/extend **from** line ... **to** line ...

(to) set the scene

(to) introduce the main characters/principal protagonists

(to) describe sb/sth **as** (being) ...

(to) give an impression **of** ...

(to) be mirrored *(widergespiegelt)* **by** the weather/landscape *(Landschaft)*

Steigende Spannung

(to) be followed **by** ...

(to) be characterised **by** ...

(to) not increase evenly *(gleichmäßig)*, but in levels/stages *(Stufe)* (to) call/term sth ...

(to) be devoted **to** ... *(gewidmet)*

(to) concern *(sich mit etwas befassen)*/be concerned **with** ...

(to) be marked/signalled **by** a key event *(Schlüsselereignis)*

(to) give rise **to** a change of direction *(Wende)*

Beschreibung der steigenden Spannung

(to) make use **of** (both) direct and indirect description *(direkte/indirekte Beschreibung)*

(to) be described/interpreted **in** detail

(to) never be left in doubt *(Zweifel)* **as to** the significance *(Bedeutung)* **of** sth

(to) employ *(einsetzen)* an indirect technique

(to) leave the reader to interpret the significance/meaning **of** sth

Höhepunkt

(to) be subdivided **into**/fall **into** ... parts

(to) be characterised **by** ...

(to) accept one's own responsibility *(Verantwortung)* **for** sth

(to) end/conclude **with** sth

(to) feel satisfaction *(Zufriedenheit)*/have a sense of satisfaction at sth

(to) overcome one's cowardice/shame/self-doubt *(Selbstzweifel)*/self-loathing *(Selbsthass)*

(to) never (ever) be quite the same again

Beschreibung der abnehmenden Spannung

(to) be characterized **by** a sudden release of tension *(abnehmende Spannung)*

(to) end **with** an event

Schritt 4: Entwerfen Sie eine vorläufige Antwort auf einem Konzeptblatt und überprüfen Sie diese sowohl auf inhaltliche Vollständigkeit als auch auf sprachliche Richtigkeit.

❸ Erzählperspektive

Die Erzählperspektive (→ point of view) bestimmt den Standort, von dem aus ein Geschehen für den Leser dargestellt wird. Hier hat ein Autor im Grunde zwei Möglichkeiten. Der Autor kann als objektiver Erzähler (third person narrator, → point of view), also aus der Sicht von außen, den Vorgang als Beobachter *(observer)* schildern oder – wie in *Just along for the ride* – als „Ich-Erzähler“ (first person narrator, → point of view) an der erzählten Welt teilnehmen.

Methode

Schritt 1: Die Geschichte wird in der ersten Person erzählt. Der Erzähler kann die Erzählsituation aus subjektiver und objektiver Perspektive darstellen. Im ersteren Fall bezieht er sich selbst ein, im zweiten beschreibt er Personen und Dinge ohne persönliche Wertung. Lesen Sie zunächst den Text, um die beiden unterschiedlichen Blickwinkel auszumachen. Beachten Sie, dass es nicht primär um die objektive Darstellung anderer Personen geht. Hier steht die Form der Wahrnehmung (→ perception) im Mittelpunkt der Analyse, also die geschilderten Gefühle, Gedankengänge *(mode of thought)* und Beweggründe *(motive)*.

COMPARE **Objektive und subjektive Darstellung**

- ▷ The man came into the waiting room and sat down next to me. After a few minutes, I heard the nurse speaking on the phone. Then she came in and said, ”The doctor can see you now, Mr Snow. This way, please.” He got up and followed her out of the room.
- ▷ The man came into the waiting room and sat down next to me. I could see he was nervous. After a few minutes, I heard the nurse speaking on the phone. Then she came in and said, ”The doctor can see you now, Mr Snow. This way, please.” He got up and followed her out of the room like a man on his way to the firing squad.

Im ersten Abschnitt handelt es sich um eine objektive Darstellung. Der Erzähler schildert Mr Snow, ohne ihn direkt oder indirekt zu charakterisieren. Er beschränkt sich auf die Rolle eines externen Beobachters *(external observer)* (→ point of view).

Im zweiten Abschnitt erfahren wir etwas über Mr Snows Gemütszustand: Er wirkt nervös, gar wie jemand, der vor ein Exekutionskommando treten muss. Hier ist der Erzähler mehr als nur ein externer Beobachter.

USEFUL EXPRESSIONS	Erzählperspektive

(to) be told **from** the point of view **of** ...

(to) take part/be involved **in** an event/a situation oneself

(to) describe one's own actions/state of mind, and those of ...

(to) function **as**/with the authority of an omniscient narrator *(allwissender Erzähler)*

(to) state the obvious/the self-evident

(to) surmise *(mutmaßen)*

(to) act **as** an external observer *(außenstehender Beobachter)*

(to) be like a/any third person narrator

(to) make the narrator report **on** ...

(to) see sb through the eyes of others

Schritt 2: Nun geht es darum, die beiden Blickwinkel zu analysieren und zu interpretieren. Charakterisieren Sie die folgenden Personen anhand des Textes: den Erzähler, Dick, Phil, Steve, Ken Benjamin und den Volvo-Fahrer. Es mag zwar umfangreich erscheinen, doch es handelt sich nur um wenige Textstellen.

USEFUL EXPRESSIONS	Charakterisierung

(to) be characterised directly and indirectly

(to) be the most important protagonist

(to) come across **as** ... *(wirken wie ...)*

(to) go along **with** sth *(sich einer Sache widerwillig anschließen)*

(to) be aware **of** what one should do

(to) confront oneself **with** one's own cowardice/weaknesses

(to) be aware **of** the implications of a situation

(to) suffer **from**/have a crucial flaw *(entscheidender Makel)* **in** one's character

(to) be relieved **of** an obligation *(von einer Verpflichtung befreit werden)* to do sth difficult/unpleasant
(to) confront sb **with** sth
(to) be the other main/principal protagonist
(to) change one's mind
(to) turn on sb viciously *(bösartig)*/aggressively
(to) put one's own interests/safety **before** that of others/all else
(to) not care **for**/have interest **in** others
(to) interest oneself (only/solely) **in** having got away with sth
(to) play a minor role
(to) be of marginal/secondary importance
(to) be responsible **for** the original idea/suggestion
(to) persuade sb to carry sth out/join in
(to) make a first reference **to** sb
(to) be repeated in line ... and line ...
(to) be the only person to do sth
(to) react immediately **to** an event
(to) be more interested **in** bringing sb **to** justice than in helping a victim
(to) be determined to do sth
(to) put oneself at personal risk
(to) fit in **with**/be consistent **with** sb's assumption/opinion **about** sb

Schritt 3: Abschließend interpretieren Sie die Rolle des Erzählers. Beachten Sie dabei, dass ein Ich-Erzähler, der **seine eigenen Gefühle** usw. einbezieht, meistens glaubwürdiger und lebendiger wirkt als ein Erzähler, der objektiv über andere Personen und Dinge spricht.

USEFUL EXPRESSIONS	Funktion der Erzählperspektive

(to) be crucial *(entscheidend)* **to** our understanding of the story/perception *(Wahrnehmung)* of the characters
(to) tend to be more direct/realistic/vivid *(lebhaft)* than ...
(to) erect a barrier/filter between the reader and people/events described
(to) make a deeper impact *(Wirkung)*/impression *(Eindruck)* **on** the reader
(to) be a direct statement of fact
(to) ensure/make sure
(to) have a primary interest **in** the main protagonist
(to) feel understanding/sympathy **for** sb's situation/predicament *(Dilemma)*
(to) spring **from**/be caused **by** a flawed character/a fatal character weakness

Schritt 4: Entwerfen Sie eine vorläufige Antwort auf einem Konzeptblatt und überprüfen Sie diese auf inhaltliche Vollständigkeit sowie sprachliche Richtigkeit. Fertigen Sie dann eine Reinschrift an.

12 Cartoon: Economy and Ecology

Beschreibung eines Cartoons
Deutung eines Cartoons

A Cartoon und Aufgaben

This cartoon by Ken Sprague, a British political cartoonist whose work is widely published in the press, is about the US-led war against the Muslim fundamentalist Taliban in Afghanistan following the Al-Qaeda attacks on New York and Washington on 11 September 2001. The Taliban were said to be helping Al-Qaeda and its leader, Osama Bin Laden in the frontier region between Afghanistan and Pakistan.

ASSIGNMENTS

(Anforderungsbereich I: Verständnis)

❶ **Describe the cartoon.**

(Anforderungsbereich II, III: Analyse und Beurteilung)

❷ **Explain Ken Sprague's message.**

USEFUL VOCABULARY

aid = help	
belly = stomach	
(to break open) **on impact** = (to break open) on hitting the ground	
desert = large area of dry land	
flour = fine powder for cooking made from grain	
humanitarian = adjective meaning 'intended to help people in need'	
loose = not firmly fixed	
parachute = umbrella-shaped cloth to make people fall slowly when dropped from an aircraft	
plank = piece of wood	
rock = small stone	
(to) starve = (to) die of hunger	
wooden crate = wooden box	

B Praktische Hilfe und Arbeitsschritte

Die Nummern ❶ und ❷ beziehen sich auf die Aufgabennummern oben.

Wir unterscheiden zwischen humorvollen und politischen Cartoons (humorous/political → cartoon). Erstere dienen vornehmlich der Unterhaltung, die zweite Gruppe ist eine pointierte satirische *(satirical)* Darstellung einer – meist aktuellen – politischen oder sozialen Situation (→ satire).

Alle politischen Cartoons sind Karikaturen. Eine Karikatur (→ caricature) lebt von einer mehr oder minder extremen Übertreibung (→ exaggeration) eines physischen Merkmales *(physical characteristic)*, in diesem Fall die aufgeschreckte Reaktion des Angesprochenen im Cartoon.

Methode

❶ Beschreibung

Schritt 1: Zunächst sollten Sie den Cartoon sorgfältig studieren und alle Einzelheiten erkennen. Beachten Sie, dass in politischen Cartoons nichts zufällig oder ohne Bedeutung ist. Die Wortliste oben wird Ihnen dabei helfen.

B Praktische Hilfe und Arbeitsschritte

Schritt 2: Im nächsten Schritt beschreiben Sie den Cartoon, ohne ihn zu interpretieren. (Zugegebenermaßen ist es schwierig, bei der Interpretation von Cartoons die zwei Phasen Beschreibung und Wertung nicht miteinander zu vermischen.) Beachten Sie, dass für Bildbeschreibungen grundsätzlich Präsensformen verwendet werden.

- Für die **Ortsbeschreibung** verwendet man das *simple present*, oft mit *there is/there are*:
  In the background **there are** bare/rocky/treeless mountains.
- Wenn wir darstellen wollen, **was in einem Bild gerade passiert** – also im Gange ist –, verwenden wir das *present progressive*:
  Two men **are looking** at a wooden crate of food aid.
  A parachute **is falling** to the ground.
- Wollen wir verdeutlichen, **was gerade passiert ist**, verwenden wir das *present perfect* (resultativer Gebrauch):
  It **has broken** open on impact.

USEFUL EXPRESSIONS	Beschreibung des Cartoons

(to) illustrate/show
(to) break open on impact
(to) comment **on** sth
(to) contain sacks of flour
(to) fall **from** the sky
(to) land in the desert/on the ground
(to) look shocked/surprised
(to) look **at** sth
(to) stand next to sth
(to) throw up one's hands in dismay/surprise
in the foreground/middle/background
in the top right-hand corner/top left-hand corner/bottom right-hand corner/ bottom left-hand corner of the cartoon
at the top/bottom/side/edge of the cartoon
on the right/left side/right-hand side/left-hand side of the cartoon

❷ Botschaft und Deutung

Üblicherweise lenkt der Karikaturist die Aufmerksamkeit des Betrachters auf einen Aspekt der Darstellung. Dieses Ziel erreicht er meist durch eine „Schockwirkung“ *(shock effect)* (→ black humour) – wie auch in diesem Fall –, was oft in Form eines Paradoxons (etwas, was einen Widerspruch in sich enthält) geschieht. Die Arbeiten vieler angelsächsischer Karikaturisten sind von dem bekannten „schwarzen Humor“ (→ black humour) der Briten gekennzeichnet.

Methode

Schritt 1: Jetzt geht es darum, Ken Spragues Botschaft *(message)* zu identifizieren und zu deuten. In diesem Fall ist es nützlich, mit den sinntragenden Wörtern *(key words)* in der Sprechblase *(speech bubble)* – also *humanitarian, full bellies, bomb* – zu arbeiten. Was will Sprague damit sagen?

USEFUL EXPRESSIONS	Die Botschaft des Cartoons
(to) assume *(vermuten)*/suppose that sb has an ulterior motive *(Hintergedanke)*	
(to) believe that sth is too good to be true	
(to) be **of** the opinion that ...	
(to) be schocked **by** a/an event/insight *(Einsicht)*/revelation *(Enthüllung)*	
(to) disguise *(verschleiern)* one's true intentions	
(to) expect sth to happen shortly	
(to) make a cynical/pessimistic/realistic/sceptical comment on one's situation	
(to) play a cruel trick **on** sb	
(to) say sth in a speech bubble	
(to) transmit a message (to the reader by means of a speech bubble)	

Schritt 2: In diesem abschließenden Schritt geht es darum, die Position des Karikaturisten zu deuten. Dies ist natürlich in gewissem Maße ein subjektives Urteil *(subjective judgement)*. Trotzdem können Sie davon ausgehen, dass der Karikaturist eine (oft äußerst) ablehnende Haltung zum Thema hat. Was ist – Ihrer Meinung nach – hier der Fall? Sehen Sie sich das Spachmaterial unten an, um Denkanstöße zu bekommen.

USEFUL EXPRESSIONS Die Deutung des Cartoons

(to) accuse *(beschuldigen)* the authorities/government **of** sth

(to) be the real victim *(Opfer)*

(to) criticise a/an decision/event/policy *(Vorgehensweise)*

(to) explain the true significance *(wahre Bedeutung)* of sth

(to) expose *(enthüllen)* the true motives of sb

(to) hold sth **up to** ridicule *(Spott)*

(to) ignore/overlook/pay no attention **to** the misery *(Elend)* of ordinary people

(to) poke fun **at** sth

(to) reject *(ablehnen)* a policy as cynical/evil *(verwerflich)*/immoral

(to) try to give a new insight into a situation

Lösungen

Einführungskurs

Anmerkung
In den Übungen 1 und 2 sollen Sie nicht unbedingt eine perfekte Entsprechung finden. Primär geht es darum, dass Sie die Ähnlichkeiten zwischen dem Englischen und dem Deutschen erkennen. Manches Deutsche mag deshalb hier „komisch“ anmuten.

Exercise 1

Seite 104

1. ... basieren auf dem Grundgedanken von Solidarität.
2. ... (aus) kulturellen und religiösen (Gründen).
3. ... etablierten riesige Teeplantagen ...
4. ... hoffen, Immigration/Einwanderung durch (engere) Kooperation zu verhindern.
5. ... haben die Sklaverei ... für illegal erklärt, (aber) sie existiert immer noch in einigen Regionen.
6. ... konservative amerikanische Politiker ..., das Schmuggeln von harten Drogen ... von Armee und Polizei ... zu stoppen.
7. Das Kabinett diskutierte eine Resolution über den Import von toxischen/giftigen Materialien ...
8. ... Soziologen haben herausgefunden, ... durch Sozial-/Klassenprivilegien geteilt.
9. ... Historiker ... , (dass) europäische Integration mehrere Generationen (dauern würde).
10. ... haben wegen der Rezession ... Bankrott gemacht/sind ... in Konkurs gegangen.

Exercise 2

Seite 106

1. kommerziellen und technologischen Zentren, 2. vor nur einer Generation, 3. hoffnungslos, 4. landwirtschaftlich geprägte Stadt/Agrarstadt, 5. die Industrialisierung der Ökonomie, 6. Metallprodukte, 7. die Produktion von Industriemaschinen, 8. exportierte seine Produkte, 9. die „Werkstatt der Welt“, 10. Industriestädte, 11. Industrialisierung der USA, 12. Verlust von Märkten, 13. geografische Position/Lage, 14. Investoren, 15. optimistisch, 16. Ödland, 17. den Ruinen von Fabriken und Lagerhäusern, 18. unbenutzten Kanälen und Güterbahnhöfen

Exercise 3

Seite 107

What <u>influence</u> do <u>genes</u> have on <u>intelligence</u>?
“When we look at good adoptive families, we know that the <u>children of more intelligent natural parents</u> will tend to be <u>more intelligent</u> than the <u>children of less intelligent natural parents</u>. This suggests that <u>genes</u> are the <u>decisive factor in intelligence</u>,” says Sandra Carr, professor of psychology at Yale University.
On the other hand, she agrees with Richard Snow, professor of education and psychology at Stanford University, that an unhappy home life <u>with little intellectual stimulation</u> can <u>keep</u> a <u>child from</u> ever using the <u>intelligence</u> she/he carries in her/his <u>genes</u>. “But such extreme cases are rare,” said Professor Carr. “The fact is that when we compare children in any given family environment – good or bad – the <u>children of more intelligent biological parents</u> always <u>perform relatively better</u> than the <u>children of less intelligent biological parents</u>.”

Exercise 4 — Seite 108

1. ~~The~~ author ~~(...) was~~ born ~~in the late 1940s in then~~ segregated Chicago, went to an integrated ~~high~~ school ~~and~~ university ~~in the 1960s and early 70s and is~~ now a professor ~~of English at an~~ integrated university ~~in California~~.
2. Something ~~in the~~ lives of Afro-Americans ~~must be~~ different ~~from that of~~ other minority groups, such as ~~the new~~ immigrants ~~from~~ Asia ~~and~~ Latin America.
3. ~~An~~ Afro-American ~~civil rights~~ activist speaks ~~to a~~ white ~~salesman~~ in ~~a hotel~~ bar. ~~He~~ makes ~~the salesman~~ feel so guilty about slavery ~~and~~ segregation ~~that the~~ white ~~man~~ gives ~~the elderly~~ Afro-American barman a $20 ~~tip~~.
4. ~~A talented~~ Afro-American university teacher tells the author ~~that he is~~ looking ~~for the~~ softest ~~academic~~ job ~~he can find~~ so ~~that he~~ has ~~as much~~ time ~~as possible to~~ go fishing.
5. ~~Mr~~ Steele reduces ~~this sad~~ catalogue ~~to~~ two ~~particular~~ problems.
6. ~~The~~ first ~~is that~~ Afro-Americans ~~have~~ less self-confidence ~~than other groups and~~ suffer ~~from~~ a fear of failure because ~~of the worldwide~~ view ~~of them as being~~ “intellectually inferior”.

Exercise 5 — Seite 112

1. The aims of the geneticist Paul Smith are .../The geneticist Paul Smith’s aims are ...
2. According to Russell Baker, the most painful side of giving up a private car was .../In Russell Baker’s opinion/view, the most painful side of giving up a private car was ...
3. Esther visited Dr Gordon because she ...
4. Mr Steele explains the paradoxical situation of Afro-Americans by (Verb + -ing-Form) that ...
5. People who want to emigrate to the USA use these/the following tricks to get round immigration laws: ...
6. The writer deals with the following/these immigration issues in his/this essay ...
7. These/The following sequence of events led to Billy’s decision (to leave home) ...
8. When the writer says (that) the export of waste to the third world is “a kind of neo-imperialism”, she means that ...

Exercise 6 — Seite 114

1. looking for, deal with; 2. came into, sat down; 3. answered, take an interest in; 4. purchased, built; 5. shown to be; 6. think about, argument; 7. damaged; 8. the death penalty, hang, kill; 9. excused, parts; 10. understand, worried

Exercise 7 — Seite 115

1. friendly; 2. bright; 3. jealous; 4. big-hearted; 5. uninterested; 6. considerate; 7. gloomy; 8. apparent; 9. argumentative; 10. mean; 11. hard-hearted; 12. committed; 13. enthusiastic; 14. lovely; 15. sceptical; 16. interesting; 17. awful; 18. childish; 19. vivacious; 20. disagreeable; 21. small-minded; 22. wealthy; 23. poisonous; 24. assorted; 25. young

Exercise 8 — Seite 115

1. jump, escape, fast-moving vehicles; 2. Supporters, more, present intake, in fact, seen, proportion; 3. wonderful gift, women, intelligent, sterile; 4. did not bother, awful, having a car, brought up the topic, look at, bought

Exercise 9

Seite 120

1. Most of the characters **are** female.
2. When we met him again, Joe Lampton **had been** married for five years.
3. Macbeth **meets** the witches on a lonely heath.
4. After Antonio had asked him for money, Shylock **made** fun of him.
5. Most politicians **exaggerate** the importance of political parties.
6. The story would be more interesting if it **reflected** real life.
7. If the report had concentrated on just one topic, it **would have been** easier to understand.
8. Joe says that Susan loves her father more than she **loves** him.
9. The witches tell Macbeth that one day he **will be** king.
10. Joe is unhappy but he **need not lead** that kind of life.
11. I can't find **anything** about this problem in the first part of the text.
12. The author says that too **many** videos are bad for children.
13. There are **pieces of evidence** for this in the final paragraph.
14. Can you give me some **information** about trains to Glasgow, please?
15. The police **are** getting worried about drug dealers in schools.
16. Susan is **Joe Lampton's wife**.
17. The front door is in fact at the **side of the house**.
18. Philosophy is about fundamental questions of **human life**.
19. He has been **in hospital** for six months now.
20. **Most** great Scottish authors wrote in English.
21. They didn't build their house **themselves**, did they?
22. Joe and Susan did not really love **each other/one another**, but they still got married.
23. This book consists **of** twelve units.
24. Compared **with/to** King Lear, Macbeth is an easy Shakespeare play.
25. I don't know if we'll go out tomorrow; it depends **on** the weather.
26. Tom has been waiting **for** his girlfriend outside the cinema for nearly an hour.
27. How long has Susan been married **to** Joe?
28. Mark's a terrible snob. He **looks down on** people less fortunate than himself.
29. The government suggested **closing** several London hospitals.
30. Nobody dares **to disagree** with Mr Davis.
31. Tom promised his doctor **to give up** smoking.
32. Can you imagine **working** with dangerous criminals?
33. Would you prefer **to stay** at home this evening?
34. It's hard but you can't avoid **meeting** your ex-girlfriend sometimes.
35. **Unfortunately we missed** the first part of the film.
36. Wendy **is still doing** her homework.
37. I'm afraid Mr Allen **has already left** the office.
38. **Of course you can come** with us to the party if you want. **(You can, of course, come ...)**
39. **We sometimes go** to the theatre in York.
40. Wendy has to visit her elderly parents **every day**.

41. **Mr Scott always gives us** homework to do at the weekend.
42. Milk **is delivered daily in** Britain, even on Sundays.
43. **We particularly enjoyed the story about** the two dogs.
44. The **girl who** was sitting next to **me gave** me a big smile.
45. The moment he spoke I **knew where** he came from.
46. The author **claims that** human rights are impossible to enforce.
47. The man you know, the one Ann met at our **party**, **phoned** her the same evening.

1 Sachtext: *Class Society*

ab Seite 122

1. Explain to what extent Olivia and Ruth's experiences support research findings into cross-class relationships.

Olivia and Ruth's experiences agree with/support research findings in that/in so far as/to the extent that they both have difficulties/problems in their marriages because their husbands come from a different social class. The two women are working class, while their husbands are middle class. For this reason, Olivia and Ruth have few shared *(gemeinsam)* childhood experiences with their husbands and (tend to) see life through different eyes/from a different angle *(Blickwinkel)*/perspective. These differences – as research findings show/suggest (here: *andeuten*) – have caused difficulties/friction *(„Reiberei")*/problems in their marriages. In the case of Ruth, class differences were made worse by a financial barrier. Her husband's father was a millionaire and her mother-in-law was certain that she had only married for money. In the end, these strains *(Belastung)*/problems caused the marriage to break down completely.

2. Point out less important examples of class-related behaviour mentioned in the text.

There are two less important/more trivial examples of class-related behaviour in the text/article. Both have to do with Olivia's marriage. Her middle-class husband's habit *(Gewohnheit)* of calling the sitting room the lounge can drive her crazy/make her very angry (l.6). The other example has to do with their parents. Olivia refers to *(erwähnen)*/speaks of/talks about her mother-in-law's middle class charity balls and her own father's working-class darts nights (ll. 47/48). Olivia says that partners should talk about such trivial things/irritants *(Reizthema)* and not let them fester *(nagen)*.

3. Describe the attitudes of the parents mentioned in the text to their child's marriage partner.

We hear about the attitudes *(Einstellung)* of Olivia's and Ruth's parents-in-law and of Ruth's father as well.

In Olivia's case, her parents-in-law objected to *(Einwände erheben gegen)*/took exception to *(an etwas Anstoß nehmen)* her attitude to the children's education. They were angry at/about her refusal *(Weigerung)* to send the children to a public school *(Privatschule)*. Olivia feels/is sure/thinks (that) her husband's parents were secretly convinced *(insgeheim davon überzeugt)* (that) she was dragging/pulling her husband/children down to her (working-class) level *(Niveau)* (ll. 14/15).

Ruth's experiences are more complex. Her own father thought (from the very beginning) that her husband's family would never accept her (ll. 30/31). Ruth says (that) her experiences show that he was right. She says that her husband's relatives and friends seem to have had a vested interest *(eigennütziges Interesse)* in keeping her in her place *(in ihre Schranken weisen)* (ll. 32/33). Her mother-in-law was certain/sure/convinced (that) Ruth was (just) a gold-digger/(that) Ruth had only married for money (ll. 31/32). This added to/complicated the class differences. In the end, Ruth just could not go on. She was worn down *(aufgerieben)* by the hostility *(Feindseligkeit)*/suspicion *(Argwohn)*. She points out (that) her husband became more and more/increasingly *(zunehmend)* like his parents as the years went by/as he became older (ll. 40/41). Ruth was terribly hurt when she became aware *(bewusst werden)* that her husband had begun seeing her through/with his mother's eyes (ll. 42/43). This was probably the real reason for the breakdown (here: *Zerrüttung)* of the marriage.

4. **Compare the two women's experiences.**

The two women's experiences are similar in that/in so far as/to the extent that they both had marriage problems for class-related reasons. In both cases, these problems had as much to do with the women's parents-in-law as with their husbands. In other ways, however, Olivia and Ruth had different experiences.

In Olivia's case, the marriage survived *(fortbestehen)* in spite of the difficulties. She obviously still loves her husband, George, and he loves her. When they clashed (here: *sich heftig streiten)* about their children's education, they were interested enough in their marriage to go to a marriage counsellor *(Eheberatung)*/to get counselling (ll. 15/16). They were both willing to compromise and they succeeded in solving the problem.

In Ruth's case things were different. To begin with, her class-related difficulties were made worse/exacerbated *(verschärfen)* by her mother-in-law's conviction *(Überzeugung)* that she had only married her son, Ian, for money. In her eyes, Ruth was a "gold digger" (l. 32). Secondly, although the marriage survived for 15 years, it ended in divorce. This was because, in Ruth's view, her husband changed. He had once been strong enough to stand up to *(sich jdm. entgegenstellen)* his parents and peer group, but as he got older he became more and more/increasingly *(zunehmend)* like them (ll. 40/41). Finally, he began seeing his wife through his mother's eyes (ll. 42/43). This is what really hurt Ruth so deeply and made her feel so bitter.

5. **Characterise Laura Marcus's article with reference to her intention.**

This text, which is in the form of two case studies *(Fallstudie)*/which presents information in the form of case studies, has many of the features *(Merkmal)* of informative texts, i.e. texts that are intended to clarify *(klären)* some topic/subject.

To begin with, except when Olivia and Ruth or the writer are speaking of past experiences, the text is written in the present tense, for example "Shared childhood experiences ... are absolutely vital to most couples" (ll. 2–4). This tense is used to express generally valid *(allgemein gültig)* ideas and is very typical of such texts.

Secondly, the text begins with a clear affirmative statement which introduces the reader to the topic (ll. 1–2). It goes on to quote/refer to expert opinion and research findings as when we are told about the results of investigations *(Untersuchung)* into cross-class relationships (ll. 2–8).
Thirdly, particularly in this case, the writer/Laura Marcus makes her article/text more credible *(glaubwürdig)* by allowing the people concerned to speak for themselves. Although she evidently *(offensichtlich)* feels some sympathy (here: *Verständnis*) for Olivia and Ruth, she does not express her own opinion or interpretation of events too strongly. It is left to the reader to reach their own conclusions.

6. **Comment on Laura Marcus's remark that there may be "even a little hyprocrisy" in Olivia's attitude.**
Laura Marcus asks this question because although Olivia is now complaining *(sich beklagen)* about George's middle-class attitudes, she fell in love with him and married him in spite of this. George has not changed; Olivia has.
Olivia says that she loves her husband as a person/for himself because he is kind and has a "wicked (here: *erfrischend respektlos*) sense of humour" (l. 22), but she admits *(zugeben)* that she also married him partly because of his background and the feeling of security this gave her. She even goes so far as to say that he "made me feel secure for the first time in my life" (ll. 24/25).
I do not think that this makes Olivia a hypocrite *(Heuchlerin)*. Her attitude may seem a little inconsistent *(inkonsequent)*, but hypocrisy is too strong. A hyprocrite is somebody who does not live according to his or her stated *(erklärt)* beliefs. For example, a person who goes to church but who does not live according to Christ's teachings. This certainly does not apply to Olivia. On the contrary *(im Gegenteil)*, she is fully aware of her attitude and speaks about it openly and honestly.

(2) Sachtext: Urban Society

ab Seite 130

1. **Point out why the congestion charge has not been as effective in solving London's traffic problems as originally hoped.**
While the congestion charge has reduced the number of vehicles entering central London by about 100,000, traffic is taking longer to travel through the area, thus making traffic congestion about the same as it was before the charge was introduced. The reason for the traffic slowing down is a big increase in roadworks and traffic-calming measures like speed humps, which have combined to reduce the road space available to drivers. Changes to traffic-light intervals to give pedestrians more time to cross the road have also had an effect.

2. **Describe what effect new measures to solve London's traffic congestion are likely to have.**
In order to solve the problem of worsening congestion, pedestrian schemes such as turning part of Parliament Square into a pedestrian zone are likely to be abandoned. Traffic-

light intervals will also be left on green for vehicles and red for pedestrians longer to allow traffic to move through central London faster. To the same end, motorbikes are to be allowed to use bus lanes. The London authorities also want to make it more difficult for utility companies to dig up roads by forcing them to get permits. The combined effect of these measures will be to make life easier for drivers at the expense of pedestrians.

3. **Summarise the text in not more than 200 words.**

London's streets are as congested now as they were before the congestion charge was introduced five years ago, in spite of a big drop in vehicle numbers. This is because roadworks, traffic-calming measures and more pedestrian zones have reduced driving space. Pedestrians are expected to suffer most from the renewed fight against congestion, with pedestrian schemes being abandoned and experts calling for shorter crossing times at traffic lights. Motorbikes will also be allowed to use bus lanes to free up road space. According to Transport for London (TfL), there has been no improvement in the congestion situation in West London since the congestion charge zone was extended to Kensington and Notting Hill, although the number of vehicles passing through the zone has dropped sharply there, too. Utility companies are to be forced to apply for permits before starting roadworks, and a plan to turn part of Parliament Square into a pedestrian zone is to be abandoned.

Supporters of the scheme argue that gridlocks and tailbacks would be even worse without the congestion charge. But TfL pointed out that a lack of road space is the biggest single cause of congestion. (190 words)

3 Sachtext: Education

ab Seite 134

1. **Explain why the power cut in Hammersmith called the government's 'wild claims' into question.**

The power cut in Hammersmith meant that the electronic tills that work out the change when paying for purchases no longer worked. Despite government claims about rising standards in schools, however, it was found that shop and restaurant staff were unable to do this simple calculation in their head or even on paper. This led to many businesses having to stop trading until electricity had been restored.

2. **Say what the author's aim in writing this article is and how it is expressed in his use of language.**

The writer's aim is to persuade the reader that government claims about rising school standards are not supported by reality.

He calls into question the government's claim that pupils are "better than ever before" (l. 28) by describing an incident in Hammersmith, London. The electronic tills in shops and restaurants were no longer working because of a power cut so staff had to calculate customers' change themselves. Many of them could not do this simple subtraction calculation with the result that businesses had to stop trading until "the 'sparkies' sorted matters out" (l. 17).

The writer expresses this intention mainly by means of his choice of words. Hence he uses strong verbs and adjectives such as "to bang on about sth" (l. 1), "wild claims" (l. 3), "dreary details" (ll. 12/13) and "complete chaos" (l. 16).
However, he also makes use of some other stylistic devices that are typical of this kind of evaluative text. For example, he uses hyperbole in such expressions as "begging to remain nameless" (l. 18) and "what an indictment" (l. 27) as well as enumeration in "including coffee bars, stationery shops, travel agents, etc." (ll. 13/14).
In addition, the writer employs irony when he speaks of present-day school pupils as "our 'hopes of the future'" (l. 27), and contrast when he tells of how different things were when he himself worked for some accountants. Then, the skill of mental arithmetic was such that he could add up columns of figures using whole numbers in pounds, shillings and pence.

4 Sachtext: The American Dream

ab Seite 138

1. **Describe what picture of Norman Mailer the reader gets from the interview and explain how it is transmitted.**

Norman Mailer is characterised partly by means of direct characterisation, i.e. concrete description by a third party, and partly by indirect characterisation, i.e. character traits are implied by what Mailer himself says or does.
Almost the whole of the introductory paragraph to the interview (ll. 1–8) is devoted to direct characterisation in the form of concrete background information about Mailer. For example, we are told that he has written 31 books, won the Pulitzer Prize twice and directed four films. We are also given some insights into his married life, for example that he was once accused of having stabbed his wife and is now married to another writer. We are even given some details of his health, such as his suffering from arthritis in the knees, which means that he can sometimes only get about with sticks.
In the body of the interview itself on the other hand, characterisation is largely indirect. Hence from what Mailer says we gather that he is against the Bush government's war in Iraq (ll. 10–13), worried about a swing to the conservative right in the USA (ll. 13–18), has strong if unconventional religious beliefs (ll. 20–25), sees some advantages in getting old (ll. 25–30) and loathes some aspects of modern America, such as plastic and the fact that America has become "loutish" (ll. 33–37).

2. **Analyse Mailer's use of language, particularly stylistic devices.**

In the interview, Norman Mailer uses several stylistic devices in order to make his position on a variety of topics clear to the reader.
Most important among these is his choice of words, i.e. his use of colloquial, everyday language. He certainly does not come across as some remote intellectual literary figure. Examples of such language, which is really characteristic of the interview as a whole, are "But I don't think that bothers our leaders very much." (ll. 12/13), "I think they kind of like ..." (ll. 13–15) and "I don't have this certainty. Thank God, that once you die you die, and

that's the end of it." (ll. 22/23). This makes what he says readily understandable to the reader and gives it an almost confiding tone. Apart from expressing himself in the language of everyday speech, Mailer also makes use of typical stylistic devices like enumeration, hyperbole and repetition. Examples of the first of these are "... all the 'frees' - free love, gay liberation, women's liberation - all the things ..." (ll. 14/15) and "plastic, superhighways, high-rise architecture, which is ..." (ll. 33/34).
Good examples of hyperbole, i.e. intentional exaggeration, are "..., which is an abomination of everything" (ll. 33/34) and "It's one of our great cultural commodities: crap." (ll. 37/38). Meanwhile, repetition is used on a number of occasions to drive home the point, as in "Leaving aside all the usual ..., forgetting all that, the fact is, that war could just go on and on and on." (ll. 10-12).

5 Sachtext: Politics and Society

ab Seite 145

1. **Pick out examples of racial discrimination given in the main extract from Martin Luther King's speech and in the other quotations from the speech.**
The main extract from Martin Luther King's speech contains only general references to (racial) discrimination. Examples are the quotation from the American constitution "We hold these truths to be self-evident: that all men are created equal", references to (the situation in) a number of southern states such as Mississippi, "a state sweltering with the heat of injustice", and Alabama "with its vicious racists" and, finally, King's call that blacks should "not be judged by the color of their skin but by the content of their character".
Other quotations (from the speech) go into more detail about the discrimination faced by blacks, such as when King complains that "the Negro lives on a lonely island of poverty in the midst of a vast ocean of material prosperity". More specifically, he refers to concrete examples of everyday discrimation such as "the unspeakable horrors of police brutality", refusal of accommodation in motels and hotels, living in ghettos and notices saying "For Whites Only".

2. **Describe King's vision of a better future for American society.**
The substance of Martin Luther King's dream is the ending of racial discrimination - particularly the form of the segregation of blacks and whites - and the realisation of social and political equality, as envisaged in the constitution.
King equates "equality" with levelling out differences between the races by the use of what may be called "topographical imagery". This is expressed in the lines "... every valley shall be exalted, every hill and mountain shall be made low, the rough places will be made plain, and the crooked places will be made straight ...".
A second demand, also echoing the constitution, is the call for freedom. Here again, King expresses this hope by referring to the topography of America as when he says "... let freedom ring from the prodigious hilltops of New Hampshire", "... from the mighty mountains of New York" and "... from the heightening Alleghenies of Pennsylvania".
Working his way through America from north to south, King goes on to allude to mountain

ranges or individual peaks in Colorado, California, Georgia, Tennessee and, finally, to "every hill and molehill of Mississippi".

3. **Analyse how Martin Luther King persuades his audience to support his civil rights campaign.**
Apart from its use of highly emotional language, which is reminiscent of gospel worship in the American South, the persuasive power of the speech depends largely on the use of three stylistic devices, namely hyperbole, enumeration and, above all, repetition.
A vivid instance of hyperbole is, for example, "... Mississippi, a state sweltering with the heat of injustice, sweltering with the heat of oppression, will be transformed into an oasis of freedom and justice". Describing Mississippi as "an oasis" is also a good example of King's use of metaphor. A further example of hyperbole is the reference to "little black boys and black girls" joining hands with "little white boys and white girls" and becoming like "sisters and brothers".
The use of enumeration is well illustrated by the passage in which King refers to a number of mountain ranges and mountains in America in the lines "... from the prodigious hilltops of New Hampshire ..." to "... every hill and molehill of Mississippi". A further powerful example of this device is "... we will be able to work together, to pray together, to struggle together, to go to jail together, to stand up for freedom together, ...".
However, the whole speech lives from King's continuous use of repetition, which comes over like the beating of a drum. Apart from the phrases "I have a dream", "I have a dream today" and "I have a dream that one day", further examples of repetition of this drumbeat type are the phraes "With this faith" and "Let freedom ring".

6 Sachtext: Economy and Ecology

ab Seite 151

1. **Give reasons why European public opinion is largely against the use of GM crops.**
Public opinion in Europe is largely against the use of GM crops for two main reasons. Firstly, the BSE scare led to worries about consumer protection and, linked to this, about the effectiveness of health and food regulation, particularly in the UK. Soon GM food was seen by consumers as "Frankenfood", which amounted to using them as guinea pigs in scientific experiments. Secondly, the fact that GM was dominated by US corporations appealed to the instinctive anti-Americanism of the European left.

2. **Summarise the author's reasons for supporting genetic manipulation in agriculture.**
According to the author, the use of GM technology could increase the European grain harvest by about 15%. Globally, increased production would lead to permanently lower food prices. In Africa particularly, cheap food is essential to the children of the urban poor, millions of whom are malnourished. But Africa's farmers can only achieve higher productivity with GM technology. Using traditional methods, the only way to increase food production is to take more and more land into cultivation. However, with the population growing fast, this option is becoming increasingly difficult and expensive. Furthermore, global warming

means that semi-desert areas will get drier, and the unreliabilty of rainfall will mean that droughts will become both more frequent and last longer. Only GM crops are hardy enough to survive these conditions.

3. **Analyse the characteristics of a popular scientific text as demonstrated in this comment on the use of GM crops.**

First of all, the present tense is characteristically used in popular scientific texts, particularly for the presentation of scientific facts, for example "GM research takes ..." (l. 12) and "a gene that gives ... is isolated ..." (ll. 33/34). Secondly, the will-future often occurs to express expectations and predictions, for example, "... will get drier ..." (l. 27), "... will mean more droughts" (l. 27).

In such texts, the passive is used for objective, impersonal description, for example, "could be increased" (l. 10), "cannot be achieved" (l. 13), "will be malnourished" (l. 22) and "can be made" (l. 36).

A further important characteristic of popular scientific texts is the replacement of technical and scientific terms with expressions likely to be known to non-specialists. Examples in this text are "can be made" (l. 36) for the more technical "can be rendered", "resistant" (l. 36) for "impervious", "reducing the need for" (ll. 37/38) instead of "minimising the application of chemicals" and, finally, "waste" (l. 38) instead of the more technical "deplete".

4. **Write a comment on the pros and cons of the widespread use of GM crops in agriculture. Give your own opinion.**

The use of genetic modification in agriculture in the form of GM crops and cloned farm animals remains highly controversial.

As a rule, supporters of GM crops point to four benefits. Firstly, GM crops and animals are said to be more productive than traditional ones. Even in Europe, it is claimed that the use of GM wheat could lead to a 15% increase in yields, for example, while cloned "supercows" could produce as much as 40 litres of milk a day.

Secondly, genetic manipulation in the laboratory leads to very much faster and more predictable results than selective breeding - which farmers have been practising for thousands of years - does.

A third big benefit claimed for GM is that it not only improves the taste and texture of food, but it also increases its nutritional value. This means that less land needs to be taken into cultivation to achieve a given level of nutrition. This is thought to be an important consideration in a world with a fast-growing population in which land is at a premium.

Finally, because GM crops require less fertiliser to grow and less pesticides and herbicides to protect them from insects and weeds, they are said to be more ecologically friendly than conventional crops.

For all that, the opponents of GM also have some rather powerful arguments at their disposal.

To begin with, and perhaps most importantly, opponents point out that in fact nobody yet knows how GM crops will react either with each other or with natural species in the longer

terms. It is simply too early to say. The potential risks to both human health and to the environment are, or at least could be, high.
Secondly, opponents of the technology fear that GM crops could create new allergies that are unknown to medicine. Related to this, it is suggested that certain GM crops and cloned animals could reduce the effectiveness of human antibiotics because of the way that they are produced in the laboratory.
A third, perhaps more concrete, fear is that GM crops can cross with natural weeds to produce so-called "superweeds" that spread very fast and in turn cross-breed with other weeds.
Even existing superweeds that have already been identified can only be destroyed and their spread controlled by the use of highly toxic herbicides that do great ecological damage such as destroying insects, including honey bees, and birds by contaminating their food. (Add a line giving your view for or against GM here.)

7 Literarischer Text: Class Society

ab Seite 158

1. **Explain "the twin deities of the world" and how they help Charles.**
   The twin deities are alcohol and nicotine. They make him feel less guilty and tired.

2. **Point out what made Charles get up and go to the bar.**
   Charles suddenly became aware of the hostility *(Feindseligkeit)* of the people around him. They evidently *(offensichtlich)* saw him as a stranger who had broken into their world. This made him feel embarrassed *(jdn verlegen machen)* and scared him. These uncomfortable feelings made him leave his seat and join the crowd at the bar.

3. **Describe the atmosphere of the extract by referring to the setting and Charles's state of mind.**
   The atmosphere of a literary text is determined (here: *bestimmt*) by the interplay *(Wechselwirkung)* between setting and the main character's state of mind.
   The incident *(Vorfall)* from *Hurry on down* takes place in a crowded bar and cannot last more than about 30 minutes or so. The setting is thus limited in both space and time. We are not given any information either about Charles's appearance *(äußere Erscheinung)* or about the other people present except that they are working-class and seem to feel some hostility towards Charles. At the bar, Charles is simply ignored. Even when he becomes more aggressive, it has little effect. The working-class feel of the place is emphasised by references to the stout-laden (l. 8) air and the bitter beer and cheap cigarettes ordered by the stocky *(stämmig)* man (ll. 18/19). Charles, by contrast, has been drinking whisky (l. 15) and wants to order gin, both typical middle-class drinks.
   At the beginning of the extract we hear that Charles manages to get rid of his guilt feelings *(Schuldgefühl)* and tiredness with the help of alcohol and cigarettes. As, however, he becomes aware of the hostility around him he feels embarrassed and frightened. This is what makes him go to the bar to order more drink. At the bar he is "curtly thrust aside"

(barsch zur Seite stoßen) (l. 14) and ignored by the landlord *(Wirt)* and his daughters. Everybody else is served promptly. This difference in treatment establishes Charles's sense of isolation and of not belonging. Soon the ebullience *(Überschwänglichkeit)* temporarily induced *(hervorrufen)* by the whisky evaporates (here: *sich in Luft auflösen*) to be replaced by renewed feelings of tiredness.

Charles's isolation is further highlighted by the reaction of the other people to his sudden show of anger. The stocky man's only reaction is to look at him "coldly for an instant" (l. 21) and then leave. It is clear that to him Charles is of no significance whatsoever. This deepens his depressed and unhappy mood. We are told that he "sank to the bottom of an Atlantic of frustration" (l. 24) and that even he, exhausted and disappointed, realised "why he was getting nowhere" (ll. 25/26).

Finally, the landlord leans across the bar and shouts at him "in his bullying way" *(auf seine tyrannische Art)* (l. 37). This makes Charles shriek back *(zurückschreien)* "with sudden violence" (l. 38). Even this, however, is only met with indifference *(Gleichgültigkeit)*.

The atmosphere is created by the strong contrast between the easy comradeship and sense of community *(Gemeinschaftssinn)* of the other customers on the one hand and Charles's intense isolation and disappointment on the other. This is finely expressed in the line "The hive *(Bienenstock)* was full of wasps, all workers and all identical; but he ... had been deprived of his sting *(Stachel)*" (ll. 34/35).

8 Literarischer Text: Urban Society

ab Seite 163

1. **Pick out factual information about Chicago given in the poem.**

Sandburg opens by saying that Chicago is the "Hog butcher for the world" (l. 1, l. 32), by which he means it is the world's biggest meat processor. He then goes on to describe the city as "Tool maker, Stacker of wheat, Player with railroads and the Nation's Freight Handler" (ll. 2/3, ll. 32/33). Here he is referring to Chicago's other main industries, i.e. the manufacture of machine tools, wheat, railways and freight handling. He closes the poem by repeating the same claim.

In the middle section we are given more information about Chicago. At the beginning of this section Sandburg describes the city's negative features. He admits that it is undeniably *(unumstritten)* marked by prostitution ("painted women under the gas lamps", l. 7), by uncontrolled crime ("... the gunman kill and go free to kill again", l. 9) and by poverty ("marks of wanton hunger", l. 11). Here he paints a very negative picture.

In the second half of this section, however, he describes some of Chicago's more positive traits. Here he gives an impression of a hard-working ("... amid the toil of piling job on job", l. 16) place with highly productive and enterprising modern industries ("... shoveling, wrecking, planning, building, breaking, rebuilding, ...", ll. 21–24).

2. **State who Sandburg is addressing and explain what he wants to achieve.**

In the first part of the poem as far as line 12 the pronoun "you" and the possessive adjective "your" refer to Chicago itself. In these lines Chicago is described as a wicked, criminal and selfish person who has done wrong and is now being judged *(beurteilen)* by Sandburg himself: "They tell me you are wicked and I believe them, for I have seen ...", "And they tell me you are crooked and I answer: Yes, it is true I have seen ...".

From line 13 onwards Sandburg changes his perspective. He is no longer addressing Chicago, but the reader. He reports what answer he gives critics ("them"). Thus in the first part of the poem Sandburg seems to take on the role of a prosecuting attorney *(Staatsanwalt)* and in the second of a defender *(Strafverteidiger)*.

Sandburg's intention is to defend Chicago against its detractors *(Verleumder)*. He does this by first admitting to *(zugeben)* the negative aspects of the situation. He wholly agrees with the adverse criticism *(ablehnende Kritik)* ("Yes, it is true I have seen ...", ll. 8/9). Then, however, he points out Chicago's good sides with great energy and conviction, setting up a contrast between Chicago and "the little soft cities" (l. 17) of its detractors.

3. **Find examples of Sandburg's use of imagery and say what effect it has on our understanding of the poem.**

The poem is built on personification and contrast.

In the first part of the middle section Chicago is personified as a "wicked" (l. 6), "crooked" (l. 8) and "brutal" (l. 10) man.

In the second part the man is further characterised as a strong, healthy young working man full of vitality, energy and humour. The image of the young man is described in solely physical terms (here: *Begriff*): "Big Shoulders" (l. 5), "Bareheaded" (l. 20), "mouth" (l. 25), "white teeth" (l. 25), "wrist" (l. 28), "pulse" (l. 28), "ribs" (l. 28), "heart" (l. 29), "half naked" (l. 31), "sweating" (l. 31).

For all his positive qualities – "husky" (l. 4), "proud" (l. 14, l. 32), "strong" (l. 15), "tall" (l. 17), "bold" (l. 17), "laughing" (l. 25 and following lines) – the young man comes across as a simple, intensely physical person without intellectual, moral or emotional qualities. In addition to being characterised as wicked, crooked and brutal – see above – he is further described as "coarse" (l. 15), "fierce" (l. 18), "cunning" (l. 18), "ignorant" (l. 27), "Bragging" (l. 28) and "brawling" (l. 31).

Sandburg deepens this image by means of similes. He compares the ferocity *(Wildheit)* of the young man to that of "a dog with tongue lapping for action" (l. 18) and his cunning to that of "a savage pitted against the wilderness" (ll. 18/19).

Sandburg makes use of this very strong contrast in order to emphasise/highlight the depth and sincerity *(Aufrichtigkeit)* of his feelings for his native city. To achieve this effect he makes use of repetition (ll. 6–10), enumeration (ll. 1–3, 20–24) and alliteration (l. 24, ll. 26/27) and – throughout the poem – very robust and emotive language.

4. **Describe your own impression of Chicago at this time in its history and say whether you can imagine living in such a place.**

Positive Meinung:

On first reading, Sandburg's use of strong words like "wicked", "crooked", "brutal", "coarse" and so on creates a negative impression of Chicago. However, I think that prostitution, crime and poverty were features *(Merkmal)* of life in all big and expanding cities at this time. I know, for example, that at this time most cities had unsafe areas which even the police avoided.

I find the other side of Chicago – its enormous vitality, variety *(Vielfältigkeit)*, enterprise and opportunity – more significant and, with hindsight *(im Nachhinein)*, we know that these qualities overcame the more negative ones and changed the city into what it is today.

I can certainly imagine living in a city like Chicago, despite the less attractive aspects of life there. These must be put against the huge advantages of life in a big city. There is much more going on there and job opportunities are much greater than in rural *(ländlich)* areas.

Negative Meinung:

I get an awful/a terrible impression of Chicago from Sandburg's poem. It is not only that prostitution, lawlessness *(Gesetzlosigkeit)* and poverty are so widespread *(weit verbreitet)* there. [Sandburg himself, who is a lover and admirer *(Bewunderer)* of the city, admits *(zugeben)* that he has seen examples of all three almost as everyday facts of life.] Much more significantly, even when Sandburg praises the vitality and strength of Chicago, it still comes across as a coarse and polluted place without any of the finer things of life. Here Chicago really does seem to be different from both many other American cities like San Francisco and New York and from European cities of the time. They also had bad social problems like prostitution and poverty, but they had a cultural life and fine parks and public buildings as well.

Although I enjoy visiting big cities from time to time, I certainly could not imagine living somewhere like Chicago. I would not feel safe on the streets and would not be able to move about freely. I would also dislike the dirt, noise, violence and pollution. On the whole, life in a smaller place may not be quite so exciting, but it is certainly more pleasant. Everybody knows their neighbours and you are not as isolated and anonymous as in a big city.

9 Literarischer Text: Education

ab Seite 170

1. **Compare schools in 2155 and "the old kind of school that they had hundreds and hundreds of years ago".**

In 2155 schools are completely automated. Each family with school-age children are equipped with computerised teaching machines ("mechanical teachers", ll. 19–20) that have been specially programmed to the age and ability of the individual child. These machines communicate with the learner by means of a screen and continuously evaluate progress *(Fortschritt auswerten)* by marking test papers written in a punch code. Each child must learn this code at the age of six (ll. 29/30).

Should the mechanical teacher break down, then a technician – the "County Inspector" (l. 22) – visits the child's home to repair it. This official is also responsible for making sure that the machine is correctly programmed. The "old kind of school" (ll. 40/41) is the same as schools today. Children leave their homes and travel to a "special building" (l. 56) where children of the same age are taught in groups by a human teacher using books.

2. **Find evidence in the text to show Margie's attitude to school.**
Margie has a highly negative attitude towards school, i.e. towards her mechanical teacher, though she does moderate *(mäßigen)* her position slightly in the second part of the story. Then her attitude becomes a little more mixed.
In the first half of the story she rejects school completely. In line 18 we hear that she was "scornful" *(verachtend)* of Tommy's old book about schools and she adds "I hate school". She repeats this one line later with increased emphasis when we are told that "Margie always hated school, but now she hated it more than ever". When the technician calls to repair her mechanical teacher, we read that "Margie had hoped that he wouldn't know how to put it together again" (ll. 24/25) and that it was "large and black and ugly" (l. 26). The whole passage *(Textabschnitt)* is full of negative language concerning the teaching machine, for example "the part she hated most was the slot" (l. 28) and that Margie "was disappointed" because "she had been hoping they would take the teacher away altogether" (l. 36). Later, she asks Tommy in a mystified way *(verblüfft)*: "Why would anyone write about school?" (l. 39).
In the second part of the story, however, her opinion of school becomes slightly less negative. When Tommy tells her that in the old schools the children were taught by a man, Margie says: "A man isn't smart enough" (l. 49) and "A man can't know as much as a teacher" (l. 51). Thinking that in the old schools male teachers visited children in their homes, Margie says "I wouldn't want a strange man in my house to teach me." (l. 54). When Tommy and Margie are talking about the effectiveness of teaching children in groups, Margie quotes her mother as saying "a teacher has to be adjusted to fit the mind of each boy and girl he teaches" and "each kid has to be taught differently" (ll. 59/60). These remarks seem to suggest that Margie does not wholly reject her teacher after all. It seems that in her opinion, a teaching machine's functional competence in comparison with a human teacher is beyond doubt.
The final section of the story is devoted to *(gewidmet)* a daydream sequence. Sitting at the screen, Margie thinks nostalgically about the social aspects of the old kind of school, when "All the kids from the neighborhood came, laughing and shouting in the schoolyard, sitting together in the schoolroom, going home together at the end of the day" (ll. 77–79) and when "They learned the same things so they could help one another with the homework and talk about it." (ll. 80/81). The mechanical teacher interrupts Margie's daydreaming and then it becomes clear to her. Computers may be more efficient, but the old schools where "the teachers were people" were more fun.

3. **Characterise the relationship between Margie and Tommy.**
The relationship between Margie and Tommy is very typical of a girl and a boy of this age. Tommy, who is two years older than 11-year-old Margie, is the dominant partner.

When Margie asks Tommy why anyone would write about school, we read that he "looked at her with very superior eyes" (ll. 39/40). When answering her question he calls her "stupid" (l. 40) and in lines 41/42 we hear that he speaks to her "loftily" *(hochmütig)*. Margie was hurt by this treatment (l. 42). Later, Tommy "screamed with laughter" at one of Margie's naive remarks and adds "You don't know much, Margie" (l. 55).
These exchanges *(Wortwechsel)* establish a hierarchy. In his own eyes, Tommy is the superior being. He is more intelligent, more knowledgeable, more experienced. Margie is inferior. Tommy – the male and the elder – acts and initiates *(in die Wege leiten)*; Margie – the female and the younger – reacts and follows. This hierarchical relationship reflects *(widerspiegeln)* the structures in society as a whole.
This seems to be confirmed by the fact that Margie "wasn't prepared to dispute" (l. 53) whether Tommy's father knows as much as a mechanical teacher, though she must be aware *(jdm bewusst sein)* that this can hardly be the case. When Tommy challenges *(infrage stellen)* Margie's position in lines 61/62 – "If you don't like it, you don't have to read the book." – Margie quickly gives way. At the end of this sequence we read that Tommy answered Margie "nonchalantly" *(lässig)* and "walked away whistling" (l. 69), thus implying *(andeuten)* that he does not care much either way. This is also a very characteristic way of establishing the 'balance of power' within a relationship, and particularly in one between people of different sexes.

4. **Present evidence from the text to show that this is a short story.**
Isaac Asimov's *The fun they had* has a number of features characteristic of this literary form.
Both the main plot and the sub-plot are set in a very limited area. The main plot takes place in a single part of Margie's garden and the sub-plot in her room. Although we are not told how long the children are reading Tommy's book, it is clear that it cannot have been very long because we read that "They weren't even half finished when Margie's mother called: ..." (l. 65). The sub-plot only lasts a short time, too. We hear in line 26 that the technician finished "after an hour or so". The number of characters involved in the story is also typical. There are two main characters, Tommy and Margie, and two minor ones, the inspector and Margie's mother, Mrs Jones.
The exterior or apparent meaning of the main plot is extremely simple. At the beginning, we hear that Tommy has found an old book about schools in the attic *(Dachboden)* of his house. At first, Margie thinks the book is about the computerised schools of her day. She cannot understand how anyone could be interested in writing such a book at all. Then Tommy explains that the book is about "the old kind of school that they had hundreds and hundreds of years ago" (ll. 40/41). This interests Margie more, and the two children begin comparing the old schools with their own kind. Margie is particularly fascinated by the idea of "all the kids from the neighborhood" (l. 77) being taught in groups in a "special building" (l. 56) in which "teachers were people" (l. 81).
The apparent meaning of the sub-plot is also very straightforward *(unkompliziert)*. Margie's mother calls the inspector, a kind of computer technician, because Margie is doing "worse

and worse" at geography (l. 21). The technician finds that the geography program is "a little too quick" and readjusts it "to an average ten-year level" (ll. 33/34). The ease with which the technician corrects the fault disappoints Margie. She has been hoping that he will take her mechanical teacher away with him.

At a deeper level the story is concerned with a conflict situation. The conflict is between Margie and her life and relationships as represented or symbolised by her mechanical teacher.

Margie has "always hated school" and now she hates it "more than ever" (l. 19). She has become "worse and worse" at geography (l. 21), which has caused her mother so much worry that she has "sent for the County Inspector" (ll. 21/22). At "the same time every day" Margie finds the "mechanical teacher on and waiting for her" (ll. 71/72). It is "large and black and ugly" (l. 26). Margie finds her own human wishes and dreams subordinated to *(untergeordnet)* the demands *(Forderung)* of a machine that dictates the rhythm of her life (ll. 72–74).

Margie's subordination to others is also reflected in her relationship to Tommy, her mother and the inspector. Tommy considers her stupid (l. 40) and laughs at her ignorance (l. 55). At the end of the episode in the garden, Tommy makes it clear that he does not care either way whether they meet again after school or not. Margie's mother is in a position of absolute authority and is not willing to allow her daughter any freedom of choice. When Margie asks if she can stay in the garden a little longer, Mrs Jones says simply "Now" and Margie obeys immediately (ll. 65–67). Her mother imposes *(auferlegen)* a strict routine because "little girls" learn better if they learn "at regular hours" (ll. 73/74). This relationship is also expressed by the inspector when he gives Margie an apple (l. 24), pats her on the head twice (ll. 31/32, l. 35) and does not refer to her by her name but as "the little girl" (l. 32). This expression is used by Mrs Jones as well (l. 73).

Margie's sense of isolation and the superior-subordinate nature of her relationships is placed in contrast to the cooperative, socialising structures of the old schools described in the book.

Margie's references to *(Bemerkung über)* these schools are as positive as her references to her mechanical teacher are negative. We read that at the old schools "the kids from the neighborhood came, laughing and shouting in the schoolyard" and that they sat "together in the schoolroom" and went home "together at the end of the day". Margie thinks it wonderful that "they could help one another with the homework and talk about it" and – above all – "the teachers were people" (ll. 76–79). In the final two lines she thinks "about how the kids must have loved it in the old days" and "about the fun they had". These highly positive words and phrases – for example "laughing", "go home together", "help one another", "love", "fun" – are in sharp contrast to words like "hate", "ugly", "bad", "sorrowfully" and "fault".

5. **Explain the function of the sub-plot.**

The sub-plot (ll. 19–38) is devoted *(gewidmet)* to Mrs Jones's worry about Margie's progress and the visit of the County Inspector, who is in effect a kind of computer technician.

We also hear of Margie's hatred of school and of her consequent *(daraus folgend)* disappointment when her mechanical teacher can be adjusted to fit her ability on the spot *(auf der Stelle)*. She had been hoping that the inspector would have to take the machine away with him.
The function of the sub-plot is to supply the reader with essential information about the education system in the year 2155. Without this information, the two children's fascination with the book Tommy has found would be hardly credible *(kaum glaubwürdig)*. We are told that in 2155 children are taught at home by a "mechanical teacher" and in isolation from their peers *(Gleichaltrige)*. When things go wrong, a technician calls. The technician looks after the machine but shows no interest in the child as a human being. The learner is expected to comply with *(sich nach etwas richten)* a prescribed *(vorgeschrieben)* program without question.

10 Literarischer Text: The American Dream

ab Seite 179

1. **Say in not more than six sentences what the extract is about.**
The salesman, Willy Loman, is talking to his employer, Howard. As a travelling salesman Willy earns commission *(Provision)* on what he sells, but now he wants to be paid a fixed salary *(festes Gehalt)*. Howard is evidently *(offensichtlich)* not interested in agreeing to this proposal *(Vorschlag)*, even at only $40 a week. Willy describes incidents from his life to arouse *(erwecken)* Howard's sympathy and interest, but Howard becomes increasingly embarrassed at this show of emotion. He finally loses patience with Willy and makes an excuse to leave the room.

2. **Explain why Willy tells the story of Dave Singleman at such length.**
Dave Singleman, now dead, was a travelling salesman of the old kind. He had a great influence on Willy and was responsible for him giving up his plan to go to Alaska so as to become a salesman, "the greatest career a man could want" (l. 23).
In his interview with Howard, Willy uses Dave Singleman as the personification of what business relationships were once like. He sets up a contrast between his own situation and that of Singleman. He does this to make his position clear to Howard, and to arouse the latter's pity.
Willy suggests that Dave Singleman was successful not only because of his skill *(Geschick)* as a salesman, but because he had the human warmth, support and friendship of those he worked with. He could make a living "without ever leaving his room" (l. 21). He could depend on *(sich darauf verlassen)* being "remembered and loved and helped" (ll. 25/26). When he died, "hundreds of salesmen and buyers" attended his funeral and "things were sad ... for months" (ll. 26–30). Willy tells Howard that "in those days" business was different: "There was respect, and comradeship, and gratitude *(Dankbarkeit)*, in it" (ll. 31/32). The implication *(Andeutung)* is that Willy's own situation has been caused by the new hard, 'inhuman' business practices that have replaced those of earlier times.

3. **Describe the elements of drama that Miller makes use of in this extract.**

We can find examples of all four elements of drama – stage setting, movement *(Bewegung)*, spoken dialogue and characterisation – in the extract.

The main setting is Howard's office. Miller also makes much use of stage directions to characterise both Willy's and Howard's present state of mind explicitly. At the beginning we are told that Willy speaks with "increasing anger" (l. 1). When Howard does not give him what he wants, Willy reacts first "desperately" *(verzweifelt)* (l. 5) and then "angrily" (l. 7). At first Howard is

"barely interested" in what Willy says (l. 13), but later we hear that he challenges Willy's claim *(eine Behauptung infrage stellen)* about his earlier earnings "impatiently" (l. 47).

Movement is also indicated in the form of stage directions. During his long speech about Dave Singleman Willy "stands up" (l. 30) to emphasise his point about the human side of business. In the final part of the extract a number of directions has Howard getting up and making his way towards the door to leave, at one point Willy "stopping him" (l. 41).

The whole text is an oral negotiation *(mündliche Verhandlung)* between Willy Loman – who asks for a fixed weekly salary – on the one hand, and his boss, Howard – who is not willing to agree to this request *(Bitte)* – on the other. The first and the last parts of the extract are in typical dialogue form, each reacting to what the other says. The middle part of the extract is, however, virtually a monologue as we hear that Howard is "barely interested" (l. 13) and "has not looked at him" (ll. 30/31). Willy is in effect speaking to himself, a device used by dramatists when they want to communicate directly with the audience *(Zuschauer)*.

Miller uses the dialogue to characterise Willy and Howard more deeply. Here we are not concerned with their present mood, but with their opposing perceptions of reality and philosophies of life.

In Willy's case this aim is achieved by means of the monologue-like speech, which is in the form of a flashback to earlier – and better – days. Using Dave Singleman as the symbol of these times, Willy refers to the more human approach to business based on "respect", "comradeship" and "gratitude" (ll. 31/32). He contrasts these to contemporary business relationships, which are "cut and dried" (l. 32) and not related to individual human needs.

Howard's position is expressed mainly in his attitude to what Willy has to say. At first he is indifferent to Willy's position, and then he becomes impatient with his exaggerated claims about his earnings (l. 47) and embarrassed at his emotional outburst (ll. 51/52). There are, however, some passages when Howard gives us some more explicit insights into his business philosophy. In the opening lines of the extract he says "... it's business ... and everybody's got to pull his own weight ..." and "... you've got to admit, business is business" (ll. 4–6). It is clear that Howard sees 'business' in the contemporary sense as an end in itself that must be efficient and run in accordance with sound economic principles:

"... where am I going to put you, kid?" (l. 2);

"... I can't take blood from a stone, ..." (l. 37).

Unlike Willy, Howard does not accept that 'business' has a social dimension as well, particularly a responsibility towards people who have given a firm many years of their life. This fundamental disagreement is expressed in Howard's remark that "... everybody's got to pull his own weight" (l. 4) and in Willy's "You can't eat the orange and throw the peel away" (l. 43/44).

4. **Analyse Miller's use of stylistic devices and say what effect they have on our understanding of Willy's situation.**

Especially in Willy Loman's part, Miller makes use of a number of/several stylistic devices, often more than once.

Repetition is used when Howard remarks that "business is business" (l. 6), and Willy echoes "business is definitely business". In Willy's long speech repetition occurs twice, first in repeating forms of the verb "go" in lines 15, 17, 19 and 24 and then of "eighty-four" years in lines 18, 22 and 24.

As Willy becomes more emotional he uses enumeration and contrast to get his point across. When speaking of Dave Singleman he says it is a wonderful thing to be "remembered and loved and helped" (ll. 25/26). Describing selling "in those days", Willy says "there was respect, and comradeship, and gratitude in it" (ll. 31/32). This is contrasted with current conditions, where relationships are "all cut and dried and there's no chance for bringing friendship to bear – or personality" (ll. 32/33).

In the same speech, Willy's emotional approach *(Ansatz)* leads him to use what we may assume *(annehmen)* is intentional exaggeration. In line 23 he says that Dave Singleman convinced him "selling was the greatest career a man could want". When referring to Singleman's death, Willy claims that "hundreds of salesmen and buyers were at his funeral" (l. 29) and that "things were sad on a lotta trains for months" (ll. 29/30).

There are two examples of personification, which is in effect a kind of imagery, in the extract. When refusing Willy's request *(Bitte)* for a fixed salary, Howard says, "I can't take blood from a stone" (l. 37), thus investing *(einer Sache etwas verleihen)*/giving a thing – the stone – the human characteristic of being able to bleed. In his bitter reply, Willy points out that "a man is not a piece of fruit" (l. 44).

A good example of metaphor – it is one of the most famous lines from the play – is Willy's pitiful cry *(Mitleid erregender Schrei)* that "you can't eat the orange and throw the peel away" (ll. 43/44). The orange represents elderly employees who are no longer as successful and productive as they once were; the peel is their now worthless bodies.

In addition to this full metaphor, one can find some instances *(Fall)* of metaphorical language in the extract, as for example when Willy tells Howard that he only needs $50 "to set my table" (l. 1), by which he means to feed his family. Later, he says that nowadays the business world is "cut and dried" (l. 32). This image comes from forestry *(Forstwirtschaft)* and means that everything has been arranged and decided in advance *(im Vorfeld)*. There is no possibility of meeting individual needs any more.

Throughout the extract Miller uses these devices to impress *(deutlich klar machen)* Willy's position on the audience as vividly *(lebhaft)* as possible.

(11) Literarischer Text: Politics and Society

ab Seite 186

1. **Summarise the story in not more than 400 words.**
Diese Zusammenfassung geht davon aus, dass der Erzähler der Autor selbst ist. Der gefährliche Zeitvertreib, den Phil vorschlägt, heißt "sweeping".
The story opens with the narrator and his four friends in a car. They are driving aimlessly round town. They feel bored and are looking for some excitement. Then Phil suggests finding "some kid" and knocking him down by driving past and opening a door/Then Phil suggests a game of sweeping. At first, the others seem to be against the idea, but they finally begin looking for "a victim". The narrator still has some doubts, but only because of the police. He keeps quiet when accused of cowardice *(jdm Feigheit vorwerfen)*.
Then they see a boy standing beneath a streetlight. Dick drives towards him and Steve prepares to open a door. The narrator shouts at them to stop and Dick loses his nerve. He tries to avoid (here: *ausweichen)* the boy, but fails and hits him. At this point the narrator sees the boy is his friend, Ken Benjamin. He tries to make Dick stop, but Dick refuses *(sich weigern)*. He is afraid of being arrested *(verhaftet werden)* for manslaughter. Then Dick notices a car behind them. It seems to be following them and a chase starts. The car tries to overtake them, but it skids off the road.
Alone at home the narrator feels terrible guilt *(Schuld)*, but he doesn't dare listen to the news to find out about his friend. He tries to find excuses for himself, but he knows that he is responsible as well. He leaves the house and drives around. He knows he should go and see Mrs Benjamin, but is too cowardly to do so. At home again, the narrator finds the others there. Dick tells him that Ken has not been badly hurt. It seems they have got away with it. At that moment he feels murderous anger against Dick. He leaves the house and drives to the Benjamins. (306 words)

2. **Describe the structure of the story.**
Exposition: Kurumada begins his story with an introductory section called the exposition. This section, which goes from line 1 to line 8, sets the scene and introduces the two main characters – the narrator ("I") and the driver, Dick – and the minor characters Phil, Reid and Steve. (Reid is not mentioned by name again.) In the exposition we hear that the five boys are driving aimlessly around the town. They are bored and are looking for some excitement. The narrator describes the evening as "crummy", though even this is better than "sitting home". This impression of aimless killing of time is mirrored by the weather, which is cold and damp.
Rising action: The exposition is followed by a long section of rising action (ll. 9–64) which is characterised by increasing tension. The tension does not increase evenly, but in four levels which we can call rising action 1, 2, 3 and 4 *(siehe Schaubild)*.
The first level (ll. 9–19) is devoted to Phil's suggestion that they play a game of sweeping and to the search for a suitable victim. Rising action 2 concerns the attack on the boy and the accident that it causes (ll. 20–36). In rising action 3 we hear how the narrator recognises the boy as his friend and how he tries to make Dick stop the car (ll. 37–46).

The fourth and final tension level is the chase ending with the Volvo skidding off the road and the boys' escape (ll. 47-64).
The transition from one level to the next is always marked by a key event which gives rise to a change of direction. Hence between rising action 1 and 2, the transition is signalled by one of the boys shouting "There's one!" (l. 20) as he spots a suitable victim. Between rising action 2 and 3, the transition is marked by the narrator saying "Ken Benjamin. I think it was Ken Benjamin!" (l. 37), and between 3 and 4 by Dick's shout "Hey!" (l. 47). Each of these transitions involves an ever steepening increase in tension by which the boys' situation becomes progressively more critical.

Just along for the ride: structural diagram

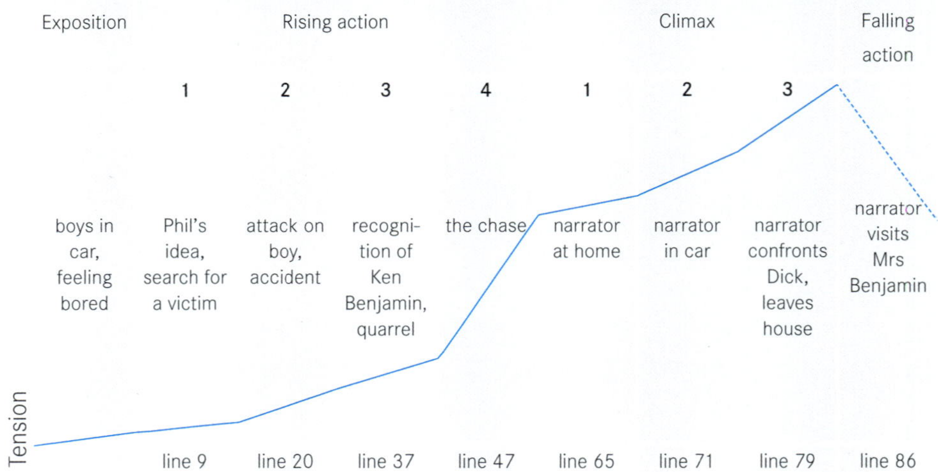

Use of direct and indirect description: Kurumada makes use of both direct and indirect description in the rising action section. Particularly the key events are described and interpreted in detail. The reader is never left in any doubt as to their significance. Hence in the accident scene we are told that "Dick got scared" (l. 33) and that the narrator himself "got all mixed up" (l. 36). Later the narrator uses direct description to tell the reader about his own feelings after the accident: "What a stupid thing to do! I got so scared that I started shivering like crazy. I just couldn't believe it. I felt sick" (ll. 45/46). At other points, however, Kurumada employs a more indirect technique. In lines 18/19, for example, we are told that one of the boys said to the narrator "Whenever we wanna have some fun, you always chicken out" and in lines 41/42 that "Tears were blobbing up in his (Dick's) eyes." In such cases, it is left to the reader to interpret the significance of these remarks.
Climax: The climax of the story (ll. 65-85) is sub-divided into three parts that are also characterised by increasing tension.
The first of these three parts (ll. 65-70) finds the narrator at home. He is assailed by feelings of guilt, fear and self-loathing. In a short sub-plot he imagines himself talking about

the incident to Ken's mother. Instead of showing remorse for what has happened to her son and confessing to his own part in it, the narrator takes the coward's way out and blames everything on his four companions. In the end, however, he finally seems to accept his own responsibility and leaves the house, the words "hit and run" drumming in his ears (ll. 69/70).

The second part of the climax goes from line 71 to line 76. Here, the narrator is driving aimlessly around in confusion. He recalls things Ken "used to say"; this use of the past tense shows us that the narrator is sure that his friend is dead. This adds to his sense of confusion and he shouts "I don't know what to do!" repeatedly to himself. This part ends with the narrator's acceptance of his own cowardice (ll. 75/76).

The final part of the climax sees the narrator back at home. His four friends are there and Dick tells him that Ken is not only alive, but isn't even badly hurt (l. 80). Dick's evident satisfaction at having got away with it (l. 82) infuriates the narrator so much that he "could have killed" Dick. At that instant, he overcomes his cowardice and shame. This is the turning point after which nothing will ever be quite the same again. Ignoring both Dick and his other three friends, the narrator leaves the house.

Falling action: The final section of the story – line 86 to the end – is characterised by a sudden release of tension that is termed falling action. This section sees the narrator driving to Ken's house. The story ends with him standing at the Benjamins' front door and ringing the doorbell.

3. State from whose point of view the incident is described and say what effect this has on our understanding

Point of view: The story is told from the point of view of one of the boys – the narrator – who himself takes part in the events. He describes both his own actions, feelings and thoughts, and also those of some of the other people involved. For example, he tells us in line 36 that he "got all mixed up" and later that he "got so scared" that he "started shivering like crazy" (l. 45). In the climax of the story he refers to his feelings of guilt and self-loathing as he struggles against his cowardice in not going to see Mrs Benjamin (ll. 68–74) and confessing to his part in her son's accident. Here he is speaking of his own state of mind. He functions with all the authority of an omniscient narrator.

When speaking of others, however, he can only state the obvious or surmise. In line 17 he says that his companions "are nuts" and in line 25 that the boys' laughter seems to have made Dick "nervous". Later, he tells us that "Dick got scared" (l. 33). In such cases the narrator is acting as an external observer like any third person narrator.

On some crucial occasions, Kurumada makes the narrator report on remarks made about himself by one of the other boys. Hence in line 18 the narrator tells us that an unnamed character said to him that he worries too much and that whenever they want to have some fun he always looses his nerve. This is the first reference to the narrator's apparent cowardice. In line 43 we hear that Dick called him a "jerk", i.e. weak and foolish. In these exchanges we are seeing the narrator through the eyes of others acting as third person narrators. The people in the story are characterised both directly and indirectly.

The narrator: The most important protagonist is the narrator himself. He comes across as a person with a conscience and a sense of right and wrong, but lacking in moral courage. He goes along with the foolish and dangerous game of sweeping rather than appear a weak spoil-sport in the eyes of his friends. Immediately after the accident, he tries to make Dick stop the car but gives up immediately when Dick challenges him. He then becomes guilty of taking part in a hit and run accident. When the Volvo driver skids off the road, he simply assumes that "he couldn't have been hurt" (l. 63). In the climax of the story he is fully aware of what he should do, but says "I couldn't. I just couldn't" (l. 75). At this moment he confronts himself with his own cowardice, but is still not able to overcome it. At every stage he is fully aware of all the implications of the situation, but does not react to them in the way he knows he should because of a crucial flaw in his character. At one point, he half hopes that the Volvo driver would catch them, thus relieving him of the obligation to reach a decision himself (l. 60). The turning point comes when he confronts Dick and the others and finally goes to see Mrs Benjamin.

Dick: Dick is the other main protagonist, although we do not receive so much information about him. As he drives towards the boy on the street corner we hear that he seemed "nervous" (l. 25). Later, he became frightened and tried - too late - to break off the game (ll. 33/34). After the accident, he at first slows down but then changes his mind and speeds away down the street. Dick turns on the narrator when he tries to make him stop (ll. 39-44). These are the reactions of a selfish and irresponsible person who puts his own safety before all else. During his confrontation with the narrator at the end of the story it is clear that Dick has no interest in Ken, only in having got away with it (l. 82).

Phil, Steve: The remaining people in the story play a minor role. The original idea comes from Phil, who is sitting in the front of the car with Dick. When the others object to his suggestion, he succeeds in persuading them to carry it out after all. Steve, who is in the back of the car, actually opens the door to sweep Ken Benjamin off his feet. There are no further references to these two characters, who come across as Dick's foolish and irresponsible followers *(Mitläufer)*.

Ken Benjamin: The first reference made to Ken Benjamin is his terror when he realises that the DeSoto is going to hit him (ll. 33/34). Later we are told that he is the narrator's friend (ll. 39/40), which is repeated in lines 59 and 68. When the narrator is driving round in confusion he "started remembering things Ken used to say" (ll. 71/72). Ken comes over as an ordinary, pleasant boy who has friends and can be interesting and even perhaps amusing.

The Volvo driver: The Volvo driver is the only person who reacts immediately to the accident - although he is more interested in bringing those responsible to justice than in helping the victim. He is clearly determined to catch Dick as he follows the DeSoto out into the country along a winding road. When he is finally "making his move" (ll. 61/62), he puts himself at personal risk. This fits in with the narrator's assumption that "a good guy would drive one of those Volvos" (ll. 58/59), i.e. a responsible citizen with a sense of right and wrong.

Significance of changing points of view: Changes in point of view are crucial to our understanding of the story and our perception of the characters. First person narration tends to be more direct, realistic and vivid *(lebhaft)* than third person narration. The latter effectively erects a barrier or filter between the reader on the one hand and the people and events described on the other. A good example of this phenomenon is the perceptual difference between the narrator's remark in line 33 that "Dick got scared" and his remark three lines later that "I got mixed up". The second example makes a deeper impact on the reader because it is a direct statement of fact made by the person concerned. These changing perspectives ensure that the reader has a primary interest in the main protagonist, the narrator. The reader feels understanding and sympathy for his predicament, although it springs from a flawed character. When the turning point comes and the narrator overcomes his cowardice and self-doubt and decides to visit the Benjamins, the reader has a satisfying feeling that right will be done.

12 Cartoon: Economy and Ecology

ab Seite 197

1. **Describe the cartoon.**
   The cartoon shows a rocky desert landscape without trees or plants with bare mountains in the background. In the centre of the cartoon there is a wooden crate that has been dropped to the ground by parachute and has broken open on impact. The crate has the words FOOD AID on its side and a sack with the words FLOUR and US for USA can be seen poking out of it. In the background top left a further crate is falling to the ground by parachute. In the foreground bottom right two people in traditional dress are looking at the crate. The taller of the two explains, "It's humanitarian so we have full bellies when they bomb us". On hearing this, his smaller companion recoils and throws up his hands in horror.

2. **Explain Ken Sprague's message.**
   On the surface, the cartoon's message is that the US government is providing people with food aid by parachuting sacks of flour into poor and remote areas of a country. The smaller of the two men is probably agreeably surprised at this apparent generosity until his companion explains what it really means. In a speech bubble, he makes a sceptical comment to his companion that transmits the message to the reader. The taller man's companion is deeply shocked by this revelation, realising that they can now expect to be bombed shortly. The cartoonist, Ken Sprague, wants to express his contempt for the US government's cynical hyprocrisy in that it 'bombs' other countries with both essential food aid to keep its citizens alive and with explosives to kill them.

Glossar literarischer Fachbegriffe

Dieses Verzeichnis beinhaltet u.a. die in den Units verwendete literarische Terminologie.
Die englischen Erklärungen sind als Formulierungshilfe gedacht.

aim *(Ziel):* Many writers have both an **overt aim** *(vordergründiges Ziel)* and a **submerged aim** *(indirektes Ziel)* when writing texts. In a press report, for example, the writer's overt aim is always to give the reader factual information about an event *(Ereignis)* or situation. By selecting particular details or quotations, and by his choice of words, the writer can, however, also make his own position clear. This is called the submerged aim. → **intention**

alliteration *(Stabreim/Alliteration):* A stylistic or literary device which involves the rhythmic repetition of the same sound at the beginning of succeeding words, e.g. *The sun sank slowly below the horizon*.

anticlimax *(Trivialisierung):* Anticlimax or **bathos** is when a writer appears to be building up towards a climax, which does not occur. Instead of the expected climax, there is a sharp letdown *(Enttäuschung)* which creates an absurd or trivial impression *(Eindruck)*.

antonym *(Gegensatzwort/Antonym):* An antonym is a word of opposite meaning, for example *big* is an antonym of *small, rich* of *poor* and *ugly* of *beautiful*. → **synonym**

assonance *(Gleichklang/Assonanz):* A stylistic device – often found in poetry – by which similar vowel sounds within succeeding words are repeated, e.g. *Player with Railroads and the Nation's Freight Handler.*

atmosphere *(Atmosphäre):* The atmosphere of a literary text is created by the interplay *(Wechselspiel)* between setting *(Schauplatz)* and the state of mind *(Gemütszustand)* of the main characters. → **setting**, → **state of mind**

autobiography *(Autobiografie):* The story of a person's life told by him- or herself. → **biography**

bathos → **anticlimax**

biography *(Biografie):* The story of a person's life told by somebody else. → **autobiography**

black humour *(schwarzer Humor):* A despairing *(verzweifelt)* and often cynical kind of humour that focuses on the absurd aspects of serious subjects such as death, mental illness, prejudice, poverty, human misery *(Elend)* and so on which are not normally thought "funny" at all. Black humour uses a **shock effect** *(Schockwirkung)* to catch and concentrate the attention of the reader or viewer. → **cartoon**

caricature *(Karikatur):* A way of ridiculing or poking fun at a person by exaggerating his or her most prominent feature or characteristic. This is done by means of extreme and sometimes cruel distortion *(Verzerrung)*. Nowadays caricature is largely visual, and is the main technique used by cartoonists. → **cartoon**

cartoon *(Cartoon):* Cartoons are divided into two main groups: humourous *(humorvoll)* and political *(politisch)*. The first of these simply entertains, while the second comments on some contemporary event or problem. Political cartoons make use of caricature - and often black humour - to highlight and/or ridicule some specific aspect of the topic *(Thema)*.
→ caricature, → black humour

case study *(Fallstudie):* A description of a real-life situation in which the people concerned are allowed to speak for themselves. Case study techniques are often used to describe social problems and personal relationships.

chain of thought → train of thought

change of direction → transition

character *(Figur):* A character is any person in a story. A **main character** *(Hauptfigur)* is somebody without whom the story could not be told. A **minor character** *(Nebenfigur)* is somebody who may have quite a lot to say, but is in fact only there to make what is happening to the main character(s) possible or plausible. An **extra** *(Statist)* is somebody who is only present for the sake of realism.

characterisation *(Charakterisierung):* Any technique used by a writer to describe and analyse a person. Characterisation does not only deal with personality, but also with outer appearance *(äußere Erscheinung)*, attitudes, state of mind *(Gemütszustand)*, mood *(Stimmung)* and lifestyle. **Direct characterisation** *(direkte Charakterisierung)* is when the writer describes what a person is like. **Indirect characterisation** *(indirekte Charakterisierung)* is when the reader must interpret what a person is like by looking at his or her actions, remarks, attitudes, relationships etc.

choice of words *(Wortwahl):* A person can make his own attitude clear to others by his choice of words. If a writer wants to give a moderate, balanced view, he will tend to avoid the use of strong words and expressions and particularly of 'loaded language' *(suggestive Sprache)*. He will also use moderators so as to avoid sounding too definite or dogmatic: *generally speaking; some people think; it might be thought* etc. If, on the other hand, a writer wants to give a strongly partisan *(parteiisch)* view, he will make use of so-called 'technicolor language' - often strong adjectives - and emphasisers: *however you look at it; it's perfectly obvious; only a fool would believe etc.* Choice of words in poetry is called diction. → diction,
→ emphasis, → style

climax *(Höhepunkt):* The point of maximum tension *(höchste Spannung)* in a story. The climax is preceded by a period of **rising action** *(steigende Spannung)* that is characterised by ever increasing tension *(ständig zunehmende Spannung)* and followed by a short phase of **falling action** *(abnehmende Spannung)*, i.e. a release of tension *(Abbau der Spannung)*. Note that the climax can be subdivided into a number of stages *(Stufe)*. This is the case in Dennis

Kurumada's short story *Just along for the ride* (Unit 11). The climax takes the form of a **turning point** *(Wendepunkt)* in a person's life when the situation confronting him or her is resolved *(gelöst)*. → **anticlimax**, → **falling action**, → **rising action**, → **turning point**

comparison *(Vergleich):* A technique which points out the similarities *(Ähnlichkeit)* between a strange or an unknown person, thing or idea and the already known or familiar *(vertraut)*. The most important stylistic device used for comparison is the simile: *The man came into the room like a crazy bull. She was as beautiful as a summer's day.* → **contrast**

conflict *(Konflikt):* All literature deals with some kind of conflict. By 'conflict' we do not necessarily mean a fight or even an argument. In literature, conflict means any kind of imbalance *(Unausgewogenheit)* or inconsistency *(Widersprüchlichkeit)* in an individual's relationships with other individuals, with his social environment *(soziales Umfeld)* or within himself. In this book you can find good examples of three kinds of conflict situation. The conflict in the poem *Chicago* (Unit 8) is between the poet - representing Chicago itself - and those who criticise the city. In the novel *Hurry on down* (Unit 7), the conflict is between the main character, Charles Lumley, and his social environment, in this case a middle-class individual in working-class surroundings. In the short story *Just along for the ride* (Unit 11) the main conflict is within the main character, the narrator. This conflict is resolved when he confronts a fatal flaw *(fataler Makel)* in his character, his cowardice. → **character**

contrast *(Kontrast):* A technique which points out the differences between persons, things or ideas in order to show the essential *(wesentlich)* qualities of one of them. → **comparison**

convention *(Konvention):* In all literature, the readers or audience have to accept certain conventions or 'rules of the game'. This is particularly true of drama, where the stage can become a ship or a battlefield or the surface of another planet from one minute to the next. Another common convention is about language. Have you noticed how everybody can suddenly understand everybody else's language? Conventions like these are essential, but they do mean that we have to be willing to 'suspend disbelief' *(sich auf die Bühnenwirklichkeit einlassen)*. → **point of view** (omniscient narration)

conversational device *(Gesprächsmittel):* A conversational device is anything that is characteristic of normal spoken language. The most common conversational devices are:

1. short forms (*isn't; hasn't; weren't*)
2. question tags (*... , doesn't it?; ... , can't she?*)
3. short answers (*Yes, it is; No, they aren't*)
4. short, simple sentences
5. 'attention catchers' (*Well, ... ; Now, ... ; Oh, ...*)
6. colloquial words (*kids* for *children; guy* for *man* etc.)

dialogue *(Dialog):* A dialogue is a spoken exchange of words between two or more characters. In prose texts it is shown by inverted commas or quotation marks ("..."). An **interior dialogue** *(interner Dialog)* is when a character speaks to him-/herself. → monologue

diction *(Ausdrucksweise/Diktion):* Originally 'diction' meant any writer's choice of words, but today it is usually used only of poetry. When talking of prose, it is better to say 'choice of words' or – more widely – 'use of language'. → choice of words

direct characterisation → characterisation

drama *(Drama; Schauspiel):* Drama tells a story to a viewer *(Zuschauer)* rather than to a reader. The playwright *(Dramatiker/in)* makes use of movement – including gesture *(Gestik)* and facial expression *(Mimik)* – and setting to show visually what other writers express in descriptive prose. In the script, they appear as stage directions. → dialogue, → monologue, → setting

emphasis *(Betonung/Emphase):* Emphasis is a stylistic device used to stress an argument, for example. In **spoken language** the commonest means of emphasis is to place an extra stress on the word or words as in *"I didn't say Harry Parker. I said Harry **Barker**."* In written texts, the emphasised words are often shown in *italics*.
Apart from stressing parts of the sentence in this way, you will also find the following means of emphasis, particularly in prose texts:

1. **Choice of words:** *In a **devastating attack** on **so-called** education experts, Prince Charles said they were talking **"unmitigated nonsense"**.*
2. Use of **qualifying adverbs** to strengthen adjectives: *The prime minister said the **disgustingly** violent behaviour of some football fans was **absolutely** unacceptable and **extremely** damaging to Britain's reputation abroad.*
3. Use of the **emphasising adverbs** *(Verstärker) certainly, definitely, really*: *There can **certainly** be no doubt that the unions **really** will strike this time.* In spoken English these special emphasisers are often replaced with *so* and *such*: *"What does Wendy see in Jack? He's **such** a fool and he's always **so** rude to her."*
4. The **emphasising expressions** *(verstärkender Ausdruck) on earth, in God's name* and *the hell* are also often used to stress whole questions: *"What **on earth**/What **the hell** are you talking about?"*
5. **Swearwords** *(Kraftausdruck)*, especially *damn, damned, bloody* and *bleeding* are very common emphasisers, especially among men: *"That's a **damn/bloody** stupid thing to do, isn't it?"*
6. Parts of sentences can also be given extra emphasis by using certain grammatical structures. You will find some information about this means of emphasis in the notes on argumentative texts in Unit 5.

enumeration *(Aufzählung/Enumeration):* This stylistic device is basically a list of three or more items as in the opening and closing lines of *Chicago* (Unit 8). It is one of the most common stylistic devices and one of the easiest to spot. → **stylistic device**

essay *(Essay):* Nowadays an essay is most usually a non-fictional prose text of several hundred words. They are often evaluative in that the writer gives his opinion on a topic of current *(aktuell)* interest and presents his arguments for it. However, the essay is a very flexible form and descriptive essays are also quite popular. They can be either humourous or serious, formal or informal. More formal essays are divided into three parts or 'structural elements', i.e. the introduction, the development and the conclusion. → **non-fictional text,** → **prose**

exaggeration *(Übertreibung):* → **hyperbole**

exposition *(Einführung/Exposition):* The introduction to a fictional work, for example a short story, in which the characters are introduced and the scene set.

falling action *(abnehmende Spannung):* The part of a fictional work that comes immediately after the climax and turning point. It is characterised by an often very sudden release of tension *(Abbau der Spannung)*. → **exposition,** → **rising action,** → **turning point**

fictional text *(fiktionaler Text):* Fictional texts are about people and events which could be real, but are in fact produced by the writer's imagination. Fictional texts can, however, be autobiographical or based on real people or events. → **cartoon,** → **novel,** → **poem,** → **short story**

flashback *(Rückblende):* A narrative technique by which a past event is pulled back into the present. A flashback is thus reliving a memory. It is used to explain a present situation and/or current *(aktuell)* attitudes. It is common in movies and TV drama.

free verse *(freie Dichtung):* A modern form of poetry that does not make use of any or all of the features *(Merkmal)* found in traditional poems, i.e. a formal rhyme scheme *(Reimschema)*, metre *(Metrik)* and a fixed number of lines per stanza *(Strophe)*. → **poem**

full metaphor → **metaphor**

hero, heroine → **character**

hyperbole *(Hyperbel):* The technical term for intentional exaggeration as in the tabloid press report in Unit 3, e.g. *"The result was* ***complete chaos****"*. However, hyperbole has become so common in the media, politics and advertising that it has lost much of its effect.

imagery *(Verbildlichung/Metaphorik):* 'Imagery' comes from the Latin word for 'making likenesses'. Hence a writer's imagery is any means used to compare one person, idea or thing with another. → **comparison,** → **symbolism**

increasing tension → **rising action**

indirect characterisation → **characterisation**

intention *(Autorenabsicht):* A writer's intention is whatever he wants to achieve with his text, i.e. his aim in writing it. In fiction, the intention is either to entertain (light literature) or to expose some general truth about the human condition (serious literature). → **aim**
Non-fictional texts fall into five groups according to their main intention, i.e. argumentative (or **evaluative**) *(wertend)*, informative, instructive, narrative or persuasive. It is, however, important to emphasise that texts seldom fall into just one category, 'informative', say. For this reason, we must often use a formulation like '*... is mainly informative with evaluative and narrative elements*'.
As a guide, here are some kinds of texts that belong to each of these categories:

- ▷ **argumentative** – essay, leading article, reader's letter, political cartoon, ...
- ▷ **informative** – travel book, guide, reference book, catalogue, press release, holiday postcard, TV magazine, theatre programme, price list, popular scientific text, feature article, lecture, ...
- ▷ **instructive** – user's manual/instructions for use, street plan/road map, product demonstration, ...
- ▷ **narrative** *(erzählend)* – press report, sports commentary, joke, anecdote, ...
- ▷ **persuasive** *(überzeugend)* – advertisement

irony *(Ironie):* A stylistic device often used in satire and critical comment. The writer appears to agree with an opinion in order to ridicule *(verspotten)* it. A primitive or unsubtle form of irony is called **sarcasm** *(Sarkasmus)*.

level of meaning *(Bedeutungsebene):* The term 'level of meaning' is mainly used when talking about poetry, i.e. **exterior meaning** *(Oberflächenstruktur)* and **interior meaning** *(Tiefenstruktur)*. The first is simply what the poet seems to be saying on the surface. The second is the hidden meaning which we discover by the interpretation of imagery and symbolism.
→ **imagery**, → **symbolism**, → **poem**

literary device *(Stilmittel):* → **stylistic device**

main character → **character**

main plot → **plot**

metaphor *(Metapher):* A **full metaphor** is a stylistic device that suggests that one person, idea or thing is not simply like another, but actually is another, e.g. *Do those boys have the same parents?* ***One's a lamb, the other a lion.*** However, in both fictional and non-fictional writing, the use of metaphorical language *(metaphorische Sprache)* is much commoner than are full metaphors. → **comparison**, → **simile**, → **stylistic device**

metre → **poem**, → **free verse**

minor character → **character**

monologue *(Monolog):* A longer speech in which a character speaks to himself or, in drama, to the audience. It is also called a **soliloquy**, which is made up of the Latin words for 'alone' and 'to speak'. → **dialogue**

mood → **state of mind**

narrator → **point of view**

non-fictional text *(Sachtext):* A text that deals with people, events and ideas in the real world and is not the product of the writer's imagination. → **fictional text**, → **intention**

novel *(Roman):* A longer fictional prose work usually involving a number of different characters and settings. Novels deal with the characters' actions and relationships over a longer period of time, sometimes over many years. A short novel that is longer than a short story but not as long as a full-length novel is called a **novella** *(Novelle)*.

perception *(Wahrnehmung):* The way people see or 'perceive' the world around them and their attitude to it. As people seldom see things in exactly the same way, differing perceptions of reality are a major source of conflict. → **conflict**

personification *(Verkörperung; Personifizierung):* A stylistic device by which things are given human characteristics. Personification is one of the commonest stylistic devices. In English, it is also easy to spot by the use of the personal pronouns *he/she, him/her* instead of *it*. → **stylistic device**

perspective → **point of view**

play → **drama**

plot *(Handlung):* This word is used for the order *(Reihenfolge)* or sequence in which events take place and its effect on characterisation. If we say that a play or novel is 'badly plotted', we mean that the sequence of events does not explain the behaviour of the characters in a satisfactory and credible *(glaubwürdig)* way. A **sub-plot** *(Nebenhandlung)* is a sequence of events that can be removed from the main plot without the story suffering *(beeinträchtigt werden)*. A sub-plot may be used to characterise the main character(s). → **flashback**

poem *(Gedicht):* The outstanding characteristic of all poems – whether traditional or free verse – is that they communicate their 'message' in a very brief and compressed *(komprimiert)* form. In order to achieve this brevity and precision, it is necessary for the poet to operate simultaneously *(gleichzeitig)* on two levels, those of exterior and interior meaning. The connection between these two levels of meaning is achieved by the use of imagery *(Metaphorik)* and symbolism *(Symbolik)*. → **free verse**, → **imagery**, → **level of meaning**, → **symbolism**

point of view *(Perspektive):* Our understanding of an event, say, is influenced by the point of view or 'perspective' *(Blickwinkel)* of the person who tells us about it. This is easy to test by looking at a road accident through the eyes of the perpetrator *(Verursacher)* and the victim *(Opfer)*. Even if both tell the truth as they see it, we usually get quite different impressions *(Eindruck)* of what happened. Concerning point of view, in literature we distinguish *(differenzieren)* between **first person narration** *(Ich-Erzählung)* - as in, for example, Dennis Kurumada's story *Just along for the ride* (Unit 11) - and **third person narration** *(beobachtende Erzählweise)* as in Asimov's *The fun they had* (Unit 9). First person narration is often used in more exciting stories with a strong storyline. Some writers claim *(behaupten)* that a **first person narrator** *(Ich-Erzähler)* comes across more vividly *(lebhaft, plastisch)* and - above all - convincingly *(glaubwürdig)*. This is because a first person narrator can obviously talk about his own feelings and thoughts in a much more direct and concrete way than a third person narrator could. In the case of a **third person narrator** *(beobachtender Erzähler)*, however, we have to differentiate *(differenzieren)* again. First, there is the narrator who seems to know absolutely everything about the people he is describing, even their most intimate thoughts and motivations. We call this kind of third person narrator an **omniscient narrator** *(allwissender Erzähler)*. In *The fun they had* (Unit 9) Asimov makes use of this sort of **omniscient narration** *(allwissende Erzählweise)*. The narrator doesn't wonder or 'surmise' *(mutmaßen)* about Margie's feelings, but seems to know all about them in a way that no outsider possibly could. For this reason, we say that this kind of narration involves the reader in a **suspension of disbelief** *(sich auf die fiktive Wirklichkeit einlassen)*. → **convention**
The second kind of third person narrator does not need this help from the reader because he comes across like any outsider. He can describe external things that can be seen, but can only surmise about a character's feelings. We call this kind of third person narrator an **external observer** *(außenstehender Beobachter)*.

popular scientific text *(allgemein verständlicher wissenschaftlicher Text):* This is a kind of mainly **informative text** about a scientific or technical topic. Specialised information is made understandable to the reader by the use of general, i.e. nonscientific, language and by visual means, such as diagrams and graphs. → **intention**

prose *(Prosa):* A prose text is any kind of text that is not poetry or a cartoon. The word comes from the Latin *prosa* meaning 'straightforward communication'.

release of tension → **falling action**

repetition *(Wiederholung):* A stylistic device which involves saying the same thing more than once, often in different words. Martin Luther King's *I have a dream* speech (Unit 5) is full of repetition. → **stylistic device**

rhetorical question *(rhetorische Frage):* Rhetorical questions are statements in the form of questions, i.e. they expect no answer. Here is an example from Unit 6: ... *how much more hunger must be endured before it (= a ban on GM crops) is faced down?* → **stylistic device**

rhyme scheme → poem, → free verse

rising action *(steigende Spannung):* The part of a fictional work that comes immediately after the exposition and builds up towards a climax. It is characterised by increasing tension which often builds up in several stages (*Stufe*). **→ climax, → exposition, → short story**

sarcasm → irony

satire *(Satire):* A means of attacking foolish or wicked behaviour, often in politics, by using sarcasm, irony and parody *(Parodie)*. **→ irony**

setting *(Schauplatz):* In literary texts, the interplay *(Wechselwirkung)* between the setting and the main characters is very important. This is because authors often use details of the setting either to reflect a character's state of mind *(Gemütszustand)* or – less often – to set up a contrast to it. Here are a few hints and ideas to help you interpret the significance *(Bedeutung)* of setting.

Space

- ▷ **limited area:** character's thoughts tend to be introverted and concerned with him- or herself; character may feel isolated or restricted *(eingeengt)* in his or her freedom of movement or thought
- ▷ **unlimited:** character's thoughts and awareness *(Wahrnehmung)* tend to be more extroverted and directed at others or the surroundings *(Umfeld)*; character may feel freer to determine *(bestimmen)* his or her own actions

Time, season

- ▷ **day, spring, summer:** state of mind or mood tends to be optimistic, positive, future orientated
- ▷ **night, autumn, winter:** character tends to be pessimistic, thoughtful, despondent *(niedergeschlagen)*, fed up, past orientated

Weather

- ▷ **stormy:** angry, excited, perhaps aggressive and violent; extremely emotional and lacking in self-control; not amenable *(zugänglich)* to reason
- ▷ **foggy, cloudy:** unclear, unfocused thoughts and feelings; uncertain and perhaps little self-confidence *(Selbstvertrauen)*; threatening *(bedrohlich)*
- ▷ **cool, wet:** unfeeling, without emotion; reserved *(zurückhaltend)*, retiring *(scheu)*; little interest in or understanding for other people and their problems
- ▷ **snow, ice:** isolated from others and social environment *(soziales Umfeld)*; incapable of making or developing human relationships; tendency *(Neigung)* to misunderstand others and to misinterpret their behaviour, often negatively; selfish, self-centred; strong tendency *(Neigung)* to self-deception *(Selbsttäuschung)*
- ▷ **sunny, dry:** carefree *(fröhlich, sorgenfrei)*; warm-hearted *(herzlich)*; understanding, tolerant; sensitive to, interested in others; outgoing *(kontaktfreudig)*

Other people

- ▷ **children at play:** innocent *(unschuldig)*; harmless; unspoilt *(unverdorben)*
- ▷ **happy people:** carefree *(fröhlich, sorgenfrei)*; exuberant, boisterous *(ausgelassen)*; free of worry, stress; outgoing *(kontaktfreudig)*, warm-hearted *(herzlich)*; extroverted
- ▷ **reserved people** *(zurückhaltende Menschen)*: shy; with little contact to others; watchful *(beobachtend)*; suspicious *(argwöhnisch)*; cold-hearted; introverted
- ▷ **loafers** *(herumlungernde Menschen)*: bored; uninterested; shallow, superficial *(oberflächlich)*; lethargic, sluggish *(träge)*

Animals

- ▷ **pets:** loyal, faithful *(treu)*; dependent; patient *(geduldig)*; substitute for people *(Menschenersatz)*; compensation *(Ausgleich)* for lack of human contact/warmth
- ▷ **farm animals:** exploitation *(Ausnutzung)*; lack of warmth, intimacy; lack of freedom of action, decision; restriction *(Einengung)*; stupidity; insensitivity *(Gefühllosigkeit)*
- ▷ **wild animals:** freedom; self-determination *(Selbstbestimmung)*

shock effect → black humour, → cartoon

short story *(Kurzgeschichte):* Short stories – particularly the American short story established by (among others) Edgar Allan Poe and Ambrose Bierce, and developed by writers like Dorothy Parker and Ernest Hemingway – have a characteristic form that makes them different from any other fictional text. These are the most important characteristics of short stories:

- ▷ Considering the complexity of the theme, short stories are relatively short, sometimes only a few hundred words and seldom more than a few thousand.
- ▷ Short stories seldom deal with a complete and fully worked out narrative. They are more a snapshot *(Schnappschuss)* of a single highly significant episode or event in the life of the main character(s). → **character**
- ▷ Short stories rarely have more than two main characters. More often they deal with just one person and his or her **perception of reality** *(Realitätswahrnehmung)*. → **character,** → **perception**
- ▷ There are few minor characters and/or extras. These characters are usually used to compress *(komprimieren)* the story in that they reflect the feelings and actions of the main characters in some way, either by comparison or contrast. → **character,** → **comparsion,** → **contrast**
- ▷ The story lasts a relatively short time, generally a few hours.
- ▷ The action takes place in a limited space, often one room. → **setting**
- ▷ There is seldom any **change of scene** *(Szenenwechsel)*. If there is a change of scene this is usually achieved in the form of a sub-plot *(Nebenhandlung)* or flashback *(Rückblende)*. → **plot,** → **flashback**
- ▷ Short stories build up towards a climax that involves a turning point *(Wendepunkt)* which has come about through the resolution of a conflict.→ **climax,** → **conflict,** → **turning point**

simile *(Gleichnis):* A stylistic device which is the main means of setting up a comparison. Here are two examples. The first is from J. B. Priestley's play *An Inspector Calls* and the second is from *Death of a Salesman*.
Notice that similes are always introduced by *like* or *as*. → **stylistic device**
But the way some of these cranks talk and write now, you'd think everybody has to look after everybody else, ***as if we were all mixed up together like bees in a hive*** *– community and all that nonsense.*
I see it (= $20,000) ***like a diamond, shining in the dark, hard and rough,*** *that I can pick up and touch in my hand. Not* ***like – like an appointment.***

soliloquy → **monologue**

stanza → **poem**, → **free verse**

state of mind *(Gemütszustand):* The main purpose of characterisation is to describe and explain a character's state of mind or **mood**. This can be done either directly or indirectly. A character's state of mind as mirrored by the setting creates the atmosphere of a scene. → **characterisation**, → **setting**, → **atmosphere**

style *(Stil):* The word 'style' is used to describe the way a person expresses himself.
The two main kinds of style are **formal**, which you generally find in written language, and **informal** – or **colloquial** *(umgangssprachlich)* – which occurs more often in spoken language. Note, however, that written communications like emails, text messages and postcards are in fact "informal spoken language in writing".
Within these two main divisions, there are several other ways of describing a person's style of speaking or writing. Thus we can say that somebody has a pompous *(gespreizt)* or inflated *(aufgeblasen)* style. At the other extreme, we sometimes speak of an easy *(locker)* style or perhaps a common or vulgar *(ordinär)* style.
Style is expressed by a person's choice of words and use of grammatical structures.
In English as in German, a formal style is characterised by a use of foreign words, generally of Latin or French origin, by complex sentences and by a non-use of conversational devices such as ellipsis and short forms.
An informal style is marked by a use of readily understandable everyday words – usually of Germanic origin –, by simple sentences and by a whole range of conversational devices *(Gesprächsmittel)* like short forms, question tags and 'attention catchers'.
Which style you use – formal or informal – is decided firstly by whether you are writing or speaking, and secondly by your relationship to the person with whom you are communicating. → **conversational device**

stylistic device *(Stilmittel):* A stylistic device is any device used by writers to make what they say clearer and more understandable to the reader or spectator. → **enumeration**, → **hyperbole**, → **imagery**, → **metaphor**, → **personification**, → **repetition**, → **simile**, → **symbolism**

sub-plot → **plot, flashback**

symbolism *(Symbolik):* A stylistic device widely used *(weit verbreitet)* in all literary fiction, particularly poetry, by which one person, idea or thing represents another.
Full metaphors are a common form of symbolism. → **imagery,** → **metaphor,** → **stylistic device**

synonym *(Synonym):* A word with the same or a similar meaning to another word, for example *big/large; buy/purchase; factory/plant; everywhere/all over the place* etc. Finding synonyms is a good way of using your own words without making too many grammatical mistakes. → **antonym**

train of thought *(Gedankengang):* A writer's train (or chain) of thought is the way one thought leads on to another so as to form a sequence or progression. It can be logical – as for example in an argumentative text – or chronological – as in a report of an event – or a combination of both.
When looking at texts, you will often be asked to expose *(freilegen)* or show the writer's train of thought. This is frequently signalled by adverbs such as: *after that, firstly/secondly/... , finally, for this reason, furthermore, hence/thus, in conclusion, later, moreover, then, to begin with* etc. → **aim,** → **intention**

transition *(Übergang):* The basic structure of a fictional story is 1) exposition, 2) rising action, 3) climax, 4) falling action. Within this structure the two parts rising action and climax can be further subdivided into stages *(Stufe)*, as in the short story *Just along for the ride* (Unit 11). We call the connecting points *(Verbindungspunkt)* between one part and the next, and between the stages within a part, **transitions**. A transition is always marked by a clear **change of direction** *(Richtungswandel)*. → **climax,** → **exposition,** → **falling action,** → **rising action,** → **short story**

turning point *(Wendepunkt):* A highly significant development in a character's life after which nothing will ever be quite the same again. A turning point in a story is always marked by a problem or a conflict being resolved *(gelöst)*. Note that there can be several turning points, particularly in the rising action part, but the climax is always accompanied *(begleitet)* by one. → **climax,** → **conflict,** → **short story**

verse → **poem**

Seite 122 f.: **Going for a bit of rough**, Laura Marcus, Options magazine, April 1994

Seite 130 f.: **Transport: London still gridlocked despite congestion charge**, Dan Milmo, The Guardian, London, 7. August 2008 http://www.guardian.co.uk/politics/2008/aug/07/congestioncharging.transport

Seite 134 f.: **Educated kids? It doesn't add up**, Daily Mirror, London, 2. November 2002

Seite 138 f.: **The last word**, aus: More craft, less smoke, Malcolm Jones, Newsweek, New York, 3. Februar 2003

Seite 151 f.: **To take on global hunger, genetic modification is crucial**, The Guardian, London, 22. August 2008

Seite 158 f.: **Hurry on down**, John Wain, Penguin Books, Harmondsworth, Middlesex, 1960; ursprünglich veröffentlicht von Martin Secker & Warburg Ltd, London, 1953

Seite 163 f.: **Chicago**, aus: Chicago Poems, Carl Sandburg, Dover Publications, New York, 1994; ursprünglich veröffentlicht von Henry Holt and Company, New York, 1916

Seite 170 f.: **The fun they had**, Isaac Asimov, aus: The Complete Stories of Isaac Asimov, 1957; Nachdruck mit Genehmigung von Doubleday, Random House, Inc., New York

Seite 179 f.: **Death of a Salesman**, Arthur Miller, Erstausgabe: Viking Penguin, 1949; Nachdruck mit Genehmigung von International Creative Management, Inc., London

Seite 186 ff.: **Just along for the ride**, Dennis Kurumada, aus: Sun and Shadow: Supplementary Reader in Contemporary American Literature for International Students of English, US Information Agency, Washington D.C., 1972

Seite 197: **Cartoon**, Ken Sprague, Nachdruck mit freundlicher Genehmigung des Ken Sprague Fund